This book develops a framework for analyzing *strategic rationality*, a notion central to contemporary game theory, which is the formal study of the interaction of rational agents and which has proved extremely fruitful in economics, political theory, and business management.

The author argues that a logical paradox (known since antiquity as the "Liar paradox") lies at the root of a number of persistent puzzles in game theory, in particular those concerning rational agents who seek to establish some kind of reputation. Building on the work of Parsons, Burge, Gaifman, and Barwise and Etchemendy, Robert Koons constructs a context-sensitive solution to the whole family of liar-like paradoxes, including, for the first time, a detailed account of how the interpretation of paradoxial statements is fixed by context. This analysis provides a new understanding of how the rational agent model can account for the emergence of rules, practices, and institutions.

T0382620

Paradoxes of belief and strategic rationality

Cambridge Studies in Probability, Induction, and Decision Theory

General editor: Brian Skyrms

Advisory editors: Ernest W. Adams, Ken Binmore, Persi Diaconis, William L. Harper, John Harsanyi, Richard C. Jeffrey, Wolfgang Spohn, Patrick Suppes, Amos Tversky, Sandy Zabell

This new series is intended to be a forum for the most innovating and challenging work in the theory of rational decision. It focuses on contemporary developments at the interface between philosophy, psychology, economics, and statistics. The series addresses foundational theoretical issues, often quite technical ones, and therefore has a distinctly philosophical character.

Other titles in the series . . .
Ellery Eells, *Probablistic Causality*

Paradoxes of belief and strategic rationality

Robert C. Koons
University of Texas at Austin

The right of the University of Cambridge to print and sell all manner of books was granted by Henry VIII in 1534. The University has printed and published continuously since 1584.

Cambridge University Press

Cambridge
New York Port Chester Melbourne Sydney

CAMBRIDGE UNIVERSITY PRESS
Cambridge, New York, Melbourne, Madrid, Cape Town, Singapore, São Paulo, Delhi

Cambridge University Press
The Edinburgh Building, Cambridge CB2 8RU, UK

Published in the United States of America by Cambridge University Press, New York

www.cambridge.org
Information on this title: www.cambridge.org/9780521412698

First published 1992
This digitally printed version 2008

A catalogue record for this publication is available from the British Library

Library of Congress Cataloguing in Publication data

Koons, Robert C.
Paradoxes of belief and strategic rationality/Robert C. Koons.
p. cm. – (Cambridge studies in probability, induction,
and decision theory)
Includes bibliographical references.
ISBN-0-521-41269-2
1. Liar paradox. 2. Games of strategy (Mathematics). 3. Belief and doubt.
I. Title. II. Title: Strategic rationality. III. Series.
BC 199. P2K66 1991
165--dc20 91-18030
CIP

ISBN 978-0-521-41269-8 hardback
ISBN 978-0-521-10059-5 paperback

To Debbie, my wife and dearest friend

Contents

Part II Solutions

Preface

My principal aims in writing this book are two. First of all, I am attempting a defense of a thesis that I call "Computationalism," namely, the thesis that the objects of psychological attitudes (like belief and intention) are abstract objects which are structured in a way that mirrors the syntactic structure of sentences. Moreover, I intend to defend a version of computationalism that is relatively "type-free" in the sense that it permits these objects of belief and other attitudes to be genuinely self-referential or self-involving. I will defend this thesis against one particular objection: the claim that such a type-free, computationalist approach to the psychological attitudes is untenable because it leads to theories afflicted by versions of the liar paradox. My defense against this objection will be twofold: I will argue that the abandonment of computationalism is neither sufficient nor necessary for averting liar-like paradoxes.

Second, I will make a case for thinking that an understanding of liar-like paradoxes is crucial to those branches of social science (like economics, game theory, public-choice and social-contract political theory, organization theory, and Gricean linguistics) that employ some form of the *rational agent model*. A notion that plays an important role in many applications of this model is that of common knowledge, or *mutual belief*. I claim that a liar-like paradox will emerge in any adequate theory of this notion that is sensitive to issues of computational complexity. Moreover, I argue that solving certain puzzles involving the notion of *reputation* depends on recognizing the role that liar-like paradoxes play in generating these puzzles. Finally, I conclude by speculating that liar-like paradoxes will play a crucial role in effecting the transition from the rational agent model to an understanding of society in terms of institutions, rules, and practices.

I argue in Chapter 1 that doxic paradoxes (liar-like paradoxes involving the notion of *rational belief*) can be formulated without relying on objects of belief that are self-referential or self-involving.

Even in an intensional logic using only modality-like operators (which identify the objects of belief with sets of possible worlds), it is possible to show that very plausible principles of rational belief come into conflict. This indicates that avoiding the liar-like paradoxes that afflict type-free computational theories of belief is not a sufficient motive for rejecting computationalism, since paradoxes afflict noncomputationalist accounts as well.

In Chapter 2, I show that the doxic paradoxes isolated in Chapter 1 are at the root of a family of puzzles in contemporary game theory. These puzzles concern the possibility of building or sustaining a tit-for-tat reputation in finitely repeated games, such as Selten's chain-store paradox. I criticize several recent attempts to solve these puzzles, including Sorensen's theory of "blindspots."

In Chapter 3, I argue that a paradox-generating epistemic logic (the logic of knowledge) can be extracted from the practice of contemporary metamathematics (the mathematical study of proofs and other formal methods in mathematics itself). Using the techniques of standard modal logic, I show that the liar paradox, the paradox of the knower, and a variety of related doxic paradoxes can be seen as special cases of a general phenomenon.

In Chapter 4, I develop a representational, computational account of the phenomenon of common belief, a notion that plays a crucial role in game theory and in linguistics. I demonstrate that an adequate theory of mutual belief that takes computational limitations into account will be afflicted with the sort of doxic paradoxes isolated in Chapters 1 through 3.

Part II takes up the question of solutions to these paradoxes. I criticize several context-insensitive solutions to the liar paradox in Chapter 5, including truth-value gap theories, oscillating extensions (Gupta and Herzberger), and recent work by Terence Parsons and Solomon Feferman. In Chapter 6, I compare three context-sensitive theories: those of Tyler Burge, Jon Barwise and John Etchemendy, and Haim Gaifman. I demonstrate that all three are special cases of a more general theory, and I propose certain specific revisions in Gaifman's algorithm for assigning indices to tokens. Finally, in Chapter 7, I adapt this algorithm to the case of the doxic paradoxes.

I presuppose some knowledge of first-order logic and elementary probability theory throughout the book. Very little else is needed for reading most of it. Although Chapter 2 includes some discussion of recent game-theoretic literature, I have tried to make it accessible to the non-game-theorist. Chapter 3 reviews some technical results in metamathematics and contains some comparisons with modal logic but should not require any special expertise in either area. Chapter 5 should probably be skipped by someone who is unfamiliar with recent work on the liar paradox. Chapters 6 and 7 contain several rather technical definitions that can be skipped, but both also contain some quite informal discussion of the nature and relevance of the context-sensitive solutions to the paradoxes.

Chapter 1 appeared as "Doxastic Paradox without Self-Reference" in the *Australasian Journal of Philosophy* 68 (1990): 168–77. Chapter 2 appeared as "A Representational Account of Mutual Belief" in *Synthese* 81 (1989): 21-45. A version of Chapter 6 appeared as "Three Indexical Solutions to the Liar Paradox" in *Situation Theory and Its Applications,* Vol. 1, edited by Robin Cooper, Kuniaki Mukai, and John Perry (Center for the Study of Language and Information, Stanford, Calif., 1990); Part of Chapter 7 appeared as "Doxic Paradox: A Situational Approach" in *Situation Theory and Its Applications*, Vol. 3, edited by J. Barwise, J. M. Gawron, G. Plotkin, and S. Tutiya (CSLI, Stanford, Calif., 1991). I thank the editors of these journals and CSLI for permission to reprint this material here.

I thank my teacher, Tyler Burge, who supervised and guided much of the research appearing here. I also thank David Charles and Robert M. Adams, both of whom helped greatly when my ideas were in the seminal stage. In addition, I thank my colleagues at Texas, especially Dan Bonevac, Nicholas Asher, and Bob Causey, who provided indispensable feedback and suggestions. I especially thank my editor, Brian Skyrms, for all of his help and encouragement, as well as his very valuable criticisms and suggestions. Much of the work was completed with the support of a National Science Foundation grant to the Center for Cognitive Science at the University of Texas (IRI-8719064) and a Summer Research Assignment from the University Research Institute of the University of Texas at Austin. Their help is gratefully acknowledged. Finally, I thank my parents, Bruce and Margaret Koons, for all their support and faith in me over many years, and my wife Debbie, without whom nothing I do would be possible.

Introduction

The following is adapted from an example of Haim Gaifman's:[1]

Rowena makes the following offer to Columna: Columna may have either box A (which is empty) or box B (which contains $100), but not both. Rowena also makes the following promise to Columna: if Columna makes an irrational choice in response to the first offer, Rowena will give her a bonus of $1,000. Let us assume that both are ideal reasoners and that Rowena always keeps her promises, and that both of these facts are common knowledge between Rowena and Columna.

How should Columna respond to this situation? If we suppose that taking box A would be irrational, then doing so would yield Columna $900 more than taking box B, which makes taking A the rational thing to do. If, alternatively, we suppose that taking box A would not be irrational, than taking box A would yield at least $100 less than taking box B, so taking box A would be irrational after all. Taking box A is irrational for Columna if and only if it is not irrational.

There is an obvious analogy between this situation and that of the liar paradox. In the liar paradox, we have a sentence that says of itself, 'I am not true.' Such a sentence is true if it is not true (since that is what it says), and it is false, and therefore not true, if it is true (since that is what it denies). Tarski (1956) demonstrated that this ancient puzzle constitutes a genuine antinomy by showing that any theory that implies every instance of an intuitively very plausible schema, convention T, is logically inconsistent. Convention T is simply the requirement that, for every sentence *s* of the language, our semantic theory should entail the claim that the sentence *s* is true if and only if φ (where '*s*' is a name of the sentence 'φ'). For example, where the sentence is 'Snow is white', our semantical theory should imply that 'Snow is white' is true if and only if snow is white.

In order to demonstrate that Gaifman's puzzle also constitutes an antinomy, I must produce intuitively plausible principles concerning

[1]Gaifman (1983), pp. 150–2.

the notion of rationality that force us into inconsistency, just as Tarski produced the intuitively plausible convention T concerning truth. Moreover, these principles should be the ones we are implicitly appealing to the informal reasoning that led to a contradiction earlier. In this book, I will produce such principles, and I will sketch out one way of resolving the antinomy, applying to this case some work on the liar paradox by Charles Parsons[2] and Tyler Burge.[3] Like other antinomies, there is no ordinary, nontechnical solution to this problem. My solution will involve a fairly radical reconstrual of the semantics of the language of justification.

THE SCOPE OF THE PARADOX

Is the Gaifman rationality paradox nothing more than a very artificial and contrived example, of no interest beyond the relatively narrow concerns of the theory of logical antinomies? No. Very close analogues of Gaifman's paradoxical situation recur in a number of heretofore unsolved puzzles in contemporary game theory and game-theoretic economics, as I will demonstrate in Chapter 2. Thus, the Gaifman paradox provides a simplified model by means of which the essential features of these puzzles can be illumined.

I will refer briefly here to three such game-theoretic puzzles: Selten's "chain-store paradox,"[4] the problem of the finite series of "Prisoner's Dilemma" games,[5] and the controversy over the game-theoretic justifiability of deterrent punishment by known act-utilitarians.[6] Selten's chain-store paradox arose from the attempt by game-theoretic economists to analyze and evaluate the rationality of predatory behavior by monopolists. I shall discuss the chain-store paradox in detail in Chapter 2.

The rationality of a strategy of punishment and reward has been discussed in the context of a finite series of Prisoner's Dilemma games by Luce and Raiffa and by Russell Hardin, among others.[7] In the Prisoner's Dilemma game, two guilty prisoners are being separately interrogated. Each faces a choice: either to confess or to hold out. Each

[2] C. Parsons (1974a).
[3] Burge (1979).
[4] Selten (1978).
[5] Luce and Raiffa (1957), pp. 100–2; Hardin (1982), pp. 145–50.
[6] Hodgson (1967), pp. 38–50, 86–8; Regan (1980), pp. 69–80.
[7] Luce and Raiffa (1957); Hardin (1982).

has the following preferences: the best outcome is when one confesses and the other holds out; the second best is when both hold out; the next best is when both confess, and the worst outcome is when one holds out and the other confesses. In a single, isolated Prisoner's Dilemma, it is in one's own interest to confess, whatever the other does. In a long series of games between two players, the issue arises of whether it is rational to try to cooperate by holding out as long as the other holds out (a policy of tit-for-tat). This policy is simply the inverse of deterrence: instead of trying to deter hurtful behavior by punishing hurtful behavior with hurtful behavior, one tries to induce helpful but costly acts by rewarding those acts with helpful but costly acts toward the other. Once again, it turns out that it is rational to be helpful in the first game of such a series if and only if it is not rational to do so.[8]

Finally, the same issue arises in the controversy between Hodgson and Donald Regan concerning whether it is justifiable for an act-utilitarian to punish criminals, given that it is common knowledge in the community that he is a rational act-utilitarian. For a utilitarian, each act of punishment is costly, since even the pain of the guilty subtracts from total utility. Thus, each act of punishment, considered in isolation, is irrational. It is justifiable if and only if it deters potential criminals from commiting future crimes. Assuming again that it is common knowledge that there is some specific, finite number of opportunities for crime, it turns out that such punishment deters crime if and only if it is not rational to think that it does, and so it is rational for an act-utilitarian to punish if and only if it is not rational for him to do so.

In order to understand the essential features of all these examples, it is expedient to examine the simplest one, Gaifman's thought experiment, which I have adapted as a story about *Row*ena and *Column*a. In order to discover the plausible but inconsistent axioms and axiom schemata that underlie our intuitive reasoning about the situation, we must first become quite clear about the meanings of the crucial expressions that appear in the story. When we say that "Columna's taking box A would be rational," we mean that it is justifiable for Columna to think that taking box A is optimal (has maximal expected

[8] Empirical psychological research (e.g., Rapoport and Chammah (1965) indicates that rational players do in fact play tit-for-tat in the beginning of long series of Prisoner's Dilemma games. I am concerned primarily, however, not with the fact of the matter concerning whether tit-for-tat is rational, but rather with the justification of the tit-for-tat policy.

utility), given Columna's total epistemic situation, that is, given the total evidence or data available to Columna in the actual situation.

What, then, do we mean by its being "justifiable" for Columna to think something, given her epistemic situation? Roughly, we mean that the evidence implying the thought in question is stronger than any evidence inconsistent with the thought. In order to make this rough idea precise, we need to develop a theory of how the rational thinker copes with a set of data that may contain unreliable information and may, therefore, be internally inconsistent.[9] Logical deduction alone is not enough, since deduction reveals the implications of a set of assumptions and informs us when that set is inconsistent: it does not tell us what to do after we have discovered that the data set we have been using is inconsistent. (Assuming the logic is classical, it "tells" us to deduce everything from such an inconsistent set, but that is not in practice the reasonable response.)

The notion of 'rational justifiability' dealt with in this book is a rather special one and must be distinguished from a number of other concepts that may be expressed by the same form of words. I am interested here in a notion of 'rationality' that is a generalization of the model of *rational economic man* (or rational political man, etc.) as it occurs in economics and related social sciences. The primary use of such a theory or model of rationality is that of predicting the choices and behavior of agents, given information about the agents' available data and values, goals, desires, and so on.

A certain degree of idealization is essential to such a theory, the assumption being that the effects of mistakes and biases can be dealt with by simply adding the relevant supplementary theories. At the same time, theoretical progress in this area consists in eliminating the unnecessary idealization of agents. A natural progression can be seen here from Ricardo's assumption of unqualified omniscience to the merely logical and mathematical omniscience assumed by the rational expectationists and finally to the resource-bounded rationality of Herbert Simon's theory. The development of a theory of rational belief in Part I of this book parallels this progression, culminating in a resource-bounded account in Chapter 4.[10]

[9] Compare the recent work of Rescher (1976) on "plausibilistic reasoning."

[10] This sort of rationality should be clearly distinguished from the juridical notion of rational justification discussed by such epistemologists as Gettier and Chisholm. Such a juridical

As ideal thinkers, we must assign to the various sources of purported information on which we are relying some degree of apparent reliability, that is, a degree of cognitive tenacity in the face of conflicting data. This degree of reliability cannot be identified with degree of probability, since it does not in general satisfy anything like the axioms of the probability calculus, nor does it have anything much to do with betting ratios. Application of the probability calculus to an individual's judgments presupposes that the individual is "logically omniscient," that is, that the sum of the probabilities of two inconsistent propositions never exceeds 1. Degrees of reliability of data have to do with an earlier, predeductive aspect of ratiocination. We want to consider cases in which two inconsistent sentences both have a very high initial plausibility or apparent reliability, which is possible if their mutual inconsistency is not immediately apparent. When a data set is revealed through logical analysis to be inconsistent or otherwise dissonant, the rational reasoner rejects the elements of the set with the lowest degree of reliability until consistency and coherency are restored.

A reasoner's epistemic situation can simply be identified with the set of sentences that are found by the reasoner to be initially plausible, together with an assignment of a degree of apparent reliability or cognitive tenacity to each such sentence. Ideally, one should accept everything that follows logically from the epistemically strongest, logically consistent subset of one's data. (The "epistemically strongest" such subset is, roughly, the one that preserves the most sentences with the greatest degree of apparent reliability.)

We are finally in a position to explicate the principles underlying Gaifman's paradox. In order to simplify this problem, I will assume that the objects of justifiable acceptance or belief can be identified, for our purposes, with sentences of some formal language that includes the language of arithmetic and a primitive predicate of sentences '$J(x)$' representing the justifiability of accepting sentence (whose code is) x. With such machinery, we can dispense with the details of the Rowena–

notion of justification may be needed in giving an account of when belief (even the belief of a cognitively idealized agent) counts as *knowledge*. It may also be needed by a theory of the ethics of belief, e.g. giving an analysis of the process of defending one's cognitive performances as having satisfied various epistemic duties. I do not wish to denigrate the importance of such research: in fact, I think that a complete theory of rational belief will need to borrow from such research when it gives an account of forming rational beliefs *about* one's own or another's knowledge. Nonetheless, these are two quite distinct sorts of rational justification.

Columna story, since we can, using diagonalization, construct a sentence σ that is provably equivalent (in arithmetic) with the sentence stating that σ is not ultimately justifiable in Columna's epistemic situation (identified with a set of weighted data sentences). Such a sentence will, in effect, say of itself that it is not justifiable in that situation.

As the first principle of justifiability, it is clear that the set of ultimately justifiable sentences, relative to any epistemic situation, is closed under deductive consequence: if a sentence is ultimately justifiable and logically implies a second sentence, then the second sentence is also ultimately justifiable (it will be accepted at some stage of the process just sketched). Let us call this the principle of deductive closure.

The so-called lottery paradox, the paradox of the preface, and similar problems have led some to doubt the principle of deductive closure for justified beliefs.[11] In particular, those who think that the black-and-white accept–reject dichotomy should always be replaced by degrees of assent (subjective probabilities) will be suspicious of this principle.

Nonetheless, the paradox of reflexive reasoning is independent of these issues. First of all, the beliefs to which this principle are to apply are theorems of arithmetic and of epistemic logic. Uncertainty about empirical facts is irrelevant. Typically, mathematical axioms are assigned a probability of 1, so there is no problem about requiring deductive closure. Second, even if we assign a subjective probability of less than 1 to the axioms of arithmetic and of epistemic logic, it is still possible to construct a version of the paradox, replacing the concept of justified acceptance with that of justified degree of belief (rational probability) and replacing the principle with an unexceptionable principle concerning the consistency of rational probabilities (see Section 1.3).

Second, we can assume that all theorems of arithmetic are justifiable (the "justifiability of arithmetic"). This principle enables us to claim that the crucial biconditional – 'σ' is not justifiable if and only if σ – is justifiable in Columna's situation. (The point of the original story was to produce such a sentence: 'taking box A is optimal' is not justifiable if and only if taking box A is optimal.)

Third, we implicitly assumed that anything that we can prove, using general epistemological principles such as these, are among the things that it is justifiable for Columna to accept. The third principle, then, is the rule of inference, which permits us to infer that anything that is provable in the system of epistemic logic we are constructing is jus-

[11] Kyburg (1970).

tifiable, relative to any epistemic situation (a rule of necessitation).

The fourth and last principle is the one that is most difficult to extract from our informal reasoning about Rowena and Columna. As a first attempt, we could produce an inconsistent logic by adding the principle of iteration: If something is justifiable in a given epistemic situation, then it is justifiable in that same situation to think that it is justifiable. Unfortunately, this principle is not very plausible in light of the explication of ultimate justifiability constructed earlier (see Chapter 4 for a fuller discussion of this point).

There is, however, an epistemological principle that is, in the presence of the other assumptions, sufficient for deriving a contradiction and for which there is strong intuitive support. I will call it the principle of negative noniteration: if something is justifiable (in a given situation), then it is not justifiable (in that situation) to think that it is not justifiable. The contrapositive of this principle is perhaps more perspicuous: if it is justifiable to think that something is not justifiable, then it really is not justifiable.

This insight can easily be incorporated into the picture of plausibilistic reasoning already sketched. The principle of negative noniteration represents the fact that there is a kind of cognitive dissonance, comparable to but distinct from logical inconsistency, in holding both *p* and that one is not justifiable in holding *p*. At each stage of the process of logical analysis, at least one of *p* and '*p* is not justifiable' will not be tentatively believed at that stage. Therefore, it is impossible for both of them to be ultimately accepted by an ideal reasoner, since if they were both ultimately accepted there would be a stage in the process after which both were accepted continuously by the ideal reasoner, which as we have seen is impossible.

The inconsistency of these four principles can be shown as follows. First, assume (for a reductio) that 'σ' is justifiable. By the justifiability of arithmetic, we know that the conditional

'If σ, then 'σ' is not justifiable'

is justifiable, and by deductive closure it follows that ''σ' is not justifiable' is justifiable. From this, by negative noniteration, it follows that 'σ' is not justifiable, contradicting our original assumption. So 'σ' is not justifiable.

This last conclusion was reached on the basis of three general epistemological principles. By necessitation, we know that this conclusion must itself be justifiable in the relevant epistemic situation:

That is, ''σ' is not justifiable' is justifiable. As the argument makes clear, the rule of inference necessitation is stronger than we need. We could use instead an axiom schema to the effect that any instance of the principles of deductive closure, the justifiability of arithmetic, or negative noniteration is justifiable in every epistemic situation. By the justifiability of arithmetic, we know that the conditional

'If 'σ' is not justifiable, then σ'

is justifiable (since it's provable in arithmetic). By deductive closure, it follows that 'σ' itself is justifiable after all. Thus, we are forced into contradicting ourselves. This paradox is closely related to the "paradox of the knower" of Kaplan and Montague (which will be discussed in Chapter 3).[12]

THE SIGNIFICANCE OF THE PARADOX

The immediate significance of this paradox is threefold. First, any attempt to construct a formal logic of justification and belief (a project of current interest among researchers in artificial intelligence and cognitive science, as well as philosophers) must take this (and certain other related paradoxes) into account, just as any set theorist must take into account Russell's paradox and any truth-theoretic semanticist must take into account the paradox of the liar. The discovery of paradoxes is one of the most important tasks of the philosopher, since through paradoxes we become aware of inadequacies in our naive conception of the relevant concept, be it that of sets, truth, or justification.

A genuine paradox, in the sense in which the liar paradox and Russell's demonstration of the inconsistency of naive abstraction are paradoxes, is more than a merely surprising result. A paradox is an inconsistency among nearly unrevisable principles that can be resolved only by recognizing some essential limitation of thought or language. The liar paradox shows that no sufficiently powerful language can be semantically closed and that, if propositions (objects of thought) possess sentence-like structure, then there can be no unitary, nonrelativized concept of truth that applies to all propositions. Similarly, the doxic paradoxes demonstrate that there can be no such concept of rational acceptability that applies to all propositions.

Second, the clear, explicit formulation of the paradox, together with the realization that it is a liar-like logical antinomy, illuminates the study of several heretofore unrelated problems and puzzles in game

[12] Kaplan and Montague (1960).

theory, moral and social philosophy, and economics. As we have seen, the structure of the paradox of reflexive reasoning recurs in such problems as the rationality of cooperation in iterated Prisoner's Dilemma games, the effectiveness of deterrence by known act-utilitarians, and the rationality of predatory behavior by monopolists. In the absence of the discovery of the paradox, each of these problems would have been handled separately and in an unavoidably ad hoc fashion. Such isolated treatment of each problem could lead to distortions of the various fields involved, due to generalizations based on too narrow a range of cases. (This implication is discussed further in Chapters 2 and 7.)

Finally, the paradox of reflexive reasoning sheds light on the general phenomenon of paradoxes or logical antinomies. Discovering a new member of the family of vicious-circle paradoxes is significant, because it enables us to test various generalizations about paradoxicality that were made on the basis of Russell's paradox and the liar paradox alone. In fact, the doxic paradox provides strong reasons for preferring some proposed solutions of the liar paradox to others. In Chapters 5 and 6, I show that context-insensitive solutions do not transfer well to doxic paradox, while context-sensitive ones do.

In the book's conclusion, I discuss some more far reaching implications of my results. First, I conclude that a materialist theory of the mind is compatible with a fully adequate resolution of the logical antinomies. Second, I indicate the implications of this model for the selection of the correct solution concept for noncooperative game theory. Finally, I suggest that the existence of rules and rule following, and, therefore, of institutions and practices, is to be explained in terms of the "cognitive blindspots" that these paradoxes generate. This has significance for ethics as well, specifically, by demonstrating the compatibility of deontic (rule-based) ethics with the rational agent model of decision theory.

PART I

Paradoxes

1

Doxic paradoxes without self-reference

1.1 PARADOX IN OPERATOR LOGIC

Both Richard Montague[1] and Richmond Thomason[2] have taken their discoveries of liar-like paradoxes in certain epistemic and doxic logics as a compelling reason for representing such notions only in languages in which no pernicious self-reference is possible. This can be achieved by representing the relevant epistemic or doxic notion by means of a sentential operator, rather than as a predicate of sentences (or of other entities with syntactic, sentence-like structure).

If it is possible to construct self-referential propositions (objects of evaluation, things that can be true or be believed), then we must consider such paradoxical sentences as 'This sentence is not true', 'This sentence is not knowable', or 'This sentence is not rationally credible'. A sentence that asserts, in effect, that it is not true is called a "liar," the traditional name of the paradox of Epimenides. If we assume that the liar is not, then it is not true, since that is what it asserts. But if we try to conclude that the liar is not true, then we seem to be forced to admit that it is true after all, since its nontruth is exactly what it asserts. Trying to evaluate the liar sentence forces us to contradict ourselves. The intensionalist seeks to avoid this contradiction by banishing self-referential objects from the domain of evaluation.

Nicholas Asher and Hans Kamp,[3] as well as Donald Perlis,[4] have shown that this strategy (called the "intensionalist" approach) alone is not enough to block the construction of paradoxes. If the language contains a binary predicate representing the relation between sentences and the propositions they express (Asher and Kamp), or if it contains a substitution operator Sub (P, Q, A) that is provably equivalent to the

[1] Montague (1963).
[2] Thomason (1980).
[3] Asher and Kamp (1986).
[4] Perlis (1987).

result of substituting the wff Q for all but the last occurrence of wff A in wff P (Perlis), then doxic paradoxes can be constructed in an intensionalist logic. Nonetheless, the intensionalist can reasonably respond that banning such expressions is a small price to pay for the avoidance of inconsistency.

If, however, it can be shown that versions of the doxic paradoxes exist that do not depend in any way on pernicious self-reference, the whole point of the intensionalist strategy will be undermined. The paradoxes will then have to be avoided or made innocuous in some other way, and they will no longer provide any reason for abandoning the syntactic or representational approach to the representation of the objects of belief. This is precisely the task I propose to take on in this chapter.

I will construct a version of Thomason's paradox of ideal or rationally justifiable belief by means of modal logic rather than by means of self-reference. In this version, the crucial expression 'is rationally justifiable' will be a statement operator rather than a sentential predicate. Thus, the semantics of the resulting formal language can represent the objects of justification (the propositions) as sets of possible worlds (as in Kripke semantics for modal logics) rather than as sentences of the language itself. In such a modal logic, it is impossible to construct a self-referential statement that is provably equivalent with a statement saying that the original statement is not justifiable.

We can nonetheless generate a paradox if it is plausible that there is some epistemic situation and some sentence 'p' such that the proposition expressed by the biconditional '$(p \leftrightarrow \neg Jp)$' is justifiable in that situation and the proposition that the biconditional proposition is justifiable is also justifiable. Without Gödelian self-reference, we cannot claim that any such biconditional is provable in Peano arithmetic, but the paradoxicality of the doxic paradoxes did not depend on that fact. It depended only on two facts: that the biconditional is justifiable and that the claim that the biconditional is justifiable is also justifiable. If we can show that it is very plausible to think that in some situations these two conditions hold with respect to sentences that are not self-referential, then such situations will constitute doxic paradoxes in intensional logic.

Thus, to construct the paradox of justifiable belief in modal operator logic, it suffices to show that in some situations and for some proposition p the following two claims are true, where 'J' is a statement operator representing the rational justifiability of a statement in some specified "epistemic situation":

(A1) $J(p \leftrightarrow \neg Jp)$,

(A2) $JJ(p \leftrightarrow \neg Jp)$.

Given these two assumptions, we can derive a contradiction within an epistemic logic consisting of the following doxic axiom schemata:

(J1) $J \neg J\varphi \rightarrow \neg J\varphi$,

(J2) $J\varphi$, where φ is a logical axiom,

(J3) $J(\varphi \rightarrow \psi) \rightarrow (J\varphi \rightarrow J\psi)$,

(J4) $J\varphi$, where φ is an instance of (J1)–(J3).

A contradiction can be derived as follows:

(1) $J(p \leftrightarrow \neg Jp)$,	(A1)
(2) $Jp \leftrightarrow J \neg Jp$,	(1), (J3)
(3) $J \neg Jp \rightarrow \neg Jp$,	(J1)
(4) $\neg Jp$,	(2), (3)
(5) $J \neg Jp$.	(A2), (J4), (J2), (J3) (see lines (1)–(4))

Given the presence of (J2) and (J3) schema (J4) could be replaced by a necessitation rule: if φ follows (in the doxic logic consisting of (J1)–(J3) from a set of premises each member of which is justifiable, then infer '$J\varphi$'. Therefore, since '$\neg Jp$' follows from (A1) in that logic (as shown by lines (1)–(4)) and since (A1) is justifiable (which is just what (A2) says), this necessitation rule would allow us to infer line (5).

(6) Jp.	(2), (5)

The schemata (J1) through (J4) are modifications of some of the schemata discussed by Montague and Thomason. They are substantially weaker than Montague's in that schema (J1) is a special case of the analogue of Montague's schema (i), '$J\varphi \rightarrow \varphi$'. This corresponds to the fact that these schemata are meant to capture the properties of justifiability of belief, as opposed to knowledge. At the same time, I suggest that (J1) through (J4) are a substantial improvement over the schemata discussed by Thomason as characterizing ideal belief. In particular, schema (J1) is much more plausible as a principle of ideal or rational belief than are the principles of Thomason's, which I omit: '$J\varphi \rightarrow JJ\varphi$' and '$J(J\varphi \rightarrow \varphi)$'.

In an article on the surprise quiz paradox, Doris Olin discussed the principle I call (J2). She argued:

It can never be reasonable to believe a proposition of the form '*p* and I am not now justified in believing *p*'. For if a person A is justified in believing a proposition, then he is not (epistemically) blameworthy for believing it. But if A is justified in believing that he is not justified in believing *p*, then he would be at fault in believing *p*. Hence, if A is justified in believing that he is not justified in believing *p*, then he is not justified in believing *p*.[5]

If one has an overwhelmingly good reason for believing that acceptance of *p* is not ultimately justifiable in one's present epistemic situation, then that fact must undermine any reasons one has for accepting *p* itself. To believe that *p* is not ultimately justifiable in one's present epistemic situation is to believe that it is inconsistent or otherwise not cotenable with data that are, by one's own lights, weightier than the data (if any) that support or seems to support *p*. This realization should undermine one's confidence in any data supporting *p*. The occurrence of this principle establishes an interesting connection between the paradox of reflexive reasoning and both Moore's paradox and the surprise quiz or hangman paradox.[6]

The other axiom schemata are equally unexceptionable. (J2) and (J3) simply ensure that the property of being rationally justifiable in a situation is closed under logical entailment. If you are persuaded by what Henry Kyburg has said against "conjunctivitis,"[7] then read '$J\varphi$' as saying that φ belongs to the corpus of subjectively certain propositions in the relevant situation. Even Kyburg admits that the conjunction of two subjectively certain propositions is itself subjectively certain.

Schema (J4) guarantees that certain obviously true axioms of doxic logic are rationally justifiable in the situation under consideration. There can be little doubt that if schemata (J1) through (J3) are rationally defensible, there must be a large and variegated class of epistemic situations in which every instance of these schemata is rationally justifiable.

It remains to be shown that there are situations in which assumptions (A1) and (A2) are intuitively true for some proposition *p*. In order to demonstrate this, I will appeal to two epistemological principles:

(I) When the evidence in some epistemic situation for every member of some consistent set *S* is stronger than the evidence for any

[5] Olin (1983).
[6] Ibid.; Wright and Sudbury (1977).
[7] Kyburg (1970).

statement inconsistent with S, then each proposition expressed by a member of S is justifiable in that situation.

(II) There are epistemic situations in which statements of the following forms are mutually consistent and are each supported by evidence stronger than any evidence supporting any statement inconsistent with their conjunction:

$$p \leftrightarrow \neg Jp,$$
$$J(p \leftrightarrow \neg Jp).$$

These two principles together imply (A1) and (A2), since principle (II) simply states that the two statements above meet all the conditions of principle (I) for justifiability. Thus, both '$p \leftrightarrow \neg Jp$' and '$J(p \leftrightarrow \neg Jp)$' are justifiable, which is exactly what (A1) and (A2) claim. I will first discuss the justification of principle (II) by constructing several scenarios exhibiting the relevant features.

1.2 PARADOXICAL SITUATIONS

The first scenario is adapted from a Gedankenexperiment suggested by Gideon Schwartz.[8] Rowena makes the following offer to Columna: Columna may have either box A (which is empty) or box B (which contains \$100), but not both. Rowena also makes the following promise to Columna: if Columna makes an irrational choice in response to the first offer, Rowena will give her a bonus of \$1,000. Let us assume that they are both ideal reasoners and that Rowena always keeps her promises, and that both of these facts are common knowledge between Rowena and Columna. For our purposes, we can define 'making an irrational choice' as choosing an action such that it is not justifiable in one's epistemic situation to think that one is acting optimally.

How should Columna respond to this situation? If we suppose that taking box A would be irrational, then doing so would yield Columna \$900 more than taking box B, which makes taking A the rational thing to do. If, alternatively, we suppose that taking box A would not be irrational, than taking box A would yield at least \$100 less than taking box B, so taking box A would be irrational after all. Taking box A is irrational for Columna if and only if it is not irrational.

There seems to be no reason why Columna cannot be apprised of the situation. If she is, then she has maximal evidence in support of a proposition that could be represented by a sentence of the form '$(p \leftrightarrow \neg Jp)$', where '$p$' represents the proposition that Columna's

[8] In Gaifman (1983), pp. 150–1.

taking box A is her optimal action, and where 'J' is relativized to Columna's epistemic situation (which is essentially the same as our own). If we assume that Columna has maximally strong evidence for the epistemic principle (I) (perhaps it counts as maximally strong evidence for itself, if it is self-evident), then Columna, by reflecting on the fact that she has maximally strong evidence for the proposition expressed by '$(p \leftrightarrow \neg Jp)$' and that the biconditional is obviously consistent, can also come to have maximally strong evidence for the proposition $J(p \leftrightarrow \neg Jp)$. Thus, the described situation is one of the sort required by principle (II).

As another example, suppose 'J' is relativized to my actual epistemic situation. Let 'p' represent the proposition that I am 'rationally humble' (i.e., I would still be humble even if I believed everything that is rationally justifiable in my present situation). Let us suppose that we understand the virtue of humility in such a way that, given my available data, I am rationally humble if and only if it is not rationally justifiable for me to accept that I am rationally humble. (I am supposing that anyone who believes of himself that he possesses such an important virtue as humility lacks humility.) Thus, we have a true and well-supported claim of the form '$(\neg p \leftrightarrow Jp)$' and another scenario satisfying the conditions of principle (II).

I will now turn to principle (I). I think that this is a very plausible principle of epistemology. If I have very good evidence for a claim, and no evidence (or much weaker evidence) against it, then ideally I should accept it.

Nonetheless, it could be objected that I am simply making inconsistent demands on the notion of ultimate justifiability, since I am simultaneously claiming that schema (J1) is also a plausible epistemological principle:

(J1) $J\neg J\varphi \rightarrow \neg J\varphi$.

Schema (J1) seems to demand that exceptions be made to principle (I): If I am justified in accepting '$\neg J\varphi$', then I cannot simultaneously be justified in accepting φ, even if I have maximally strong evidence for both '$\neg J\varphi$' and φ and despite the fact that the two are logically consistent with one another.

Principle (I) and schema (J1), however, are consistent with one another if we suppose that it is impossible to have evidence simultaneously for both of two claims of the form φ and '$\neg J\varphi$' (where 'J' is relativized to one's own epistemic situation). Evidence for two claims so related is mutually antagonistic: evidence for the second undermines the evidential character of what would otherwise be evidence for the first. Anything that could really count as evidence for a claim of the form '$\neg J\varphi$' must be sufficient to undermine as evidence for φ anything available in that epistemic situation that would otherwise be overwhelming evidence for φ. Conversely, if there is clearly overwhelming evidence for φ available in the situation, reflection on that fact should constitute conclusive evidence against the claim that φ is not ultimately justifiable.

Finally, as an alternative to principles (I) and (II), there is a third epistemological principle to which I can appeal:

(III) If φ is justifiable in situation E and E' differs from E only in having more evidence for φ, then φ is justifiable in E'.

In the Columna–Rowena scenario, we assumed that Columna possesses a very weighty body of apparent evidence for the biconditional: taking the box is optimal if and only if it is not justifiable in situation E to think that taking the box is optimal (where 'E' is some self-referential description of Columna's epistemic situation). Suppose that Nemo is in situation E^*, which differs from E only in having slightly less evidence for this very same biconditional (i.e., the one concerning situation E). Unlike situation E, situation E^* is not self-referential. Consequently, we can derive no contradiction from the supposition that this biconditional is justifiable in E^*. Since the weight of apparent evidence, by hypothesis, in E^* favors the biconditional, we seem to be forced to admit that the biconditional is justifiable in E^*. Then, by principle (III), we are forced to admit that the biconditional is justifiable in E as well, leading to the paradox.

1.3 A PROBABILISTIC SOLUTION?

The doxic paradoxes I have presented so far concern when it is rational to accept a proposition. It might be thought that the generation of the paradox depended on working with the black-and-white dichotomy of accepting–rejecting. One might hope that replacing this dichotomy with a scheme of degrees of belief (represented as conforming to the probability calculus) would dissolve the paradox, especially if we insist that all nonmathematical statements are always believed with a probability some finite distance both from 1 and from 0. In fact, a reexamination of the putatively paradoxical situations from this perspective does not lead to a nonparadoxical solution, if self-reference via syntax is forbidden.

We can replace each of the principles used in generating the paradox of justifiability with the corresponding principles concerning rational probability instead of justifiable acceptability. The following two schemata are consequences of the probability calculus:

(B1) $J(\varphi/\psi) \cdot J(\psi) = (J(\varphi \,\&\, \psi)$,

(B2) $J\varphi + J\neg\varphi = 1$.

'$J\varphi$' is a function operator that, when applied to a statement φ, yields a real number between 0 and 1, inclusive, representing the rational probability of φ in the relevant epistemic situation.

We also need a principle expressing the relationship between second-order and first-order probabilities. I will occasionally refer to (B3) as "Miller's principle," from an article by D.Miller:[9]

(B3) $J(\varphi/J\varphi \geq x) \geq x$.

B3′ is an equivalent formulation of Miller's principle:

(B3′) $J(\varphi/J\varphi \leq x) \leq x$.

We can replace $\geq$ with $>$ in (B3), and $\leq$ with $<$ in (B3′), if $x < 1$ and $>$ 0. In the case of the inequality '$J\varphi > 0$', we can appeal to the closely related principle (B3*):

(B3*) If $J(J\varphi > 0) > 0$, then $J\varphi > 0$.

The claim that (B3) holds whenever the relevant probabilities are defined is simply the generalization of schema (J4): if φ is justified, then that φ is not justified is not justified. If we interpret 'ψ is justified' as 'the rational probability of $\neg\psi$ is zero', then (J4) is simply an instance of (B3*).

Van Fraassen has produced a Dutch book argument in favor of the (B3) principles.[10] The principle has also been endorsed by Haim Gaifman and Brian Skyrms.[11] I will briefly give the Dutch book argument for principle (B3). We can assume that $J(J\varphi \geq x) > 0$, since otherwise the conditional probability is undefined. Suppose for contradiction that this conditional probability is less than x. Then the agent is vulnerable to a Dutch book. He is willing to do simultaneously the following: (i) bet for $J\varphi \geq x$, at some positive odds, (ii) place a conditional bet against φ on the condition that $J\varphi \geq x$ at the odds x. If $J\varphi < x$, then the agent loses the first bet and the second conditional bet is called off. If the agent wins the first bet, then he is willing to bet for φ at the odds x (since, ex hypothesi, $J\varphi \geq x$), that is, he is willing to buy back

[9] Miller (1966).

[10] Van Fraassen (1984).

[11] Gaifman (1986); Skyrms (1986).

his first bet at a net loss. If the proportion between the stakes of the two original bets is chosen correctly by the bookie, the agent is sure to suffer a loss.

Transposing the Columna–Rowena story into probabilistic terms, we must assign for Columna some rational conditional probability corresponding to the two directions of the biconditional: p if and only if $Jp \le \frac{1}{2}$ (where 'p' stands for 'Taking the box is optimal for Columna'). I will take '$J_c\varphi > \frac{1}{2}$' as expressing 'Columna accepts φ' in probabilistic terms. Miller's principle entails

$$J_c(p/J_i p \le \tfrac{1}{2}) \le \tfrac{1}{2},$$
$$J_c(p/J_i p > \tfrac{1}{2}) > \tfrac{1}{2}.$$

where 'i' represents a special mode of presentation: the way in which each thinker is presented to herself as herself. This corresponds to the use of the first-person-singular pronoun in natural language.

Let the lambda abstract '$\lambda x q(x)$' represent the property of being in the sort of epistemological predicament into which we have hypothetically placed Columna. Thus, the description of this predicament entails that

$$\forall y(\lambda x q(x) y \rightarrow [p \text{ iff } J_y p \le \tfrac{1}{2}]).$$

Let us suppose that Columna is aware of this entailment. Consequently, where 'd' is any individual constant,

$$J_c(p/q(d) \,\&\, J_d p \le \tfrac{1}{2}) \approx 1,$$
$$J_c(p/q(d) \,\&\, J_d p > \tfrac{1}{2}) \approx 0.$$

It is clear that it is epistemically possible that some person should be in such a predicament. So for all individual constants 'd' such that 'd' 'i',

$$J_c(q(d)) = \epsilon, \quad \text{for some } \epsilon > 0.$$

Moreover, evidence could be acquired that would confirm that the individual named 'd' is in such a predicament – evidence that a very intelligent and well-informed agent has made the relevant offer to d and that this agent reliably fulfills such offers. Let '$E(d)$' represent such evidence:

$$J_c(E(d)/q(d)) = \beta, \qquad \beta \approx 1,$$
$$J_c(E(d)/\neg q(d)) = \gamma, \qquad \gamma \approx 0.$$

This entails by Bayes's theorem that $J_c(q(d)/E(d)) = (\beta \cdot \epsilon)/[(\beta \cdot \epsilon) + \gamma \cdot (1 - \epsilon)]$. Consequently, if Columna should actually acquire such evidence and should update her probabilities by what is known as "Bayesian conditionalization," her resulting probability function would be such that $J_c(q(d)) = (\beta \cdot \epsilon)/[(\beta \cdot \epsilon) + \gamma(1 - \epsilon)]$, and

$$J_c(p/J_d p \leq \tfrac{1}{2}) \geq (\beta \cdot \epsilon)/[(\beta \cdot \epsilon) + \gamma \cdot (1 - \epsilon)],$$

$$J_c(p/J_d p > 2) < \gamma \cdot (1 - \epsilon)/[(\beta \cdot \epsilon) + \gamma \cdot (1 - \epsilon)].$$

By hypothesis, the first conditional probability is close to 1 (certainly, much greater than ½), and the second is close to 0 (much less than ½).

Now, suppose that 'd' = 'i' that the person about whom Columna gained this evidence is none other than herself (and recognized by Columna to be herself). There are three possibilities:

(1) Columna violates Miller's principle.

(2) Columna has an asymmetric prior probability function such that $J_c(q(i))$ is, for all practical purposes, zero, despite the fact that $J_c(q(d))$ is, for all 'd' ≠ 'i', nonnegligible.

(3) Columna systematically violates Bayesian conditionalization.

I have already alluded to the case for Miller's principle as a condition of rationality. If we embrace possibility (2), we must make a very bizarre and implausible assumption a prerequisite for rationality. Someone whose prior probability function fulfilled possibility (2) would in effect be assuming that he is uniquely and inexplicably exempt from the possibility of finding himself in the sort of predicament I have described, that he enjoys a uniquely charmed existence. The principle of Bayesian conditionalization is based on essentially the same foundation as are the axioms of the classical probability calculus or Miller's principle. David Lewis (as reported by Paul Teller) has constructed a dynamic Dutch book argument for conditionalization.[12]

In grappling with the surprise quiz paradox, Doris Olin[13] and Roy Sorenson have in effect embraced the third possibility, the necessity of deviating from Bayesian conditionalization. Olin concludes that we must give up what she calls epistemological principle P5:

(P5) If A is justified in believing $p_1, \ldots, p_n$, $p_1, \ldots, p_n$ strongly confirm q, A sees this and has no other evidence relevant to q, then A is justified in believing q.

If we take 'A is justified in believing $p_1, \ldots, p_n$' to mean that the joint probability of $p_1, \ldots, p_n$ approaches 1, we take '$p_1, \ldots, p_n$ strongly confirm q' to mean that the conditional probability of q on $p_1, \ldots, p_n$ approaches 1, and finally we take "A is justified in believing q" to mean

[12] Teller (1976), Gärdenførs (1988).
[13] Olin (1983).

the A's posterior probability for q approaches 1, then Olin's (P5) is simply a consequence of updating by Bayesian conditionalization.

Similarly, Sorensen apparently rejects the universality of Bayesian conditionalization by positing the existence of what he calls "consequential blindspots":

Given that a proposition is a consequential blindspot to you, it is possible for you to know the proposition and it is possible for you to know the antecedent. However, it is impossible to know both the consequential blindspot and its antecedent.[14]

If we interpret this definition probabilistically, a consequential blindspot would be a pair of propositions p and q such that, even if (i) initially, the conditional probability $J(p/q)$ is high, and (ii) subsequently, one learns q by observation, and consequently $J(q)$ is 1, and (iii) one learns nothing else relevant to p, nonetheless, the posterior probability of p cannot be high. To assert that such consequential blindspots exist is to insist that the ideal reasoner occasionally violates the principle of Bayesian conditionalization.

The Olin–Sorensen solution, as applied to the Rowena–Columna story, entails the following. Even though Columna recognizes that it is quite possible for someone to be in the predicament as described, and even though she recognizes that the conditional probability of an arbitrary individual d's being in such a predicament conditional on possible evidence $E(d)$ is very high (much greater than $\frac{1}{2}$), nonetheless, were she actually to acquire such evidence, she would never assess the probability of some particular person's actually being in such a predicament as greater than $\frac{1}{2}$. This strikes me as patently unreasonable on Columna's part, and consequently I believe that the Rowena–Columna scenario is paradoxical in the very strong sense of constituting an antinomy based on virtually undeniable principles of rationality.

[14] Sorensen (1988).

2

Doxic paradoxes and reputation effects in iterated games

A Bayesian approach to game theory seeks, as the solution of a game, the rational decision for each agent to make at each decision point. A rational decision is one that maximizes the utility of the agent, given his beliefs, which are themselves rationally generated from the information available to the agent. Therefore, such an approach must rely on a formal theory of rational belief.[1] This suggests the possibility that doxic paradoxes arise in some game-theoretically described situations. In this chapter, I will argue that this possibility is in fact the case. Doxic paradoxes arise in any game in which all of the Nash equilibria involve noncentroid mixed strategies. I will discuss one example of such games: iterated games involving reputation effects.

In Section 2.1, I will discuss the problem about correctly characterizing the rational choices in such iterated games, which Selten labeled the chain-store paradox. In Section 2.2, I will isolate the doxic paradox that arises in such games. By replacing the notion of rational belief with that of rational subjective probabilities, one can avert this paradox by means of probabilistically mixed strategies. In Section 2.3, I argue that solutions involving noncentroid mixed strategies are not in general satisfactory, and in Section 2.4 I show how the doxic paradox can be reinstated if such strategies are ruled out. Section 2.5 contains a comparison of the notion of doxic paradox with Roy Sorensen's notion of doxic blindspot. Unlike my account, Sorensen's leaves the possibility of such blindspots unexplained.

2.1 SELTEN'S PARADOX OF REPUTATION

Game theorists have discovered several scenarios involving the finite repetition of a noncooperative game that give rise to a certain kind of "paradox." These include Selten's chain-store paradox,[2] the problem of the finite series of Prisoner's Dilemma games,[3] and the controversy

[1] See Bacharach (1987), Binmore (1987) and (1988), and Tan and Werlang (1988).
[2] Selten (1978).
[3] Luce and Raiffa (1957), pp. 100–2; Hardin (1982), pp. 145–50.

over the game-theoretic justifiability of deterrent punishment by known act-utilitarians.[4] In each of these cases, a "backward-induction" argument is used to prove that it is futile to try to establish a reputation for cooperative or punitive behavior through appropriate action in the early stages of the game, despite the fact that nearly all agree that it is intuitively "reasonable" to do so.

Selten's chain-store paradox arose from the attempt by game-theoretic economists to analyze and evaluate the rationality of predatory behavior by monopolists. The name derives from a standard example, that of a firm which monopolizes retailing in a region through ownership of a chain of stores. In order to simplify the problem, economists made several unrealistic but innocuous assumptions, in particular that it is *common belief* (the doxic analogue of "common knowledge") that the monopolist faces some fixed number of potential competitors,[5] that each potential competitor has only a single moment of opportunity to enter the retail market, and that these moments occur one at a time at regular intervals.

As each moment of opportunity arrives, the corresponding potential competitor has to decide whether to enter into competition with the monopolist. If the potential competitor does enter the market, the monopolist faces a choice between two alternatives: (i) engage in predatory pricing, driving the competitor out of business, at a great cost to both the competitor and the monopolist, or (ii) reach an accommodation with the competitor (e.g., by buying her out), which yields the competitor a profit and which costs the monopolist less than the first alternative does.

Initially, one might assume that rational monopolists would always choose the second, less costly alternative. Many economists, however, have argued that this view ignores the deterrent effect of predatory behavior on future potential competitors. Predation, although more costly in the short run, would be lucrative in the long run if it dissuaded a sufficient number of potential competitors from entering the market at all.

4 Hodgson (1967), pp. 38–50, 86–8; Regan (1980), pp. 69–80.

5 It might be thought that the assumptions that there are only a finite number of competitors and that this number is common knowledge are extremely fantastic, reducing the value of the example as a model of real-life situations. As a matter of fact, there are real-life cases (such as nuclear strategy) in which the number of possible retaliatory stages is finite and known. Moreover, it is possible to construct closely analogous paradoxes that involve infinite or indefinite series by introducing some uncertainty on the part of the potential competitors as to whether the monopolist has preyed on earlier competitors who entered the market.

Selten demonstrated the following paradoxical result. If we assume that the exact number of potential competitors is a matter of common belief, then it is irrational for the monopolist ever to engage in predatory behavior. Clearly, it would be irrational for the monopolist to prey on the very last potential competitor, should he enter the market, since there are no further competitors to deter. If the last potential competitor is rational, therefore, he will enter the market no matter what the monopolist has done in the past, so long as he still believes that the monopolist is a rational maximizer of his own interest. For this reason, it would be irrational for the monopolist to prey on the next-to-last potential competitor, since he has no hope of deterring the last competitor. This argument can be repeated indefinitely, demonstrating (by backward induction) that it is irrational for the monopolist to prey on any potential competitor.

2.2 DOXIC PARADOX IN GAMES OF REPUTATION

Selten believed that this is paradoxical in the weak sense: a surprising, unexpected result of game theory. I would argue that it is paradoxical in the strong sense: a logical antinomy of rational belief, analogous to the paradox of the liar. To simplify matters, let us suppose that there are only two potential competitors and that, for whatever reason, the first potential competitor does enter the market. Suppose it is true that it would be irrational for the monopolist to prey on the first competitor should she enter the market. Then preying on the first competitor would convince the second potential competitor that the monopolist is not a rational maximizer of his self-interest and therefore that he may prey on the second competitor. If we suppose that under these conditions the second competitor would be deterred from entering the market, then we have a compelling argument for preying on the first competitor's being in the monopolist's best interests. An intelligent monopolist would be aware of this argument, so preying on the first competitor would not be irrational, contrary to our original assumption.

Therefore, preying on the first competitor would not be an irrational thing for the monopolist to do. However, this means that the monopolist's preying on the first competitor would not be inconsistent with the belief that the monopolist is a rational maximizer. Thus, if the monopolist did prey on the first competitor, the second potential competitor would still be able rationally to believe that the monopolist is a rational maximizer who would certainly not prey on the second competitor. Preying on the first competitor would not, therefore, deter the second potential competitor and so would not be in the monopolist's interest. The monopolist is aware of all the facts we used to reach this conclusion, so it would be irrational for the monopolist to prey on the first competitor.

Thus, the monopolist's preying on the first competitor is irrational if and only if it is not irrational. Let us represent the rational belief by player i ($i = m, c$) of proposition p by '$J_i p$' and the subjunctive proposition that, if the monopolist were to prey on the first competitor, the second competitor would stay out by 'K'. As a first approximation, let us suppose that the monopolist believes that $K \leftrightarrow \neg JcJmK$, that is, that the second competitor would be deterred from entering unless he believes that the monopolist believes in K. If the monopolist also believes that the competitor believes 'JmK' if and only if the monopolist will (rationally) believe it, then the monopolist will infer $K \leftrightarrow \neg JmJmK$. As I have argued elsewhere, any proposition of the form $Jm(K \leftrightarrow \neg JmJmK)$ is inconsistent with the axioms and rules of a very plausible theory of rational belief:[6]

(J1) $J \neg J\varphi \rightarrow \neg J\varphi$,

(J2) $J\varphi$, where φ is a logical axiom,

(J3) $J(\varphi \rightarrow \psi) \rightarrow (J\varphi \rightarrow J\psi)$,

(J4) $J\varphi \rightarrow JJ\varphi$,

(J5) From φ, infer $J\varphi$.

The inconsistency can be proved as follows:

(1) $J(K \leftrightarrow \neg JJK)$,	Assumption
(2) JK,	Assumption
(3) $J \neg JJK$,	(1), (2), (J2), (J3) {(1), (2)}
(4) $\neg JJK$,	(3), (J1) {(1), (2)}
(5) $JK \rightarrow \neg JJK$,	{(1)}
(6) $J(K \leftrightarrow \neg JJK) \rightarrow [JK \rightarrow \neg JJK]$,	
(7) $J[J(K \leftrightarrow \neg JJK) \rightarrow [JK \rightarrow \neg JJK]]$,	(6), (J5)
(8) $JJ(K \leftrightarrow \neg JJK)$,	(1), (J4) {(1)}
(9) $J(JK \rightarrow \neg JJK)$,	(7), (8), (J3) {(1)}
(10) JJK,	Assumption
(11) $J \neg JJK$,	(9), (10), (J3) {(1), (10)}
(12) $\neg JJK$,	(11), (J1) {(1)}
(13) $J(K \rightarrow \neg JJK) \rightarrow \neg JJK$,	

[6] See Chapter 1.

(14) $J[J(K \leftrightarrow \neg JJK) \rightarrow \neg JJK]$, (13), (J5)

(15) $J \neg JJK$, (8), (14), (J3) {(1)}

(16) JK, (1), (15), (J2), (J3) {(1)}

(17) JJK, (16), (J4) {(1)}

(18) $\neg J(K \leftrightarrow \neg JJK)$. Reductio, (1), (12), (17)

Philip Reny[7] and Cristina Bicchieri[8] have argued that retaliatory play makes the players' "theory of the game" inconsistent, where a player's "theory of the game" is a set of assumptions about the game tree and about the beliefs and rationality of the other players. If the competitor begins in a state of certainty about the rationality and beliefs of the monopolist, then, given the soundness of Selten's backward induction argument, if the monopolist were to retaliate against the first competitor, then adding this information to the competitor's original stock of beliefs results in inconsistency. Suppose, as Reny suggests, that the competitor would respond to this inconsistency by assuming that the monopolist is irrational (or that the monopolist's payoffs are such as to make retaliation worthwhile even in one-shot interactions). Then, the competitor would in fact be deterred from entering. If the monopolist knew this, then the monopolist could realize that retaliating in the first game is rational after all, despite the backward induction argument! But if retaliating in the first game can be rational after all, how can learning that the monopolist has done so be inconsistent with the competitor's original theory of the game?[9]

Bicchieri attempts to solve this paradox by using the theory of belief revision developed by Isaac Levi and Peter Gärdenførs[10] to constrain the reaction of the second competitor to the monopolist's act of retaliation. Bicchieri points out that the competitor cannot update his beliefs by Bayesian conditionalization, since the prior probability of the monopolist's retaliating was zero (i.e., it was not a "serious possibility"). According to the Levi–Gärdenførs theory of belief revision, the competitor should give up those beliefs that had the least epistemic importance for him. If the theory of the game (including the competitor's beliefs) and the rules of belief revision are initially matters of common belief between the two players, then Bicchieri argues that the competitor should give up his assumption that "the

7 Reny (1988).

8 Bicchieri (1988a, 1988b and, 1989).

9 The same criticism applies to the solution proposed by Pettit and Sugden (1989).

10 Levi (1977) and (1979), Gärdenførs (1978) and (1984).

players always play what they choose to play at all nodes."[11] The competitor should assume that the retaliation was the result of an unintentionally "trembling hand," a failure by the monopolist to carry out his true intentions. The competitor will suppose such errors to be rather rare exceptions, and consequently he will not be deterred from entering. Therefore, the monopolist should not retaliate, and the backward induction argument is apparently vindicated.

But what if the competitor is not initially certain about the monopolist's rationality and/or payoff function? What if the probability that the monopolist is a rational player for whom retaliation is costly is close to but not equal to 1? Then the competitor should, if the monopolist does retaliate, update his belief function by Bayesian conditionalization on the new evidence, and Bicchieri's resort to Levi-style belief revision would not be justified.

Reny and Bicchieri did not consider this possibility because they took the work of Kreps, Milgrom, Roberts, and Wilson[12] as establishing that the backward induction argument does not work once any exogenous source of doubt about the monopolist's rationality or payoffs is introduced. However, it is important to realize that the solution of Kreps et al. depends crucially on the use of *mixed-strategy equilibria* and, in the general case, on *noncentroid* mixed strategies.

In order to explain this point, a brief excursus into some of the technicalities of game theory (specifically "noncooperative" game theory) is necessary. A "pure strategy" is a function that assigns, for a given player, a choice to be made at each of that player's "information sets" (an "information set" for a player being a collection of possible states of the game between which that player is unable to discriminate). A "mixed strategy" is a particular probabilistic mixture of simple or "pure" strategies. A "Nash equilibrium" is an assignment of strategies (pure or mixed) to each of the players in a game that satisfies the following condition: given knowledge of the other players' strategies at the equilibrium, no player can improve her own payoff by choosing a different one than is assigned to her by the equilibrium. In a Nash equilibrium, each player's strategy is a best response (not necessarily the best response) to the other players' strategies (Nash 1951).

The notion of a Nash equilibrium can be illustrated by a very simple game: that of Matching Pennies. Each player chooses to turn his

11 Bicchieri (1988a), p. 392.

12 Kreps, Milgrom, Roberts, and Wilson (1982); Kreps and Wilson (1982).

concealed penny face-up or tails-up. Both pennies are then unveiled. If they match, the first player wins both pennies; if they do not match, the second player wins. If the first player is known to turn his penny face-up consistently, the second player can win consistently by turning his tails-up. Thus, the first player's pure strategy cannot be part of a Nash equilibrium. In fact, the only Nash equilibrium is for both players to choose the mixed strategy ($\frac{1}{2}$, $\frac{1}{2}$), that is, to turn the penny heads-up one-half the time, as determined by some random variable. If the other player is known to be playing this mixed strategy, a given player cannot positively improve his chances of winning by deviating from it.

In a Nash equilibrium, all the random variables that determine the actual results of each player's mixed strategy are independent of one another: it is as if each player privately consults a separate randomizing device when executing a mixed strategy. In a correlated equilibrium, a closely related idea recently developed by Aumann,[13] the random variables need not be independent: the players may correlate or coordinate their mixed strategies by reference to a common randomizing device.

I will define a "mixed-strategy equilibrium" as a Nash or correlated equilibrium in which one or more players play a mixed (impure) strategy. It is an elementary theorem of game theory that, at a mixed-strategy Nash equilibrium, any player playing a mixed strategy is indifferent between any of the pure strategies involved in it, and therefore indifferent also between any two mixed strategies composed of these same pure strategies. A Nash equilibrium contains a "noncentroid mixed strategy" if it contains a mixed strategy in which the player does not play these equally valued pure strategies with equal probabilities.

A correlated equilibrium assigns a probability to each combination of strategies, and thus assigns to each strategy of each player a probabilistic distribution over the strategies of the other players. (For simplicity's sake, I will discuss a two-player game.) The notion of a 'noncentroid mixed strategy' can also be extended to correlated equilibria: we can say that a correlated equilibrium q calls for a noncentroid mixed strategy on the part of player 1 if and only if there are strategies j and k of player 1 such that (i) the equilibrium q assigns distribution p to strategy j, (ii) player 1 is indifferent between responding to p by strategy j and responding to it by strategy k, and (iii) there is a strategy m of player 2 such that equilibrium q assigns different probabilities to the pairs (j, m) and (k, m). In many games, all

[13] Aumann (1987).

correlated equilibria contain noncentroid mixed strategies in this sense. In particular, this is true of the chain-store game. Therefore, the argument to follow against equilibria involving noncentroid mixed strategies applies also to correlated equilibria with this property.

2.3 A CRITIQUE OF MIXED-STRATEGY EQUILIBRIA

It is difficult to justify the use of noncentroid mixed-strategy equilibria in the solution of games. The problem is that, in a mixed-strategy equilibrium, each player having a mixed strategy is in a state of complete indifference between any of the pure strategies involved in her equilibrium strategy and between any random distribution over those pure strategies. Although she has no reason to prefer any such strategy to her equilibrium strategy, she also has no reason to select the equilibrium strategy from among the infinitely many indifferently valued strategies available. This fact is often expressed by calling mixed-strategy equilibria "weak equilibria." However, in most cases, unless the other players can confidently expect the player whose equilibrium strategy is mixed to choose exactly the right probabilistic mixture of pure strategies, the game will move out of equilibrium.

There are certain special cases in which such mixed-strategy equilibria do make sense. First, some mixed strategies are "centroid strategies," strategies in which every pure strategy involved is assigned equal probability. It makes sense to expect that a player who is perfectly indifferent between several possible actions will have an equal probability of performing any one of them. Most mixed-strategy equilibria, however, have noncentroid mixed strategies.

Another case in which a mixed strategy makes sense is one in which deliberate randomization according to the correct probability distribution can be motivated as the rational thing for the player to do. One such case is that of a constant-sum game in which the only equilibrium strategy (in this case, the maximin strategy) available to a player is a mixed strategy. In constant-sum games, if another player can predict that you will deviate from the equilibrium in a certain way, he may be able to exploit that knowledge to his gain and your loss. In order to ensure that the other players, no matter how much they know about the idiosyncrasies of your own psychology, cannot know anything more precise about your own future action than your equilibrium probability distribution, you have sufficient reason to have recourse to a randomizing device calibrated to the correct probabilities.

In non-constant-sum games, however, you might even expect to benefit from being thought to be about to deviate from your equilibrium mixed strategy. For example, Martin Shubik discusses the following case:

	C_1	C_2
R_1	−9, +9	+9, −10
R_2	+10, −9	−10, +10

The only Nash equilibrium is the pair of mixed strategies (.5, .5), (.5, .5), which gives each player an expected payoff of zero. Suppose Row deviates to (.51, .49). If Column does not anticipate this deviation, then Row's expected payoff is still zero. However, if Column does anticipate the deviation, then his best response would be to choose C_1 with probability 1, yielding Column an expected payoff of +.18 and Row with an expected payoff of +.31. Thus, as Shubik observes, "If the deviation isn't found out, it doesn't matter; if it is found out, the natural reaction of the other player benefits both players."[14]

J. Howard Sobel has also argued that current game theory offers no satisfactory solution for games with only mixed-strategy equilibria.[15] Consider a modification of the preceding game that has only noncentroid mixed strategies in equilibrium:

	C_1	C_2
R_1	+1, −2	−2, +2
R_2	−3, +5	+6, −1

The unique equilibrium is ($\frac{2}{3}$, $\frac{1}{3}$) for Row and ($\frac{2}{3}$, $\frac{1}{3}$) for Column. Sobel argues that this game does not resolve for "hyperrational" utility maximizers.

> Suppose the structure resolves in its equilibrium. Then ($\frac{2}{3}R1$, $\frac{1}{3}R2$) is selected by Row's [decision-guiding principle] and has greater informed expected utility than does any other strategy open to him [that is, at least as much expected utility as the alternatives]. Column knows this: in a hyperrational community there is no private relevant information. So Column expects ($\frac{2}{3}R1$, $\frac{1}{3}R2$). Which means that Column's informed expected utility for each of his strategies, pure or mixed, is+1. Column's principle does not single out ($\frac{2}{3}C1$, $\frac{1}{3}C2$) or any other strategy, and Column is indifferent as to what strategy he employs. Knowing this, as he would, Row judges that each of Column's strategies is equally probable. But then $R2$, not the mixed strategy ($\frac{2}{3}R1$, $\frac{1}{3}R2$) has greatest informed expected utility and is selected by Row's principle.[16]

[14] Shubik (1982), p. 250.
[15] Sobel (1975), p. 682n4.
[16] Ibid.

Sobel makes the very plausible point that there is no explanation of rationally expecting a rational player to use a particular noncentroid mixed strategy, given that the other player has no motivation to produce the equilibrium probability distribution deliberately.

John C. Harsanyi has developed a reinterpretation of mixed strategies that does make mixed-strategy equilibria comprehensible as a solution, given certain assumptions about the game situation being analyzed. Harsanyi has suggested that a player's mixed strategies be interpreted as consisting solely of uncertainties in the minds of other players as to what he will in fact do, uncertainties that are consequences of fundamental uncertainties in their minds as to the exact payoff function of the player in question (or as to other parameters of the game situation, such as what actions are in fact available to the player). Harsanyi calls his framework a theory of games of "incomplete information," meaning that the players are not certain about exactly what game they are playing.[17] Harsanyi shows how to construct, given a game of incomplete information, a theoretically equivalent conventional game of complete information.[18]

Harsanyi's defense of mixed-strategy equilibria is certainly ingenious, but it is not fully general in scope. It requires us to assume that the game situation in question is one of incomplete information. It is true, as Harsanyi argues, that real-life situations are typically best modeled as situations in which the precise parameters of the game being played are not known with certainty by the players. However, it does not seem correct to say that they are invariably so best modeled. It is at least conceivable that the parameters of a given game situation (alternatives available, prior probabilities, and payoff functions of the players involved) might be known by all beyond a shadow of a doubt; we need some theory about how rational players would cope with such a situation. [19]

Moreover, Harsanyi's theory requires that the uncertainty involved be of a very special kind: it must be representable as a continuous

[17] Harsanyi (1967–8).

[18] See also Aumann (1987).

[19] R. Aumann (1987) generalizes Harsanyi's reinterpretation of mixed-strategy equilibria so as to apply it to games in which all the relevant parameters are common knowledge. Aumann achieves this generalization by considering correlated equilibrium, rather than Nash equilibria. Like Harsanyi, Aumann thinks of a player's mixed strategy as representing the other players' state of uncertainty about what that player will actually do. In many games, like the chain-store game or the games discussed by Shubik and Sobel, all the correlated equilibria contain noncentroid mixed strategies. Aumann has not provided any plausible rationale for the other players' having such asymmetric expectations about the relevant player's actions. If they believe that he is, given his expectations and utilities, indifferent between two strategies, then why should they assign unequal probabilities to the player's actually carrying them out?

probability distribution over some random variable. If, instead, all uncertainty in the minds of the players can be represented only as a distribution of probability values over finitely many propositions, then expectations will not in general converge to a Nash equilibrium. Suppose, for example, that the other players are uncertain about player i's payoff function, but they believe that her payoff function is one of U_1, U_2, U_3, and U_4. To each possibility they assign a probability of .25. Suppose that the only Nash equilibrium of the game assigns to i the mixed strategy ($\frac{2}{3}$, $\frac{1}{3}$). Since $\frac{1}{3}$ is not a multiple of .25, Harsanyi's procedure cannot bring the other players to the equilibrium-sustaining probability distribution over i's pure strategies.[20]

To understand this point, consider again the mixed-strategy equilibrium game we examined earlier, letting Row play the role of player i:

	C_1	C_2
R_1	$+1+\epsilon, -2$	$-2, +2$
R_2	$-3, +5$	$+6, -1$

The possible payoff functions U_1, U_2, U_3, and U_4 assign the values $-.2$, $-.1$, $+.1$, and $+.2$ to ϵ, respectively. Column assigns each payoff function the probability .25. The only mixed strategies for Row that correspond to possible probability distributions on Column's part are (0, 1), (.25, .75), (.5, .5), (.75, .25), and (1, 0), depending on how many of the U_n's Column concludes would lead Row to select R_1. The equilibrium strategy ($\frac{2}{3}$, $\frac{1}{3}$) is not included. The two closest available distributions are (.5, .5) and (.75, .25). But if Column's probability distribution is (.5, .5), then Column's best response (by a wide margin) is C_1, and Row's best response to C_1 is R_2, whether his payoff function is U_1, U_2, U_3, or U_4. Similarly, if Column's distribution is (.75, .25), then Column's best response is (by a wide margin) C_2, and Row's best response to C_2 is R_1, independently of the U_n's. An approximation to the equilibrium distribution does not approximate the sort of stability possessed by the equilibrium itself.[21]

2.4 A PROBABILISTIC VERSION OF THE PARADOX

Let me illustrate the way in which the solution of Kreps et al. depends on noncentroid mixed strategies. The following is a game tree for a two-stage chain-store game:

[20] The criticism in this paragraph applies also to the view of Aumann (1987).

[21] See McClennen (1978) for an early attack on mixed equilibria and Stahl (1988) for some very sophisticated results on the instability of mixed-strategy Nash equilibria.

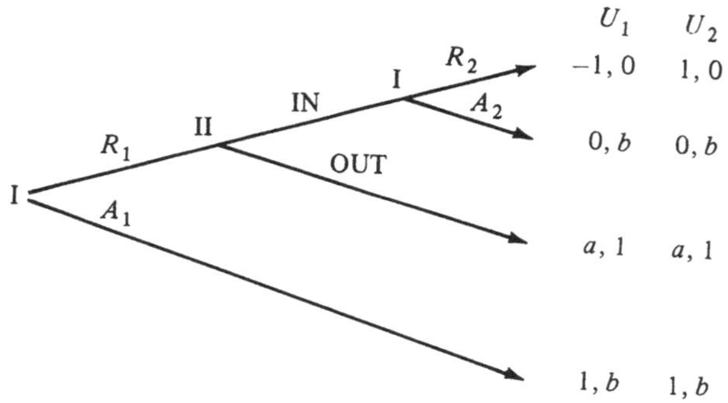

U_1 represents the actual payoffs to the monopolist and the second competitor; U_2 assigns different payoffs to the monopolist, making it worthwhile for the monopolist to retaliate against the second competitor should he enter. U_1 and U_2 are the two hypotheses about the structure of the game entertained by the second competitor. The initial probability for the competitor of U_1 is $1-\epsilon$, with ϵ close to but not equal to zero.

In the following arguments, I do not assume that the players share a common prior probability function. I do not even assume that each player knows the other player's prior. In fact, I do not assume that each player knows his own probability function. In most treatments of probability in the economic literature, these assumptions (especially the last one) are made. The last assumption is a consequence of the semantics for probability that has become the standard among economists, the Savage information-partition theory. This standard semantics forces us to assume a kind of perfect introspection on the part of the players: each player knows with certainty which member of his information partition contains the actual state of the world, and therefore he knows his own a posteriori probability function in the actual world. Some economists, unaware of the existence of alternatives to this semantics, do not realize that they are making a theoretically substantial assumption by using it.

The standard information-partition semantics guarantees that all higher-order probabilities are trivial: if the operator 'P' represents the probability function of a given player at a given state, then $P(P(\varphi) > k)$ is always either 0 or 1. If, instead of adopting the standard semantics, we simply require that for each player i and each state w there is a probability function P defined over some set of worlds A, then we open up the possibility of nontrivial higher-order probabilities, so long as we do not require that the same probability function P be assigned to i at every state in A. This is the more general approach, and the one I will follow here. Of course, the results I prove, using this very weak game theory, will hold a fortiori under the stronger, standard assumptions.

Let 'K' stand for the subjunctive conditional 'If the monopolist were to play R_1, the second competitor would play OUT'. If the probability of K for the monopolist is greater than $1/a$, then the monopolist should play R_1; if the probability of K is less than $1/a$, then the monopolist should play A_1; otherwise, the monopolist should be indifferent. If the monopolist does play R_1, then the competitor should play IN if his posterior probability of U_1 is greater than $1/b$. He should play OUT if his posterior probability of U_1 is less than $1/b$, and he should be indifferent otherwise. Assuming that the second competitor updates by Bayesian conditionalization, he should play IN if his prior probability $P_2(U_1/R_1)$ was greater than $1/b$.

The Kreps et al. solution to this game consists of the following equilibrium. The monopolist plays R_1 with probability $\epsilon/(1-\epsilon)(b-1)$, and the competitor plays OUT with probability $1/a$. Given the competitor's mixed strategy, the monopolist is clearly indifferent between R_1 and A_1. Bayes's theorem yields the result that the competitor's probability $P_2(U_1/R_1)$ is equal to $1/b$, so the competitor will be indifferent between IN and OUT:

$$P(U_1/R_1) = P(U_1) \cdot P(R_1/U_1)$$

$$[P(U_1) \cdot P(R_1/U_1) + P(\neg U_1) \cdot P(R_1/\neg U_1)]$$

$$= (1-\epsilon) \cdot P(R_1/U_1)/[(1-\epsilon) \cdot P(R_1/U_1) + \epsilon \cdot 1]$$

$$= 1/b.$$

If either $1/a$ or $\epsilon/(1-\epsilon)(b-1)$ is not equal to ½, then the solution is a noncentroid mixed-strategy equilibrium. If we rule out noncentroid equilibria, for instance, by stipulating that the players suffer from no further uncertainties about the structure of the game tree and perhaps that a huge penalty will be exacted for resorting to noncentroid mixed strategies, then a probabilistic version of the backward induction paradox can be created.

If both players are fully apprised of the game situation (including the ban on noncentroid strategies), then the following probability statements are true (where 'P_1' stands for the monopolist's prior and 'P_2' for the second competitor's prior).

(1) $P_1(K/P_2(U_1/R_1) > 1/b) = 0$,

(2) $P_1(K/P_2(U_1/R_1) < 1/b) = 1$,

(3) $P_1(K/P_2(U_1/R_1) = 1/b) = \frac{1}{2}$,
(4) $P_2(U_1/R_1 \ \& \ P_1(K) > 1/a) = 1 - \epsilon$,
(5) $P_2(U_1/R_1 \ \& \ P_1(K) < 1/a) = 0$,
(6) $P_2(U_1/R_1 \ \& \ P_1(K) = 1/a) = (1 - \epsilon)/(1 + \epsilon)$.

Statements (1) and (2) reflect the monopolist's certainty that the competitor will play a strategy if it is uniquely utility maximizing. Statement (3) is justified by the ban on noncentroid mixed strategies: if the competitor is indifferent, he will play either pure strategy with a probability of $\frac{1}{2}$. Statement (4) is a consequence of the fact that, if $P_2(R_1/U_1) = 1$, then $P_2(U_1/R_1) = P_2(U_1)$. Statement (5) is a consequence of the fact that, if $P_2(R_1/U_1) = 0$, then $P_2(U_1/R_1) = 0$. Finally, statement (6) is a consequence of Bayes's theorem, given that $P_2(R_1/U_1 \ \& \ P_1(K) = 1/a) = \frac{1}{2}$ (again reflecting the ban on noncentroid strategies).

If we assume that the monopolist believes statements (4) through (6) with certainty and that the monopolist is certain that $P_1(\varphi) = P_2(\varphi)$ whenever φ is a P_1 formula,[22] then it can be shown that statements (1) through (3) are in conflict with a fundamental principle of higher-order probability theory, the so-called Miller's principle.[23] The principle can be stated in its general form thus:

(M) If $P(P\varphi) \geq x \ \& \ \psi) \neq 0$, then $P(\varphi/P(\varphi) \geq x \ \& \ \psi) \geq x$, where ψ is any conjunction of probabilistic formulas.[24]

Miller's principle corresponds closely to the axiom schema R_1 presented earler.

I will now establish that each of the statements (1) through (3) is contradicted by Miller's principle. Since we are assuming that the monopolist is certain that $P_1(\varphi) = P_2(\varphi)$ whenever φ *is* a P_1-formula, we can replace 'P_2' with 'P_1' throughout the argument. For simplicity's sake, I will use 'P'. Given the monopolist's certainty of statements (4) through (6), we can replace in statements (1) through (3) the quantity expression '$P(U_1/R_1)$' by the following equivalent expressions:

$$P(U_1/R_1) = P(U_1/R_1 \ \& \ P(K) > 1/a) \cdot P(P(K) > 1/a) + P(U_1/R_1 \& \ P(K) < 1/a) \cdot P(P(K) < 1/a) + P(U_1/R_1 \ \& \ P(K) = 1/a) \cdot P(P(K) = 1/a)$$
$$= (1 - \epsilon) \cdot P(P(K) > 1/a) + 0 \cdot P(P(K) < 1/a) + (1 - \epsilon)/(1 + \epsilon) \cdot P(P(K) = 1/a) = P(P(K) > 1/a) \cdot (1 - \epsilon) + P(P(K) = 1/a) \cdot (1 - \epsilon)/(1 + \epsilon).$$

[22] An equation or inequality involving only numerical constants and P1-terms.
[23] Miller (1966); see Chapter 1, this volume.
[24] Equations or inequalities involving only numerical constants and probability items.

Let Q stand for the quantity $P(P(K) > 1/a) \cdot (1 - \epsilon) + P(P(K) = 1/a) \cdot (1 - \epsilon)/(1 + \epsilon)$. Consequently, the proposition '$P(U_1/R_1) < 1/b$' can be replaced by the proposition '$Q < 1/b$' and similarly for the propositions '$P(U_1/R_1) > 1/b$' (K_1) and '$P(U_1/R_1) = 1/b$' (K_2). Thus, statements (1) through (3) can be restated thus:

(1) $P(K/Q > 1/b) = 0$,
(2) $P(K/Q < 1/b) = 1$,
(3) $P(K/Q = 1/b) = \frac{1}{2}$.

Let us begin with statement (1). Assuming that $\epsilon > 0$, the probability calculus guarantees that if $Q > 1/b$, then $P(P(K) < 1/a) < 1 - 1/b(1 - \epsilon)$, and so $P(P(K) \geq 1/a) > 1/b(1 - \epsilon)$. Moreover, using the standard rules of probability, we can calculate that

$$P(K/Q > 1/b) \geq P(K/Q > 1/b \;\&\; P(K) \geq 1/a) \cdot P(P(K) \geq 1/a/Q > 1/b)$$
$$\geq P(K/Q > 1/b \;\&\; P(K) \geq 1/a) \cdot P(P(K) \geq 1/a/Q > 1/b \;\&$$
$$P(P(K) \geq 1/a) > 1/b(1 - \epsilon)).$$

Assume for the moment that $P(Q) > 1/b > 0$. By Miller's principle, it follows that

(i) $P(K/Q > 1/b \;\&\; P(K) \geq 1/a) \geq 1/a$, and
(ii) $P(P(K) \geq 1/a/Q > 1/b \;\&\; P(P(K) \geq 1/a) > 1/b(1 - \epsilon)) > 1/b(1 - \epsilon)$.

Consequently, $P(K/Q > 1/b) \geq 1/a \cdot 1/b(1 - \epsilon)$. This is certainly greater than zero.

In the case of statement (2), we observe that, if $Q < 1/b$, then $P(P(K) > 1/a) < 1/b(1 - \epsilon)$. The standard rules of probability entail

$$P(K/Q < 1/b) = P(K/P(K) > 1/a \;\&\; Q < 1/b) \cdot P(P(K) > 1/a/Q < 1/b \;\&$$
$$P(P(K) > 1/a) < 1/b\,(1 - \epsilon)) + P(K/P(K) \leq 1/a \;\&$$
$$Q < 1/b) \cdot P(P(K) \leq 1/a/Q < 1/b \;\&\; P(P(K) > 1/a)$$
$$< 1/b(1 - \epsilon))$$

Again, assume momentarily that $P(Q) < 1/b > 0$.The following are consequences of Miller's principle:

(i) $P(P(K) > 1/a/Q < 1/b \;\&\; P(P(K) > 1/a) < 1/b(1 - \epsilon)) < 1/b(1 - \epsilon)$,
(ii) $P(K/P(K) \leq 1/a \;\&\; Q < 1/b) \leq 1/a$.

Consequently, it is easy to calculate that

$$P(K/Q < 1/b) \leq 1/b(1 - \epsilon) + 1/a \cdot (1 - 1/b(1 - \epsilon))$$
$$= (a + b - b\epsilon - 1)/ab(1 - \epsilon)$$

The quantity $(a + b - b\epsilon - 1)/ab(1 - \epsilon)$ is less than 1 (given $\epsilon < 1$), contradicting statement (2).

By similar arguments, it is easily established that, if $P(Q = 1/b) > 0$, then

(a) $P(K/Q = 1/b) \geq 1/ab(1 - \epsilon)$, and

(b) $P(K/Q = 1/b) \leq (a + b - b\epsilon - 1)/ab(1 - \epsilon)$.

By choosing suitable values of a and b, it can be guaranteed that $1/ab(1 - \epsilon) > \frac{1}{2}$, contradicting statement (3).

At least one of the conditional probabilities $P(K/Q > 1/b)$, $P(K/Q < 1/b)$, and $P(K/Q = 1/b)$ must be well defined, since it is impossible for all three conditions to be given zero probability. I have demonstrated that Miller's principle so constrains the subjective probabilities of the monopolist (and, similarly, that of the competitor) that there are definite limits to the extent to which the subjective conditional probabilities can approach the true or objective conditional probabilities (contained in statements (1) through (6)). Thus, Miller's principle forces the monopolist to make grossly inaccurate estimates of these crucial conditional probabilities. Consequently, these higher-order probability constraints entail that the monopolist has wildly inaccurate beliefs about the nature of the game situation he is entering, since statements (1) through (3) are simple consequences of the actual game tree and of the competitor's probability function.

2.5 FROM DOXIC BLINDSPOTS TO DOXIC PARADOX

What I have established is that the monopolist suffers from what Roy Sorensen has called a doxic "blindspot" with respect to the theory of the game.[25] A proposition p is a doxic blindspot for person x if p is possibly true but it is impossible for x to be in a position of rationally believing p. Sorensen has analyzed the very same iterated supergames discussed here, but without, I think, correctly applying his notion of a blindspot. Sorensen has claimed that the competitor is in a blindspot with respect to the monopolist's rationality after the monopolist has played R_1.[26] Sorensen has not recognized that, before play has begun, the monopolist is already in a blindspot with respect to the conditions of the game. The theory of rational belief entails that the monopolist cannot recognize the truth of the biconditional '$K \leftrightarrow \neg JmJmK$'.

Although I think that it is essentially correct to classify the monopolist's predicament as one involving a doxic blindspot (in

[25] Sorensen (1988).

[26] Ibid., pp. 355–61; also Sorensen (1986).

Sorensen's sense), I do not think that this level of analysis can be the final word on the subject, for the following reason. Let the predicate '$M(x)$' represent the state of being in the sort of doxic predicament the monopolist as I have described him is in. The property of satisfying '$M(x)$' includes such features as the following:

(1) Being player I in the game tree U_1 as given earlier.

(2) Playing against a player II who is a rational Bayesian player and who believes initially with probability $1 - \epsilon$ that he is playing in game tree U_1 (against a player who knows that U_1 is the game tree) and with probability ϵ that he is playing in game tree U_2 (against a player who knows that U_2 is the game tree).

(3) Playing against a player II who updates by Bayesian conditionalization.

(4) Playing against a player II who believes that player I is Bayesian rational.

(5) Playing against a player II whose probability function P_2 is such that $P_1(\varphi) = P_2(\varphi)$, for any P_1 formula φ.

(6) Playing against a player II whose probability function P_2 assigns equal probabilities to all of player I's strategies on the condition that all of the strategies maximize player I's expected utility.

It is clear that it is epistemically possible for someone to be in such a predicament. Consequently, for an arbitrary new constant c, $P_1(M(c)) = \delta$, $\delta > 0$. Moreover, surely evidence could be acquired that would confirm that the individual named 'c' is in such a predicament. Let '$E(c)$' represent such evidence. Then

$$P_1(E(c)/M(c)) = \alpha, \qquad \alpha \approx 1,$$
$$P_1(E(c)/\neg M(c)) = \beta, \qquad \beta \approx 0.$$

This entails, by Bayes's theorem, that $P_1(M(c)/E(c)) = \delta\alpha/(\delta\alpha + \beta\,[1 - \delta]$. Consequently, if the monopolist were to acquire evidence $E(c)$ and were to update by Bayesian conditionalization, this quantity would be the posterior probability $P_1(M(c))$. Let us abbreviate his quantity by 'γ'. Thus, $P_1(M(c)) = \gamma, \gamma \approx 1$. Now, let '$i$' represent the distinguished constant in the monopolist's language of thought that represents himself qua *himself*. Suppose 'c' = 'i', that is, that the evidence acquired was '$E(i)$', evidence that the monopolist himself is in the predicament as described. The arguments used to support statements

(1) through (3) also support the conclusions:

(1') $P_1(K/Q > 1/b \,\&\, M(i)) = 0$,

(2') $P_1(K/Q < 1/b \,\&\, M(i)) = 1$,

(3') $P_1(K/Q = 1/b \,\&\, M(i)) = \frac{1}{2}$.

If $P_1(M(i)) = \gamma$ and the monopolist updates by Bayesian conditionalization, then

(1") $P_1(K/Q > 1/b) \leq 1 - \gamma$,

(2") $P_1(K/Q < 1/b) \geq \gamma$,

(3") $\gamma/2 \leq P_1(K/Q = 1/b) \leq 1 - \gamma/2$.

But as we have seen, Miller's principle may constrain these conditional probabilities to be far from these values.

There are therefore only three possibilities. Either (i) the monopolist must have an asymmetric prior such that the prior $P_1(M(i))$ is practically zero, despite the fact that, for all 'c' ≠ 'i', the prior $P_1(M(c))$ is nonnegligible, (ii) the monopolist violates updating by Bayesian conditionalization, or (iii) the monopolist violates Miller's principle.[27] This is indeed an antinomy, in the strongest possible sense.

A solution of this antinomy would give us the resources to describe this predicament adequately without falling into self-contradiction ourselves. In Chapter 7, I will make use of recent work on the paradox of the liar in order to produce just such a coherent description of this paradoxical predicament. In particular, I will be able to explain exactly why a perfectly rational agent in these circumstances is forced to violate Bayesian conditionalization, as well as its nonprobabilistic counterpart, deductive closure.

Aumann (1987) and Brandenburger and Dekel (1987) have established that whenever the Bayesian rationality of the players and the other parameters of a game are matters of common knowledge, each player will choose a strategy that is part of a correlated equilibrium. That is, each player will play as if guided by a correlated equilibrium solution to the game. If a game has an extensive form (a game tree) involving reputation effects (like the chain-store game), and all of the correlated equilibria involve noncentroid mixed strategies, then the argument of this chapter gives us reason to believe that these correlated equilibria solutions are not available and, therefore, that common

[27]See the discussion at the end of Chapter 1.

knowledge of the sort stipulated to exist by Aumann, Dekel, and Brandenburger is, in such games, impossible in principle, no matter how well informed and rational the players may be. The exact nature of this impossibility will be clarified in Chapter 4.

3

A study of liar-like epistemic paradoxes

In this chapter, I conduct a survey of the territory of epistemic and doxic paradoxes and investigate the parallels between them and the paradox of the liar. In so doing, I demonstrate that the paradox developed in the last two preceding chapters is a genuinely new result as well as make clear the strong family resemblances that bind all of these paradoxes together. In Section 3.1, I introduce what I call the "paradox of the disprover," a close relative of Kaplan and Montague's paradox of the knower discovered by Richmond Thomason. This paradox provides an important bridge between the doxastic paradox of Chapters 1 and 2 and the more familiar paradox of the knower. In Section 3.2, I compare the theorems that constitute the doxastic and epistemic paradoxes with theorems by Gödel and Löb. Finally, in Section 3.3, I use standard modal logic to bring to light the common basis of the paradoxes (including the liar) and to classify the paradoxes into subfamilies.

3.1 THE PARADOX OF THE DISPROVER

The paradox of the disprover is not a new formal result: it is a reinterpretation of a well-known result, the Kaplan–Montague paradox of the knower, discussed in their paper "A Paradox Regained."[1] I will use a new version of that formal result, developed by Richmond Thomason.[2] In place of the notion of 'knowledge', I will suggest in this section that we interpret this formal paradox by means of the notion of 'subjective provability', which I will explain in due course.

Kurt Gödel showed in 1931 how to create a formal theory of syntax using number theory. His approach can be generalized to provide a "syntax" of any domain of propositions whose internal structure mirrors that of the sentences of a language. Gödel first defined a numerical code for the expressions of the language under examination. He then showed how to define, in number theory, operations that

[1] Kaplan and Montague (1960).
[2] Thomason (1980).

correspond to all of the familiar syntactic operations, such as forming the conjunction of two formulas, substituting one term for another in a formula, and so on. It is a result of Gödel's accomplishment that any language powerful enough to describe the system of natural numbers is also powerful enough to express its own syntax. In fact, the language need only be powerful enough to express a first-order, finitely axiomatizable fragment of arithmetic known as "Robinson arithmetic" (after Raphael Robinson).

The property of being a proof in a given formal system (like Robinson arithmetic) is itself a syntactic property and so is representable in number theory by Gödel's method. Consequently, the property of being a sentence that is provable in a given system is also definable in this way. For any formal system T, we can define a predicate 'Bew_T' (for *beweisbar*, "provable" in German) that is demonstrably true of exactly those numbers that are codes of sentences provable in T.

One of the most important of Gödel's results is known as the "self-reference lemma". Suppose that $\mathcal{L}$ is a language powerful enough to express Robinson arithmetic. Let us imagine that we have assigned unique numbers to each of the basic symbols of $\mathcal{L}$ and that we have defined numerical operations corresponding to each of the syntactic operations in $\mathcal{L}$. Then each formula of $\mathcal{L}$ will be assigned a unique number, known as its "code." If φ is a formula of $\mathcal{L}$, let 'φ' be the number that is φ's code. Gödel proved that, for each formula $\varphi(x)$ of $\mathcal{L}$ with a single free variable x, there is a formula ψ such that we can prove, in Robinson arithmetic, the biconditional '$\psi \leftrightarrow \varphi$('$\psi$')'. Such a formula Ψ is, in effect, self-referential: it is provably equivalent to a sentence which asserts that the code of ψ has the property expressed by the open formula $\varphi(x)$.

A consequence of Gödel's self-reference lemma is the undefinability of truth in any formal system T consistent with Robinson arithmetic (a result proved independently by Alfred Tarski [1956]). Suppose, for a contradiction, that we can define truth by means of the open formula $\tau(x)$. If $\tau(x)$ is an adequate definition of truth, then, for any sentence Ψ in $\mathcal{L}$, T should include the biconditional τ('ψ') $\leftrightarrow \psi$, that is, the code of the sentence ψ should have the property that corresponds to truth if and only if ψ itself is the case (this condition is known as Tarski's "convention T"). But by the self-reference lemma, there is a sentence λ such that we can prove in Robinson arithmetic that $\sim\tau$('λ') $\leftrightarrow \lambda$. (Let $\sim\tau(x)$

be the open formula to which we apply the lemma.) Thus, T must be inconsistent, since it contains both $\sim\tau(`\lambda') \leftrightarrow \lambda$ and $t(`\lambda') \leftrightarrow \lambda$.

Richard Montague (1963) generalized Tarski's result, proving that truth is not the only interesting property that can be shown to be inexpressible by the self-reference lemma. He proved that, if T is a formal system that meets the following four conditions, then T is inconsistent: (i) T contains the axioms of Robinson arithmetic, (ii) T is closed under logical consequence, (iii) T contains all instances of the conditional $\nu(`\varphi') \rightarrow \varphi$, and (iv) $T$ contains every instance of the schema $\nu(`(\nu(`\varphi') \rightarrow \varphi)')$. We can think of $\nu(x)$ as representing knowability or necessity. If something is knowable, then it is the case, and presumably every instance of this truism is itself knowable. To prove the inconsistency of any such T, Montague used the self-reference lemma to produce a knower paradox sentence κ, about which it is provable in Robinson arithmetic (and so in T itself) that $\kappa \leftrightarrow \nu(`(R \rightarrow \sim\kappa)')$, where R is the conjunction of the axioms of Robinson arithmetic. The sentence κ, asserts, in effect, that it is knowable that κ is not the case, under the assumption of Robinson arithmetic. Since the biconditional is a theorem of Robinson arithmetic, it is provable in logic alone that $R \rightarrow (\kappa \leftrightarrow \nu(`(R \rightarrow \sim K)'))$. Montague's result can be proved as follows:

(1) $\vdash_T \nu(`(R \rightarrow (\kappa \leftrightarrow \nu(`(R \rightarrow \sim\kappa)')))')$,	condition (ii)
(2) $\vdash_T \nu(`(\nu(`(R \rightarrow \sim\kappa)') \rightarrow (R \rightarrow \sim\kappa))')$,	condition (iv)
(3) $\vdash_T \nu(`(R \rightarrow \sim\kappa)')$,	(1), (2), and condition (ii)
(4) $\vdash_T R \rightarrow \sim\kappa$,	(3), and condition (iii)
(5) $\vdash_T \sim\kappa$,	(4), and conditions (i) and (ii)
(6) $\vdash_T \sim\nu(`(R \rightarrow \sim\kappa)')$,	(5), self-reference lemma, and conditions (i) and (ii)
(7) $\vdash_T \bot$.	(3), (6), and condition (ii)

Now I would like to present Thomason's version of Montague's result. Beginning with the language of Robinson arithmetic, we add the primitive one-place predicate $P(x)$. Thomason proved that, if a theory contains every instance of the following schemata, then it also contains $P(`\Psi')$, for every sentence Ψ of the language:

(P1) $P\,`(P(\varphi) \rightarrow \varphi)'$,

(P2) $P\,`\varphi' \rightarrow P`P\,`\varphi''$,

(P3) $P`\varphi'$, if φ is a logical axiom,

(P4) $P`(\varphi \rightarrow \Psi)' \rightarrow [P`\varphi' \rightarrow P`\Psi']$,

(P5) P'R', where R is the axiom Robinson arithmetic.

The result is proved by constructing a sentence a that is provably equivalent (in R) with the sentence 'P'$\neg a$''.

$$\vdash_R (a \leftrightarrow P\text{'}\neg a\text{'}).$$

By sentential logic, this biconditional implies the following formula:

$$\vdash_R [(P\text{'}\neg a\text{'} \rightarrow \neg a) \rightarrow \neg a].$$

By axioms (P3), (P4), and (P5), we can use this result to derive:

(1) P'$[(P$'$\neg a$' $\rightarrow \neg a) \rightarrow \neg a]$'.

The following sentence is an instance of axiom (P1):

(2) P'$(P$'$\neg a$' $\rightarrow \neg a)$'.

From (1), (2) and axiom (P4), we get

(3) P'$\neg a$'.

From (3) and (P2), it follows that

(4) P'P'$\neg a$''.

From (P1), (P2), (P3), and the fact that the biconditional '$(a \leftrightarrow P$'$\neg a$'$)$' is provable in R, we can prove

(5) P'$(P$'$\neg a$' $\rightarrow a)$'.

From (4), (5) and (P4), we arrive finally at

(6) P'a'.

From (3), (6), (P3) and (P4), we can prove P'Ψ', for any sentence Ψ whatsoever.

In the original Kaplan–Montague paradox, the predicate 'P' was interpreted as representing *knowledge*. Thomason has suggested interpreting 'P' in his version as *ideal belief*. For the paradox of the disprover, we must interpret 'P' as representing a notion I will call "subjective (or inter subjective) provability."

Subjective provability is different from the sort of provability or formal derivability studied by Gödel and by proof theory, in that I am not trying to formalize the notion of 'provable in Q', or of provability relativized to any particular system or calculus. By saying that a sentence is subjectively provable, I am saying that it is derivable from subjectively self-evident axioms by means of self-evidently valid rules.

There is, however, an element of relativity in this notion of provability, since what is subjectively self-evident to one person (or community) at one time need not be subjectively self-evident to others or even to the same person (or community) at a later time. Thus, provability (I will hereafter drop the qualifier "subjective," for brevity's sake) is a relation between a sentence and an epistemic situation or state. We can avoid the problem of characterizing such epistemic states by instead relativizing provability to a particular individual or community of individuals at a particular time (implicitly relativizing to the epistemic state that those individuals share at that time). The picture is something like this: We are to imagine well-known Martian anthropologists to be isolating a time slice of some community of human mathematicians, extracting from it all the axioms and rules that are self-evident to the group at that time and then building a Turing machine that, with unlimited memory and computing time, derives everything derivable by means of those axioms and rules.

When I describe provability as consisting in the possibility of deriving a sentence from self-evident axioms by means of self-evident rules, I mean the possibility of deriving it in a finite number of steps (constructively). I do not intend to include any kind of infinitary process as a possible proof; for example, I will not count checking each of the natural numbers for a given property as describing a procedure by means of which it could be proved or disproved that all the natural numbers possess the property in question (Rosser's ω-rule).[3] I also do not want to count any process that involves supplementing the set of axioms that are now self-evident to us with additional truths that might someday become self-evident to us or to other competent mathematicians.

The self-evident sentences and rules need not be thought of as analytically true or in principle unrevisable (although some of them may be). What seemed self-evident at one time may later be rejected altogether (e.g., the parallel postulate of Euclid, Frege's naive comprehension axiom). In fact, I am not committed to claiming that the self-evident sentences of mathematics are a priori in any nontrivial sense. I need not deny that they are derived from experience or by means of empirical scientific methods. Self-evident sentences are "general laws, which themselves neither need nor admit of proof," as Frege describes them.[4] They must be general laws, not about particular, observable objects and not containing egocentric indexicals or demonstratives, so that their self-evidence can be shared by all the

[3] Rosser (1937).
[4] Frege (1978), p. 4.

members of the mathematical community (thus, sentences like'I think' and 'I am' do not count as self-evident in this sense).[5]

Moreover, the self-evident sentences must have a subjective probability of 1, or at least infinitesimally close to 1,[6] since the rational credibility of a mathematical theorem does not in fact depend on the number of different axioms from which it is derived, or on the number of steps by which it is derived. In practice, mathematicians rely just as confidently on theorems whose proofs are very complex, relying on a large number of instances of logical axiom schemata and consisting of a large number of applications of modus ponens and other inference rules, as on theorems whose proofs are much shorter, so long as the possibility of computational error is equally excluded. This practice can be rationalized only by assigning a subjective probability of 1 (or infinitesimally close to 1, if infinitesimals are admitted) to the axioms and to the chance that each application of an inference rule has preserved truth.

Finally, unlike the set of provable sentences, the set of self-evident sentences must be effectively decidable, and decidable by a known mechanism. This mechanism is simply to ask a competent mathematician or, if one is a competent mathematician oneself, simply to reflect upon one's own intuitions. The mathematical community has, with respect to the question of what is now self-evident, the sort of first-person authority we all have with respect to our own present sensory experience.

The point of the notion of self-evidence is to explain the conclusiveness of mathematical proof. If self-evidence is not itself effectively recognizable by all competent mathematicians, then any account of the conclusiveness of proof faces any infinite regress. As Alonzo Church has argued:[7]

> Consider the situation which arises if . . . there is no *certain* means by which, when a sequence of formulas has been put forward, the auditor may determine whether it is in fact a proof. He may then fairly demand a proof, in any given case, that the sequence of formulas put forward is a proof; and until this supplementary proof is provided, he may refuse to be convinced that the alleged theorem is proved. This supplementary proof ought to be regarded, it seems, as part of the whole proof of the theorem [my emphasis].

5 Indexicals that reflexively refer to the mathematical community itself as its present state of development (the Wittgensteinian "we") can, however, occur within self-evident sentences, since they can have the same epistemic status for all members of the community. Thus, an expression like 'what is self-evident to us (mathematicians)' may appear in self-evident sentences.

6 See Appendix A on how to apply the notion of subjective probability to the necessary truths of mathematics.

7 Church (1956), p. 53.

The set of proofs is, therefore, effectively decidable by a known mechanism (consulting competent mathematical intuition). The set of proofs is effectively decidable if and only if the applicability of all self-evident rules is decidable (as is, e.g., the applicability of all the rules of predicate calculus) and if the set of self-evident rules and axioms is itself decidable. Thus, the set of self-evident sentences is effectively decidable, which would not be the case if our confidence in the truth of a self-evident sentence depended on our having a proof of the sentence (the set of provable sentences is effectively enumerable, not decidable). This condition embodies the traditional idea of self-evidence as "undemonstrability."[8]

We can now return to a consideration of the axioms by which the formal result was derived:

(P1) $P`(P`\varphi' \rightarrow \varphi)'$,

(P2) $P`\varphi' \rightarrow P`P`\varphi''$,

(P3) $P`\varphi'$, if φ is a logical axiom,

(P4) $P`(\varphi \rightarrow \psi)' \rightarrow [P`\varphi' \rightarrow P`\psi']$,

(P5) $P`R'$, where R is the axiom of Robinson arithmetic.

I will argue that the class of subjectively provable sentences, relative to any rational mathematician who is sufficiently sophisticated, will satisfy each of these five conditions. Given that '*P*' represents some kind of provability, the truth of axioms (P3) through (P5) is a trivial matter. The axioms of first-order logic and of Robinson arithmetic will be subjectively self-evident to any fairly sophisticated mathematical intuition, and if they are self-evident, they are of course provable. Axiom (P4) merely says that the set of provable things is closed under modus ponens, which is surely undeniable.

I will try to show that a rational mathematical intuition will necessarily satisfy (P1) by showing that every instance of the following schema is self-evident:

(P*) $P`\varphi' \rightarrow \varphi$.

I will show that instances of P^* are self-evident by showing that it would be irrational for us not to give P^* a subjective probability of 1. I will demonstrate, in other words, that

(1) Prob $[P^*] = 1$.

[8] Frege (1978), p. 4, and (1979), p. 205; Aristotle, *Metaphysics* 1005b 10–12; and Aquinas, *Summa Theologica*, I–II, Q. 94, A. 2.

By the definition of conditional probability, (1) is equivalent to

(2) Prob [φ/P'φ'] = 1, or Prob [P'φ'] = 0.[9]

To prove (1), I need only prove that the first disjunct of (2) is true whenever the relevant conditional probability is defined. I will show that it would be irrational, for any sentence φ, to have a conditional probability of φ on P'φ' other than 1.

Remember that 'P'φ'' implies that our subjective probability for 'φ' is 1. Thus, the first disjunct of (2) can be restated as

(3) Prob [φ/(Prob [φ] = 1)] = 1.

(3) is an instance of what is known in probability theory as Miller's principle, a widely accepted rationality condition.[10] As I mentioned in Chapter 2, a probability distribution that violates (3) would be vulnerable to a Dutch book strategem. If you make conditional bets on the basis of assigning the conditional probability in (3) some number other than 1, everyone who bets against you can quite easily make a Dutch book. If it turns out that your subjective probability of φ is not equal to 1, then you cannot win anything from such conditional bets. If your subjective probability for φ is equal to 1, then you will be willing to make straight bets that directly contradict your conditional bets, resulting in a certain loss.

Another argument for (P1) is based on an instance of actual mathematical practice. Gödel's informal argument that the self-

9 First of all, the conditional '(P'φ' → φ)' is logically equivalent to the disjunction '(¬P'φ' or φ)'. The following equations are consequences of the probability calculus:
(4) Prob[P'φ' → φ] = Prob[¬P'φ' *or* φ],
(5) Prob[¬P'φ'or φ) = Prob[¬P 'φ'] + Prob [φ] – Prob[¬P'φ' & φ].
Condition probability is defined by the following formula:
(6) Prob [φP'φ'] = Prob[φ & P'φ']/Prob[P'φ'].
To prove that (1) is logically equivalent to (2), we will first show that (2) implies (1). If Prob [P 'φ'] is equal to 0, then the probability of the conditional '(P'φ' → φ)' is obviously equal to 1. Suppose that [Prob [φ/P'φ'] = 1. Then,
(7) Prob [φ & P'φ'] = Prob [P'φ'].
It is a consequence of the probability calculus that Prob[φ] can be expressed as follows:
(8) Prob[φ] = Prob[φ & P'φ'] + Prob [φ & ¬P'φ'].
Equations (7) and (8) together imply
(9) Prob [φ & ¬P'φ'] = Prob [φ] – Prob [P'φ'].
Using (9), together with (4) and (5), we can prove the following equation:
(10) Prob [P'φ' → φ] = Prob [¬P'φ'] + Prob [P'φ'] = 1.
Now, to prove that (1) logically implies (2), we can begin by assuming that Prob [P'φ' → φ] is equal to 1. By (4) and (5), it follows that
(11) Prob [¬P'φ'] + Prob [φ] – Prob [¬P'φ' & φ] = 1.
From (8) and (11), we get
(12) Prob [¬P'φ'] + Prob [φ & P'φ'] = 1.
Since Prob [¬P'φ'] = 1 - Prob [P'φ'], (12) is equivalent to
(13) Prob [P'φ'] = Prob [φ & P'φ']
Finally, (13) and (6) imply that Prob[φ/P'φ'] equals 1.

10 Miller (1966).

referential sentence he constructed was true but unprovable in Peano arithmetic was based implicitly on the use of the (P*) schema

(P*) P'φ' → φ.

As I discussed previously, Gödel constructed a self-referential sentence (call it 'G') that can be proved in Peano arithmetic to be equivalent to the sentence that G is unprovable in Peano arithmetic (more precisely, that the number coding 'G' has the number-theoretic property that codes *provability in Peano arithmetic*). Gödel provided, in effect, an informal proof of G by arguing that it cannot be provable in Peano arithmetic, because if it were provable in Peano arithmetic, then it would be provable tout court (since all of the axioms of Peano arithmetic and first-order logic are self-evident); and by the appropriate instance of the (P*) schema, we could infer G itself, from which it follows that G is unprovable in Peano arithmetic, contrary to the original assumption. So, we have proved (by means of (P*) and Peano arithmetic) that G is unprovable, from which the Gödel sentence itself is derivable (in Peano arithmetic).

It could be argued that the plausibility of Gödel's argument depends not on the self-evidence of (P*), but rather on the weaker principle that whatever is provable in Peano arithmetic is in fact the case, which we can call schema (P*PA):

(P*PA) Prov_{PA} 'φ' → φ.

However, it is clear that Gödel's argument can be convincingly reiterated indefinitely, which is in effect what the Feferman construction involves.[11] Since we can convince ourselves of the truth of the Gödel sentence G, we could add it to Peano arithmetic as a new axiom, producing a new system PA', which is intuitively sound in the sense that, for any given sentence φ, we would accept the conditional '$\text{Prov}_{\text{PA}'}$ 'φ' → φ', where '$\text{Prov}_{\text{PA}'}(x)$' encodes the provability property in PA'. We can now repeat Gödel's argument and convince ourselves to accept a new Gödel sentence G'. The iteration can even be carried into the transfinite. The reiterations of the argument require more than instances of (P*PA), however. We would require infinitely many different axiom schemata, one for each new theory as it is generated. I find it impossible to believe that each of these schemata is independently self-evident. As very complicated sentences of number theory, the new axioms would be far from evident had they not been generated

[11] Feferman (1962).

by means of a kind of reflection principle from an axiom system already established as sound. It is clear that a single, implicitly self-referential schema, namely (P*), is in fact being relied upon. Each additional Gödel sentence is derivable by means of (P*) from the previous one, so all of them are provable in the single system consisting of Peano arithmetic plus (P*).

A final argument for the self-evidence of (P*) will be taken up in Chapter 4 of this book. There I will argue that an adequate account of common knowledge and of game-theoretic rationality must attribute reliance on (P*) to all rational agents.

Axiom schema (P2) states that, if something is provable, then it is provably provable. Since it is provable in Robinson arithmetic whether or not a sentence is an instance of a given schema and whether or not a sentence follows from two other sentences by modus ponens, the plausibility of (P2) turns on the question of whether every sentence that is self-evident is self-evidently self-evident. We have seen that the set of self-evident sentences is effectively decidable by a known procedure, namely, consulting competent mathematical intuition. It seems reasonable to assume that, for each sentence that such intuition confirms, it is self-evident that it is so confirmed and, therefore, also self-evident that it is self-evident.

In any case, I do not believe that giving up schema (P2) offers a viable escape route from the paradox, because (P2) is in fact much stronger than is needed to generate the paradoxical result. Suppose '$\mathrm{Prov}_S(x)$' is an arithmetical predicate encoding the property of being derivable in system S, consisting of first-order logic plus the instances of schema (P1). Then the following schema is still strong enough to generate the paradox:

(P2') $\mathrm{Prov}_S`\varphi' \rightarrow P`P`\varphi''$.

In other words, all that is needed is that the axioms of logic and instances of (P1) be self-evidently self-evident.

Thomason's theorem seems to show, therefore, that any rational and reasonably sophisticated mathematical intuition leads to inconsistency. Since I take this to be an unacceptable consequence, and yet I think that (P1) through (P5) are virtually undeniable, I claim that we have here an antinomy as deserving of serious attention as is the liar paradox itself. We can get an actual contradiction by adding the axiom (P6):

(P6) $\neg P`\bot'$.

Here '$\bot$' represents an arbitrary absurdity. The paradox depends not on interpreting (P6) as saying that our present system of intuitive mathematics is consistent, but on interpreting 'P' as representing provability in an ideal intuitive mathematics. The inconsistency of (P1) through (P6) shows that any intuitive mathematics that meets certain minimal requirements of rationality is inconsistent.

There is an even simpler version of the paradox.[12] Let '$S(x)$' represent the statement that the sentence named by 'x' is self-evident. Consider the following axioms:

(S1) $S`a' \rightarrow S`S`a''$,

(S2) $\neg S`a' \rightarrow S`\neg S`a''$,

(S3) $S`\neg a' \rightarrow \neg S`a'$.

Here 'a' stands for some standard name of a sentence. Standard names include, but need not be limited to, numerals (naming sentences via a fixed Gödel code). Let us suppose that we can also introduce standard names by stipulation, as a result of a public dubbing ceremony, for instance. Suppose we introduce the name 'σ' as follows (analogous to Kripke's "Jack"):[13]

$$\sigma: \quad \neg S`\sigma'.$$

A contradiction quickly ensues. If we suppose that σ is self-evident, then we get $S`S`\sigma''$ by axiom (S1), but we also have $S`\neg S`\sigma''$, by virtue of the fact that $\sigma = `\neg S`\sigma''$. So σ is not self-evident. By axiom (S2), it follows that it is self-evident that σ is not self-evident ($S`\neg S`\sigma''$). But, again, since σ is identical to '$\neg S`\sigma'$', it follows that σ *is* self-evident. This is a contradiction.

I have already discussed and defended axiom (S1). Axiom (S2) states that, if a sentence is not self-evident, then the sentence asserting that it is not self-evident (using a standard name for it) is self-evident. The argument I gave above for (S1) applies equally to (S2). Appeal to competent mathematical intuition is an effective procedure for deciding whether a sentence is selfevident. If a sentence is not so validated by intuition, it is surely self-evident that it is not self-evident. Normally, this procedure does not involve any vicious circularity, since it

[12] A paradox very similar to this one was first discussed by Burge (1978). See also Burge (1984).

[13] Kripke, in Martin (1984), p. 56: "Let 'Jack' be a name of the sentence 'Jack is short', and we have a sentence that says of itself that it is short. I can see nothing wrong with 'direct' self-reference of this type. If 'Jack' is not already a name in the language, why can we not introduce it as a name of any entity we please? In particular, why can it not be a name of the (uninterpreted) finite sequence of marks 'Jack is short'? (Would it be permissible to call this sequence of marks 'Harry', but not 'Jack'? Surely prohibitions on naming are arbitrary here.) There is not a vicious circle in our procedure, since we need not interpret the sequence of marks 'Jack is short' before we name it. Yet if we name it 'Jack', it at once becomes meaningful and true."

is not normally self-evident that a self-referential sentence is self-referential. If a sentence refers to itself by means of containing a definite description that picks out its own Gödel number, it will not be self-evident that that description does pick out the sentence's own number. However, if self-reference is achieved directly, by means of a new standard name introduced à la Kripke's "Jack," vicious circularity is possible, as the preceding paradox demonstrates.

It might be argued that the possibility of self-evident self-reference introduces an element of circularity that undermines the decidability of the set of self-evident sentences. The existence of the paradoxical sentence 'σ' undermines the intuition we appealed to in justifying (S1) and (S2). Merely pointing out this fact does not solve the paradox, however. We need to reconcile the requirement of the decidability of self-evidence with the possibility of self-evident self-reference. That is precisely the problem that the paradox poses.

Axiom schema (S3) simply states that there are no cases in which both a sentence and its negations are simultaneously self-evident. This is a far weaker claim than asserting that our naive proof procedure is consistent. A sentence's seeming self-evident must exclude its negation's also seeming self-evident. Avoiding explicit contradiction is a basic condition of rationality.

3.2 A HISTORICAL INTERLUDE

I shall briefly compare the epistemic paradoxes discussed in Section 3.1 with the earlier results by Gödel and Löb, concerning the predicate 'Bew' (for *beweisbar*), which represented (by means of the Gödel numbering technique) the proof relation of Peano arithmetic within the language of Peano arithmetic. Corresponding to Gödel's incompleteness theorem, there are paradoxes in epistemic logic that replace Gödel's 'Bew' predicate with a primitive predicate symbol representing intuitive provability.

For example, Gödel's incompleteness theorem can be transposed into epistemic logic. Gödel used the following facts about 'Bew' and Peano arithmetic in order to derive his result:[14]

(1) If $\vdash_{PA} \varphi$, then $\vdash_{PA}$ Bew ('φ'),

(2) $\vdash_{PA}$ [Bew('($\varphi \rightarrow \Psi$)') $\rightarrow$ (Bew('φ') $\rightarrow$ Bew('Ψ'))],

(3) $\vdash_{PA}$ [Bew('φ') $\rightarrow$ Bew ('Bew('φ')')].

From these three facts, he proved that '$\neg$Bew($\perp$)' cannot be proved in

[14] In fact, Gödel used not Peano arithmetic, but a closely related system, P.

Peano arithmetic, unless it is inconsistent. If we replace 'Bew' with the primitive predicate symbol 'P' (representing intuitive provability), replace PA with a theory T that includes PA plus the three axioms governing the extension of 'P' that reproduce the three properties of 'Bew' used by Gödel, and add a fourth axiom that states that what is provable is consistent (that the absurdity '$\bot$' is not provable), we produce the following set of plausible but inconsistent principles:

(G1) If $\vdash_T \varphi$, then $\vdash_T P$ 'φ' (where PA is a subtheory of T),

(G2) $\vdash_T [P`(\varphi \rightarrow \Psi)' \rightarrow (P`\varphi' \rightarrow P`\Psi')]$,

(G3) $\vdash_T [P`\varphi' \rightarrow P`P`\varphi''']$,

(G4) $\vdash_T \neg P`\bot'$.

Axioms (G2) and (G3) are identical to axioms (P4) and (P2) of Thomason's theorem, discussed in Section 3.1. Axiom (G4) is a single instance of the axiom schema we called (P*):

(P*) $P`\varphi' \rightarrow \varphi$.

If we replace S with $\bot$ in (P*), (G4) follows by sentential logic. Axioms (G1) and (G4) together imply $P`\neg P`\bot''$, which is virtually an instance of Thomason's (P1):

(P1) $P`(P`\varphi')'$

Again, if "$\bot$" is used as an instance of S in this formula, we get the instance $P`(P`\bot' \rightarrow \bot)'$, and since "$(P`\bot' \rightarrow \bot)$" is equivalent in the propositional calculus with "$\neg P`\bot'$", it is easy to show that, this instance of (P1) is equivalent with $P`\neg P`\bot''$.

Axiom (G1) is not a consequence of any of the assumptions of Thomason's theorem. Thomason needs only to assume that, if a sentence is derivable in Peano arithmetic or if it is an instance of (P*), then it is provable. (G1) says that, if a sentence is derivable in the system consisting of PA plus instances of (G1) through (G4), then it is provable. We have seen that (G4) is a consequence of (P*), but schemata (G1), (G2), and (G3) are independent of Peano arithmetic and of (P*). (G1) can be considerably weakened without eliminating the inconsistency. Let (G1') be the following rule:

(G1') If $\vdash_{PA} \varphi$, then $\vdash_T P`\varphi'$.

Since T includes PA, axiom (G1') is strictly weaker than (G1) Let T^* be the theory consisting of Peano arithmetic plus all instances of the schemata (G1'), (G2), (G3) and (G4) (but not (G1)). Then the following axiom is strictly weaker than (G1), since T includes T^*:

(G1*) If $\vdash_{T^*} \varphi$, then $\vdash_T P`\varphi'$

Nonetheless, (G1*) is sufficient for the derivation of a contradiction. (G1*) has the advantage over (G1) of not being self-referential, a fact about (G1) that might be thought to cast doubt on its self-evidence.

In order to derive the paradox, we use Gödel's method to construct a sentence 'a' such that the following biconditional is derivable in Peano arithmetic:

$$\vdash_{PA} [a \leftrightarrow (P`a' \rightarrow \bot)]$$

We can prove both $P`a'$ and $\neg P`a'$ as follows:

(1) $P`[a \leftrightarrow (P`a' \rightarrow \bot)]'$,	(G1*) (or (G1'))
(2) $P`a' \rightarrow P`(P`a' \rightarrow \bot)'$,	(1), (G2)
(3) $P`(P`a' \rightarrow \bot)' \rightarrow [P`P`a'' \rightarrow P`\bot']$,	(G2)
(4) $P`a' \rightarrow P`P`a''$,	(G3)
(5) $P`a' \rightarrow P`\bot'$,	(2), (3), (4)
(6) $\neg P`a'$,	(5), (G4)
(7) $P`(P`a' \rightarrow P`\bot)'$,	(1)–(5), (G1*)
(8) $P`\neg P`a''$,	(7), (G2), (G4)
(9) $P`a'$.	(1), (8), (G2)

Nonetheless, (G1) is a very plausible assumption. The very considerations in Section 3.1 that supported the self-evidence of the axiom corresponding to (G3) also support (G1). If a sentence can be proved, then it can be proved to have been proved. Thus, we have an independent and very plausible epistemic paradox, which could be called "Gödel's paradox."

Gödel's paradox can also be compared with the Kaplan–Montague paradox. Transposing the assumptions of the Kaplan–Montague paradox into our notation, we get

(K1) If φ is a logical axiom, then $\vdash_T P`\varphi'$,
(K2) $\vdash_T [P`(\varphi \rightarrow \Psi)' \rightarrow (P`\varphi' \rightarrow P`\Psi')]$,
(K3) $\vdash_T P`(P`\varphi' \rightarrow \varphi)'$,
(K4) $\vdash_T P`\varphi' \rightarrow \varphi$.
(K5) PA is a subtheory of T.

Axiom schema (K2) is identical to (G2). Kaplan and Montague, however, do not need anything corresponding to (G3). Axiom (G4) is an instance of (K4) (which is identical to (P*)). That leaves (G1), which entails (K1) and (K5), but which entails only one instance of (K3) (namely, $P`(P`\bot' \rightarrow \bot)'$). At the same time, (K1) through (K5) do not entail (G1) (or (G1*)).

Another related fact concerning the properties of Gödel's 'Bew' predicate that can be transposed into an epistemic paradox is a theorem of Löb's.[15] In effect, Löb showed that the following set of axiom schemata are inconsistent:

(L1) There exists some σ such that $\vdash_T P`(P`\sigma' \rightarrow \sigma)' \ \& \ \neg P`\sigma'$,

(L2) $\vdash_T [P`\varphi' \rightarrow P`P`S\varphi']$,

(L3) $\vdash_T P`\varphi'$, where φ is a logical axiom,

(L4) $\vdash_T [P`(\varphi \rightarrow \psi)' \rightarrow (P`\varphi' \rightarrow P`\psi')]$,

(L5) $\vdash_T P`R'$, where R is the axiom of Robinson arithmetic,

(L6) $\vdash_T P`\varphi'$, where φ is an instance of (L2) through (L5).

Schemata (L2), (L3), (L4), and (L5) are identical to assumptions (P2), (P3), (P4), and (P5) (respectively) of Thomason's theorem. There is no assumption of Thomason's theorem corresponding to (L6). Schema (L1), however, is strictly weaker than the conjunction of (P1) and (P6):

(P1) $\vdash_T P`(P`\varphi' \rightarrow \varphi)'$,

(P6) $\vdash_T \neg P`\bot'$.

(L1) states only that T includes some instance σ of the (P1) schema such that T also includes '$\neg P`\sigma'$'. This is logically entailed by the combination of (P1) and (P6), the absurdity '$\bot$' being the σ whose existence is asserted by (L1). (L1) is weaker in two ways: it does not require more than one instance of (P1) being included in T, and it does not require that '$\bot$' in particular be the sentence whose (P1) instantiation and whose unprovability are included in T.

Löb's paradox is proved by constructing a sentence 'a' such that the biconditional '$(a \leftrightarrow [P`a' \rightarrow \sigma])$' is provable in Peano arithmetic, where '$\sigma$' is the name of the sentence satisfying (L1). Both '$P`a'$' and '$\neg P`a'$' can be proved using (L1) through (L6). A slight modification of Löb's assumptions yields a notational variant of what I called "Gödel's paradox." Replace (L1) with (L1') and (L6) with (L6'):

(L1') There exists a σ such that $\vdash_T \neg P`a'$,

(L6') $\vdash_T \neg P`\varphi'$, where $\varphi$ is an instance of (L2) through (L5), or where $\varphi$ is the sentence $\neg P`\sigma'$, for some σ satisfying (L1').

We can still derive a contradiction, picking up the proof of Gödel's paradox at line (6):

(6) $\neg P`a'$,	(5), (L1')
(7) $P`\neg P`a''$,	(1)–(6), (L6')
(8) $P`(P`a' \rightarrow \sigma)'$,	(7), (L3), (L4)
(9) $P`[(P`a' \rightarrow \sigma) \rightarrow a]'$,	(L3), (L4), (L5)
(10) $P`a'$.	(8), (9), (*L*4)

[15] Löb (1955).

(L6'), together with (L3) and (L5), corresponds to (G1*). (L4) is identical to (G2), and (L2) is identical to (G3). (L1') is simply the existential generalization of (G4):

(G4) $\vdash_T \neg P$'$\bot$'.

(G4) therefore entails (L1'). Because of the special nature of '$\bot$', (L1') is true only if (G4) is, given assumptions (L2) through (L5) and (L6'). If T includes, for some sentence 'σ', the sentence '$\neg P$'σ'', then, since '$\bot$' logically implies 'σ', and (L3) and (L4) imply that the extension of '*P*' is closed under logical implication, it follows that *T* includes '$\neg P$'$\bot$''. Thus, the assumptions of this modification of Löb's paradox are logically equivalent with the assumptions of Gödel's paradox.

3.3 MODAL LOGIC AND THE LIAR

The use of modal logic can assist in the understanding of the formal features of liar-like paradoxes. By replacing the predicates 'is true', 'is knowable', 'is rationally believed', and so on, by the modal operator and by using standard Kripke-style model theory, we can examine the relationships between the various paradoxical theories already produced, as well as discover a recipe for generating new paradoxes.

As mentioned in Chapter 1 (and much emphasized by Montague), theories that are inconsistent when the notion of truth, rational belief, or whatever is represented by means of a predicate of sentences (or of sentence-like representational structures) may be consistent when the theory is transcribed by replacing such predicates with modal operators. Each of the paradoxical systems discussed in this chapter, for instance, corresponds to a consistent modal logic. We can therefore use standard modal logic to examine the relations of implication, equivalence, and independence among the relevant semantic, epistemic, and doxic axioms.[16]

All liar-like paradoxes have a common feature: the use of a diagonalization argument to produce a sentence φ for which it is provable that $\varphi \leftrightarrow \neg P$'$\varphi$' (where the predicate '*P*' stands for 'is true', 'is provable,' or any other suitable predicate). The modal transcription of this theorem of arithmetic would be $\varphi \leftrightarrow$'φ. If we assume that whatever is a theorem of arithmetic is true, knowable, provable, rationally believable, and so on, then we should recognize that this diagonalization really gives us the following family of formula schemata:

[16] In this chapter, I will use only normal modal logics, logics containing the rule of necessitation and the axiom schema (K): $(\varphi \rightarrow \psi) \rightarrow (\varphi \rightarrow \psi)$.

$(L^n)^n\ (\varphi \leftrightarrow \neg\varphi), \qquad n \geq 0.$

Suppose normal modal logic Σ has as a theorem schema the negation of a conjunction of formulas from the family (L^n). Suppose theory Σ^* results from Σ by (i) replacing by some predicate of sentences P, (ii) adding an axiomatization of the syntax of the language to Σ^*, and (iii) closing the result under a rule of necessitation: from $\vdash_{\Sigma^*} \varphi$, infer $\vdash_{\Sigma^*} P$ 'φ'. Then Σ^* will be inconsistent due to the presence of a liar-like sentence, producible by the usual diagonalization. Therefore, there is a precise definition of those systems of modal logic that are "paradoxical" in this sense.

A normal system of modal logic is *paradoxical* if and only if it has as a theorem schema a finite disjunction each of whose disjuncts is of the following form:

$$\Diamond^n\ (\varphi \leftrightarrow \varphi), \qquad \mathrm{n} \geq 0.$$

An order of paradoxicality can also be defined. Let us call a system that has $(\varphi \leftrightarrow \varphi)$ *as* a theorem schema zeroth-order paradoxical, one that has $(\varphi \leftrightarrow \varphi) \vee \Diamond (\varphi \leftrightarrow \varphi)$ first-order paradoxical, one that has $(\varphi \leftrightarrow \varphi) \vee \Diamond (\varphi \leftrightarrow \varphi) \vee \Diamond\Diamond (\varphi \leftrightarrow \varphi)$ second-order paradoxical, and so on.

Tarski's convention T, when transcribed into modal logic, produces a system that is zeroth-order paradoxical. The resulting normal modal logic has the characteristic axiom schema $\varphi \leftrightarrow \varphi$. The accessibility relation for any standard frame of this system is the identity function: each world is accessible to itself and only itself.

The modal systems corresponding to the assumptions of the Kaplan–Montague paradox, the Gödel paradox, and the Thomason paradox are all first-order paradoxical. All have the schema $\Diamond (\varphi \leftrightarrow \varphi)$ as a theorem. The characteristic axioms of the Kaplan–Montague system are:

(T) $\varphi \rightarrow \varphi$,

(U) $\varphi\ (\varphi \rightarrow \varphi)$.

In a normal modal logic, instances of (U) are all entailed by instances of (T) (together with necessitation).[17] Thus, the Kaplan–Montague paradox corresponds to the familiar modal logic (T). The standard frames of (T) are those in which the accessibility relation is reflexive.

17 The use of normal modal logics blurs some distinctions among paradoxical theories. For instance, in the Kaplan–Montague paradox, it is not necessary to assume that the axiomatization of syntax is itself knowable, while such an assumption is needed in the case of the Gödel and Thomason paradoxes. The presence of a rule of necessitation in the normal modal logics forces us to gloss over this distinction.

Thomason's assumptions correspond to the axiom schemata (U), (D), and (4):

(D) $\neg\bot$,

(4) $\varphi \rightarrow \varphi$.

Standard frames corresponding to the resulting system (DU4) are those in which the accessibility relation is transitive, serial, and secondarily reflexive (i.e., $\forall x \forall y(Rxy \rightarrow Ryy)$). These three conditions do not jointly entail reflexivity, and reflexivity entails seriality and secondary reflexivity, but not transitivity. The Gödel paradox depends on schemata (D) and (4) only. In the presence of a rule of necessitation, the axiom schema (U) is redundant. Therefore, the condition of secondary reflexivity is not needed.

Another first-order paradoxical system contains the schemata (U) and (5c):

(5c) $\varphi \rightarrow \Diamond\varphi$.

Frames for this system are secondarily reflexive and have a property that might be called weak transitivity: $\forall x \exists y \forall z(Rxy \,\&\, (Ryz \rightarrow Rxz))$. This system, like the previous ones, is "canonical" and therefore complete.[18] To show that the system (U5c) is canonical, I must show that the canonical standard model is secondarily reflexive and weakly transitive. The worlds in a canonical standard model consist of maximal (U5c)-consistent sets of sentences. First, I will show that the model is secondarily reflexive. Let α be a maximal consistent set, and let $\Gamma = \{\varphi\colon \varphi \in \alpha\}$. Suppose there is a world β such that $R\alpha\beta$. Therefore, Γ is consistent. Let $\Delta = \{\varphi\colon \varphi \in \beta\}$. I claim that $\Delta \subseteq \beta$. Suppose $\varphi \in \Delta$. Then $\varphi \in \beta$ and $\varphi \in \alpha$. Since a contains theorem (U), $(\varphi \rightarrow \varphi) \in \alpha$. By axiom (K) and modus ponens, $\varphi \in \alpha$. So, $\varphi \in \beta$. Thus, $R\beta\beta$. *QED*.

To show that the canonical model for (U5c) is weakly transitive, let α be a maximal consistent set. Let $\Gamma = \{\varphi\colon \varphi \in \alpha\}$. Let $\Delta = \{\varphi\colon\varphi \in \alpha\}$. First, I claim that Γ and Δ are each consistent. For Δ, this is obvious, since α is consistent. For Γ, suppose that both φ and $\neg\varphi$ belong to Γ. Then $\bot \in \alpha$. By axiom $5c$. $\Diamond\bot \in \alpha$. But, by (U), so does $\neg\bot$ and so α is inconsistent, contrary to assumption. Next, I claim that $\Gamma \cup \Delta$ is consistent. Suppose it were not. Then for some φ, $\varphi \in \alpha$ and $\neg\varphi \in \alpha$. Since α contains axiom *(5c)*, $\Diamond\varphi \in \alpha$., and so α is inconsistent, contrary to assumption. By Lindenbaum's lemma. $\Gamma \cup \Delta$ can be expanded into a maximal consistent set β such that $R\alpha\beta$ and $\forall z(R\beta z \rightarrow R\alpha z)$.

18 See Chellas (1984), pp. 171–4, for a description of canonical standard models.

Of course, the weakest system that is first-order paradoxical has the single-axiom schema $(\varphi \leftrightarrow \varphi) \vee \Diamond(\varphi \leftrightarrow \varphi)$. Further investigation is needed to determine whether this axiom corresponds to any first-order definable condition on frames. If it does, the axiomatization of the theory of that class of frames would give us the weakest complete theory that is first-order paradoxical. Moreover, the axiomatization might be more intuitively plausible than $(\varphi \leftrightarrow \varphi) \vee \Diamond(\varphi \leftrightarrow \varphi)$. Unfortunately, I suspect that the class of frames for this axiom is not first-order definable, in which case the best we can do is look for still weaker and more plausible sets of axioms that have this schema as a theorem.

The paradox developed in Chapter 1 is the only paradox I know of that corresponds to a second-order paradoxical system. The single-axiom system of the corresponding system is (5c), which, as previously mentioned, corresponds to a kind of weak transitivity property. As already shown, this system is canonical.

4

A computational account of mutual belief

I argued in Chapter 1 that doxic paradox cannot be averted simply by blocking self-reference through some sort of rigid Russellian or Montagovian type theory. In this chapter, I want to reinforce that argument by contending that, in any case, the loss of the capacity for significant self-reference is too high a price to pay. I will develop an account of the phenomenon of common or mutual belief that is representational or computational, thereby illustrating the crucial importance of the kind of reflective reasoning that generates the paradoxes.

The notion of 'common knowledge' appears in several theoretical contexts: in linguistics (the pragmatics of definite reference),[1] in social philosophy (the theory of conventions),[2] and in certain branches of game theory (noncooperative Nash equilibrium theory).[3] To be more precise, the notion that these disciplines employ would be more aptly described as "mutual belief," since Gettier-like distinctions between knowledge and justified true belief are quite irrelevant.

Herbert H. Clark and Catherine R. Marshall, drawing on work by H.P. Grice, argue that the presence of mutual belief is essential to the pragmatics of expressions of definite reference: expressions like 'the mess I made' or 'that animal'.[4] They discuss a vignette in which Ann asks Bob, 'Have you seen the movie at the Roxie tonight?' Let '*t*' abbreviate 'the movie at the Roxie', and let *R* be *Monkey Business*, the movie actually playing at the Roxie that night. In order for Ann to make '*t*' refer to *R* felicitously in her conversation with Bob, she must believe that Bob believes that '*t*' refers to *R*, that Bob believes that Ann believes that '*t*' refers to *R*, that Bob believes that Ann believes that Bob believes that Ann believes that '*t*' refers to *R*, and so on ad infinitum.[5]

1 Clark and Marshall (1981).
2 Lewis (1969), pp. 51–5; Schiffer (1972).
3 Armbruster and Böge (1979); Böge and Eisele (1979); Mertens and Zamir (1985); Harsanyi (1975); Kreps and Ramey (1987); Tan and Werlang (1988).
4 Clark and Marshall (1981).
5 Ibid., pp. 11–15.

Similarly, David Lewis argues that, for a behavioral regularity B to be a true convention, it must be a matter of mutual belief that everyone conforms to B.[6] Suppose, for example, that everyone drives on the right because everyone expects everyone else to drive on the right. But suppose that everyone has the false belief F: except for myself, everyone drives on the right by habit, for no reason, and would go on driving on the right no matter what everyone else did. Lewis argues that under such conditions driving on the right would not be a convention. Likewise, even if no one actually had the false belief F but everyone believed that everyone else had that false belief, then the regularity B would still not count as a convention. To count as a convention, B must be a matter of mutual belief.

Formal theories of belief and other propositional attitudes fall into two large classes: computational and noncomputational accounts. Noncomputational accounts of the attitudes assume that the objects of the attitudes are pieces of information (or would-be information) about the world, where logically or otherwise necessarily equivalent sentences are to be taken as corresponding to the same piece of information. For this reason, noncomputational accounts operate on a level of abstraction at which problems of computation disappear: the human mind as described by the theory is logically and mathematically omniscient. The prototypical example of such an account is the use of a Kripkean possible-worlds semantics as the basis for a theory of belief and knowledge, as pioneered by Hintikka.[7] The economist Robert Aumann constructed the first account of common knowledge along these lines.[8]

In this chapter, I will develop a computational account of mutual belief. In computational accounts of the attitudes, the objects of the attitudes are taken to have a structure that is mirrored by the grammatical structure of sentences. Thus, two logically or mathematically equivalent but grammatically distinct sentences can correspond to two distinct objects of belief. A computational account is not, therefore, implicitly committed to treating the human mind as logically and mathematically omniscient, and such an account can deal in a direct and natural way with problems of computational tractability. Computational theories of the attitudes have been developed by Carnap,[9] Davidson,[10]

[6] Lewis (1969), pp. 58–9.
[7] Hintikka (1962).
[8] Aumann (1976).
[9] Carnap (1947), pp. 53–5, 61–4.
[10] Davidson (1967).

Konolige,[11] and Kamp and Asher.[12] Montague,[13] together with Kaplan, discovered a paradox similar to Tarski's version of the liar paradox that afflicts computational theories of knowledge, which he, and others such as Thomason,[14] have taken as a motivation for abandoning the computational account altogether. We will encounter a version of the Kaplan–Montague paradox later in this chapter, where I will argue that recent work on solutions to the liar paradox has opened the way to rendering the paradox innocuous to the computational approach.

4.1 TWO PROBLEMS

The point of a theory of mutual belief is to describe the state of mind of one who believes that a certain proposition is a matter of mutual belief among the members of a certain group. A computational theory of mutual belief must explain how, given a finite set of informational inputs, the cogiter can generate each of an infinite series of beliefs in a finite amount of time and with finite resources. The beliefs in question are of the following form: A believes that *p*, B believes that *p*, A believes that B believes that *p*, B believes that A believes that *p*, and so on.

A number of philosophers have begun to tackle this problem: David Lewis,[15] S.R. Schiffer,[16] Gilbert Harman,[17] and Jon Barwise.[18] All of their theories have the same structure. Clark and Marshall have extracted the following schema from Lewis's book, which is also an apt summary of the definitions of Schiffer and Barwise:

A and B mutually know that *p* iff some state of affairs *G* holds such that:

(1) A and B have some reason to believe that *G* holds.

(2) *G* indicates to A and B that each has reason to believe that *G* holds.

(3) *G* indicates to A and B that *p*.[19]

Harman's fixed-point definition is obviously closely related to this but involves more explicit self-reference:

[11] Konolige (1985).
[12] Asher and Kamp (1986). Asher and Kamp build on earlier work by Kamp (1981) and (1983) and Heim (1982); See also Asher (1986).
[13] Montague (1963); Kaplan and Montague (1960).
[14] Thomason (1980).
[15] Lewis (1969).
[16] Schiffer (1972).
[17] Harman (1977).
[18] Barwise (1985).
[19] Clark and Marshall (1981), p. 33.

A and B mutually know that *p* if and only if A and B know that *p* and *q*, where '*q*' is the self-referential sentence 'A and B know that *p* and *q*'. The connection between the two definitions is this: in order to know such a proposition as *q*, one must be aware of some such state of affairs as *G*.

These accounts leave a central question unanswered: what is it for a state of affairs to 'indicate' something to someone? If we interpret '*G* indicates to *x* that *p*' as meaning that the situation *G* provides *x* with some evidence or warrant for the truth of *p*, then the Lewis–Schiffer definition cannot be wedded to a computational account of belief because of two problems: bounded or limited deduction (the lack of logical omniscience) and the possible inconsistency of the available data. First, the state of affairs *G*, if taken as a finite set of sentence-like representations, may provide *x* with the information that *p*, in the sense that *p* may be deduced from *G*, without *x*'s being able, given limitations of time and other resources, to recognize this logical entailment. Second, the state of affairs *G* might provide *x* with prima facie evidence for a logically inconsistent set of sentences. For example, *G* might contain conflicting testimony from two apparently reliable witnesses. The state of affairs *G* might give *x* some reason for accepting *p* while simultaneously giving *x* even stronger reason for accepting $\neg p$.

These two problems are not independent: the second is dependent on the first. Since human beings are not logically omniscient, they may be unable to detect the presence of inconsistency in the available data. Therefore, the solutions of the two problems must ultimately be interrelated. I will address the second problem first (in the Section 4.2) and then gradually relax the assumption of logical omniscience until a satisfactory approximation to reality can be reached.

4.2 THE PROBLEM OF INCONSISTENT DATA

Given an inconsistent set of data, the ideal (logically omniscient) reasoner believes the logical closure of the *weightiest* subset of the data that is consistent and otherwise coherently cotenable. Nicholas Rescher has described in some detail a system of "plausible reasoning" that incorporates this intuition in the simplest possible way.[20] Rescher's system employs a weakest-link principle: the various sources of data are graded according to degree of reliability, or "probitive solidity" and the ideal reasoner eliminates first from an inconsistent set of data those elements having the lowest ranking. More precisely, Rescher

[20] Rescher (1976). See the Introduction for an extended discussion of Rescher's construction.

defines the "maximal subsets" of an inconsistent data set:
S' is a maximal subset of data set S iff
(1) S' is not inconsistent, and
(2) for every other subset S'' of S that satisfies (1), if S'' contains more elements of S of rank k than does S', then there is some rank $k + n$ such that S' contains more elements of S of $k + n$ than does S'',

where rank 1 is the rank of lowest probitive solidity and S is a finite set. If the data set S is consistent, then S is its own maximal subset. The ideal plausible reasoner with data set S accepts just the propositions in the logical closure of the *intersection* of the maximal subsets of S (there may be more than one such maximal set).[21]

There are a number of interesting alternatives to Rescher's system. Rescher's system requires one to restore consistency by eliminating first the sentences of lowest rank, no matter how many must go. For example, one must prefer the elimination of thousands of sentences of rank k to the elimination of even one sentence of rank $k + 1$. We could replace Rescher's ranks with a set of additive weights and require that, in choosing between two routes to consistency, one must choose the subset that conserves the greater amount of weight. Another alternative would be a probabilistic system in which each source of data were assigned some probability of error. Assuming that these probabilities are mutually independent, one could assess each consistent subset of the data set by multiplying together the error probabilities of the data sentences that are excluded. The preferred subset would have the largest such product. Obviously, there are an endless number of possible modifications and combinations of these ideas. For our present purposes, it does not matter which is selected.

We can identify the epistemic state of a human reasoner with a set of data sentences, where each sentence is tagged according to its source and each source is assigned a rank, a weight, an error probability or some other measure of epistemic trustworthiness. We can use Rescher's system or one of the alternatives to define the sentences that are *ultimately justifiable* given epistemic state E. Now we are in a position to say something about what it is for a state of affairs G to 'indicate' something to someone:

G indicates to x that p iff G includes the fact that x is in an epistemic state E such that p is ultimately justifiable in E.

21 Ibid., pp. 49–56.

Using this definition, we can now take a second look at the Lewis–Schiffer definition of common knowledge, in particular at clause (2) of the definition:

(2) G indicates to A and B that each has reason to believe that G holds.

By eliminating some unnecessary detail, we can replace (2) with the more explicit and perspicuous (2'):

(2') A and B are in epistemic state E_A and E_B respectively, such that it is ultimately justifiable in both E_A and E_B to accept that A and B are in epistemic states E_A and E_B, respectively.

Therefore, the data sets of E_A and E_B must each be self-referential.

Suppose that clause 3 of the Lewis–Schiffer definition is also satisfied; that is, suppose that accepting that p is ultimately justifiable in both E_A and E_B. Does it follow that p is a matter of mutual belief between A and B? Only if both A and B are logically and mathematically omniscient, and recognition of this fact is itself ultimately justifiable in E_A and E_B. In order for the fact that p to be a matter of mutual belief between A and B it must be the case that A and B believe that p, A and B believe that A and B believe that p, and so on. From the fact that p is ultimately justifiable in E_A and E_B, it follows that A and B will ultimately believe that p, *if* A and B are logically infallible reasoners who reason for eternity. Any inconsistencies in any of the subsets of the data of E_A and E_B will eventually come to light, so A and B will eventually reach the maximal subsets of each state, and each logical consequence of the intersection of these maximal subsets will eventually be deduced. Some sentences may switch back and forth between acceptance and nonacceptance: by 'A ultimately accepts that p', I mean that A eventually reaches a point of permanent acceptance of p. (It does not follow that A will ever realize that she has reached such a point: at each point in her logical analysis of her epistemic state, she may be unsure whether any undetected inconsistency remains in the subset of data she has tentatively accepted. The set of ultimately justifiable sentences is Σ_2, not even recursively enumerable.)

We can assume that A must be able to recognize that B will eventually believe that p, given that B is in state E_B, only if we assume that A is also *mathematically* omniscient. A would have to be able to recognize, of an arbitrary set of sentences S, whether or not S is consistent. Gödel demonstrated that even logical infallibility and limitless time do not suffice for this task: there are sets of sentences whose consistency (relative to any axiomatizable background theory) cannot be proved. Therefore, to assume that A can be counted on eventually to realize that accepting p is ultimately justifiable in E_B is to ascribe truly godlike powers to A.

In order to be able to deduce each of the infinite series of beliefs present in a situation of mutual belief, we need a schema of the following form:

(JJ) $J_x`\varphi' \rightarrow J_y`J_x`\varphi''$,

where 'φ' is any sentence built up from 'p' by iterations of 'J', x and y are any two members of the group sharing the mutual belief that p, and 'J' represents the attitude of believing (or 'judging'). In the present context, we must interpret '$J_x`\varphi''$' as representing the eventually unvarying acceptance of 'φ' by a logically infallible x with infinite time, memory, and patience. As already explained, this schema would readily follow if the members of the group were mathematically omniscient. However, there is way in which schema (JJ) could be justified without resorting to the assumption of mathematical omniscience. Reasoner A could reproduce B's reasoning within E_B, and whenever A found himself tentatively accepting (in his impersonation of B) that φ, A could add to her own tentative beliefs the sentence $J_B`\varphi'$. If A later discovers that the subset of $E_B$ from which she deduced $\varphi$ is inconsistent, then she will give up $J_B`\varphi'$, just as B at that point would give up φ itself. If B eventually stabilizes at the acceptance of φ (deducing φ from the maximal, truly consistent subset of E_B), then A will likewise eventually stabilize at the acceptance of $J_B`\varphi'$.

This notion of ultimately justifiable belief can therefore provide a basis for a formally adequate characterization of mutual belief. However, since this notion concerns which beliefs of an ideal reasoner *ultimately* stabilize, its range of application is quite limited. We are typically interested in the beliefs of a person as a factor in the explanation of his actions. We can never predict with any confidence that all and only those beliefs that are ultimately justifiable in a person's present epistemic state will affect his behavior. We cannot even predict that he will have pursued the logical analysis of his data to the greatest extent possible in the available time; since time, memory, and mental energy are scarce resources that must be economized, he is unlikely to have devoted all of his available resources to a given problem without some special reason for thinking that this task warrants such priority by offering a reasonable prospect of recognizable success.

At this point, we must turn to the first of the problems discussed in Section 4.1: taking into account the absence of mathematical and logical omniscience. Before discussing a series of successively more realistic approximations, I want to describe some of the desiderata of a limited deduction theory of mutual belief.

4.3 DESIDERATA OF AN ACCOUNT

In Section 4.4, I will construct several definitions of a state of mutual belief, each of which entails all of the beliefs that are commonly taken to constitute such a state, namely, A and B believe that *p*, A and B believe that A and B believe that *p*, and so on. Before doing that, however, I want to consider carefully what are the desirable features of a computational account of mutual belief taking into account both the resolution of inconsistent data and the limitations of computationally feasible deduction. I contend that there are two principal desiderata: that mutual belief, as defined, be iterable (i.e., if it is mutually believed that φ, then it is mutually believed that it is mutually believed that φ) and that a computationally feasible algorithm for generating each of the beliefs in the series be described.

First, let us consider iterability. Within a computationalist framework (in contrast to the more familiar noncomputationalist or possible-worlds approach), if we define a state of mutual belief that *p* to be a state in which everyone believes that *p*, and everyone believes that everyone believes that *p*, and so on, it does not follow that, if *p* is mutually believed, then it is mutually believed that *p* is mutually believed. In the absence of assumed mathematical omniscience, it is quite possible for a reasoner to believe, of each member of an infinite set, that it has a certain property, without believing that every member of the set has that property. One might believe every member of the series: we all believe *p*, we all believe that we all believe *p*, and so on, to be true, without believing *that* every member of the series is true. Thus, a state of mutual belief might exist without its being recognized as existing by any of the members of the group, to say nothing of its being *mutually believed* by the group. Is such a noniterating definition of mutual belief defective?

Yes. In the absence of an iteration principle (such as schema (JJ)), it is impossible for every member of the infinite series of beliefs to be deducible from a finite data base. But without a finite data base, nothing would be computationally feasible. Without something equivalent to the iteration principle, each individual in a situation of mutual belief would have to have distinct sets of data from which he could deduce each member of the infinite hierarchy $p, J`p', J`J`p'', \ldots$ He would therefore have to have infinitely many data sentences and infinite memory in which to store them.

Even if we are concerned with only a finite segment of the mutual-belief hierarchy, there are problems from a computational point of view with abandoning the iteration principle. Let me illustrate this point by means of a more concrete example: a finite, two-person game of pure coordination (a game in which the payoffs to each player are always equal) with a unique pure-strategy Nash equilibrium. Here is a simple example:

	C_1	C_2
R_1	0, 0	1, 1
R_2	-1, -1	2, 2

In any such game, there is at least one action of one of the players that is strictly dominated, meaning that there is some alternative action that yields that player more utility, no matter what the other player does.[22] The deletion of the dominated action results in another, smaller game which also has a unique pure-strategy equilibrium. By repeatedly eliminating dominated actions, we eventually reach a trivial game in which each player has only one available action, the very action that belonged to the unique equilibrium in the original game.[23] If we assume that the game in question is a $k \times k$ game (each player has k actions available), then the two players will infer the correct solution only if the parameters of the game are common knowledge at least up to degree k.[24] Without the iteration schema (JJ), the data sets of the two players would have to include sentences in which the 'J' predicate is nested to a depth of $2k$, for instance, $J_1`J_2`J_1`\ldots J_{2p}\ldots'''$. It seems probable that there is a very low upper bound on the complexity of data sentences that can be delivered either by sense perception or by testimony. For any k greater than 3 or 4, it is unlikely that any such sentence could be indicated by any amount of sense data or could be communicated successfully by means of language. In fact, it seems doubtful that the content of such a sentence is even a possible object of thought for the human mind.

22 Lewis (1969), pp. 17–20.

23 Ibid., p. 19.

24 Let action a_{1k} (the kth action of the first player) be strictly dominated in the original game and let it be the case that, when action $a_{1(i+1)}$ is eliminated, a_{2i} is dominated in the remaining game,

Second, let us consider the desideratum for a more realistic account of mutual belief that it include the description of a computationally efficient algorithm for generating each of the sentences that are a matter of mutual belief within a given group. Otherwise, we cannot count on each member's actually holding each of the supposedly mutual beliefs. Of course, there is an obvious problem in accomplishing what I have just described: in a state of mutual belief, there are always infinitely many sentences that are mutually believed. Therefore, there is obviously no finite computation that can generate all of them. What we need, I think, is a concept of 'virtual belief'. A virtual belief is a sentence that is accepted as true *if* the question of its truth-value is raised. The algorithm for generating virtual beliefs should be

and when action a_{2i} is eliminated, a_{1i} is dominated in the remaining game, for every $i > 1$. Let $Z(i, n)$ represent the proposition that player i will not perform any action a_{im}, for $m \geq n$. We need the following assumption about the epistemic states of players 1 and 2: for all n such that $2 \leq n \leq k - 1$,

$(1, n)\ J_1$'$[J_2$'$Z(1, n+1)$' $\rightarrow Z(2, n+1)]$',

$(2, n)\ J_2$'$[J_1$'$Z(2, n+1)$' $\rightarrow Z(1, n)]$',

$(2, k)\ J_2$'$Z(1, k)$'.

These assumptions reflect the fact that each of the players understands the progressive elimination of feasible actions already described.

We also need two axiom schemata for the belief predicate:

(JJ) J_x'φ' $\rightarrow J_y$'J_x'φ''

(JMP) J_x'$(\varphi \rightarrow \psi)$' $\rightarrow [J_x$'φ' $\rightarrow J_x$'ψ']

The (JJ) schema represents the assumption that rational belief always iterates: if it is rational for one player to believe something, then it is reasonable for the other player to believe that it is rational for the first player to believe it. The (JMP) schema represents the principle that rational belief is closed under modus ponens: if it is rational for someone to believe both a conditional and its antecedent, then it is reasonable for him to believe the consequent. From these assumptions, it is straightforward to prove that each of the two players will expect the other to choose that action of his that belongs to the unique equilibrium (namely, a_{11} and a_{21}). Here is how the proof begins:

(1) J_2'$Z(1, k)$',	$(2, k)$
(2) J_1 'J_2'$Z(1, k)$'',	(1), (JJ)
(3) J_1'$Z(2, k)$',	(2),$(1, k-1)$, (JMP)
(4) J_2'J_1'$Z(2, k)$'',	(3), (JJ)
(5) J_2'$Z(1, k-1)$',	(4), $(2, k-1)$, (JMP)

etc. finally reaching:

$(4k-8)$ J_2'J_1'$Z(2, 2)$'',	$(4k-9)$, (JJ)
$(4k-7)$ J_2'$Z(1, 2)$',	$(4k-8)$, $(2, 2)$, (JMP)
$(4k-6)$ J_1'J_2'$Z(1, 2)$'',	$(4k-7)$, (JJ)
$(4k-5)$ J_1'$Z(2, 2)$'	$(4k-6)$, $(1, 1)$, (JMP)

To reach the conclusion 'J_2'$Z(1, 2)$'& J_1'$Z(2, 2)$'' (i.e., the conclusion that each player expects the other to play his equilibrium strategy) requires only $(4k-5)$ steps and $(2k-3)$ separate assumptions (plus the two schemata).

In the absence of the (JJ) schema, this deduction would be quite formidable. The number of premises needed would be a linear function of k^2, and the average length of the premises would be a function of k, so the complexity of the proof would be a function of k^3, a feasible computation but one that is much less efficient than that involved in producing is proof (the complexity of which is a linear function of k).

query-driven. We can then define a given sentence *p* as virtually believed in epistemic state *E* just in case the appropriate algorithm, when given *E* and queried about *p*, delivers the answer 'yes'.

Our second desideratum, therefore, amounts to the requirement that the specified algorithm always give the correct answer. The set of mutually believed sentences must therefore be recursively enumerable. In the Section 4.4, I will construct a definition of mutual belief that meets an even stronger requirement: that the computation be completed within a length of time that is a polynomial function of the complexity of *E* and of *p*. In the language of computational-complexity theory, such computations are described as completable in "polynomial time." Polynomial time is the accepted formal equivalent of the intuitive notion of 'feasibility'.

4.4 TOWARD AN ACCOUNT OF VIRTUAL BELIEF

My first definition will be of what I shall call "weak virtual belief". A sentence 'φ' is weakly virtually believed in epistemic state *E* if and only if it is provable in *M* that accepting 'φ' is ultimately justifiable in *E*, where *M* is some axiomatizable mathematical theory all of whose axioms are self-evident in *E*, and where *M* contains a description of *E* from which it can be proved that the axioms of *M* are self-evident in *E*:

$$W_E\text{`}\varphi\text{'} \leftrightarrow_{df} (\exists M)\ (P_M\text{`}J_E\text{`}\varphi\text{''}\ \&\ S_E(M)\ \&\ P_M\text{`}S(M, E)\text{'}).$$

This notion is stronger than that of ultimately justifiable belief, since, as we have seen, a sentence can be ultimately justifiable without its being provably so, in any axiomatizable system. If *M* includes Robinson arithmetic, then this account satisfies the iterability constraint of the preceding section. 'Provable in *M*' can be defined in the language of *M* in such a way that, whenever a sentence 'φ' is provable in *M*, it is provable in *M* that it is provable in *M*.

If, however, we intend *M* to represent all of the intuitively acceptable mathematics for one in a given epistemic state, reflection on the implications of Gödel's incompleteness results, as Benacerraf has shown,[25] provides good reason for supposing that, if one's beliefs are consistent, they cannot include a belief as to which formally axiomatizable theory *is* one's own intuitive mathematics. "Epistemic arithmetic" (the supplementation of ordinary mathematics with the logic of mathematical knowledge) should validate a logic analogous

[25] Benacerraf (1967).

to a normal modal logic.[26] Therefore, it should include a schema asserting, in effect, its own soundness (P‘φ’ $\rightarrow \varphi$, for all φ), as well as a necessitation principle (from $\vdash\varphi$ to deduce $\vdash P$‘φ’). If it does so by specifying which axiomatizable theory it is and asserts of that system that it is sound (and therefore consistent), then Gödel's second incompleteness theorem entails that the system is inconsistent.

Consequently, we should add to our language a *primitive* predicate ‘$S_E(x)$’, representing the self-evidence of sentence x to someone in the given epistemic state. ‘Provable in M’ will then coincide with ‘deducible from self-evident-in-E sentences’. Therefore, we should omit any reference to the specific axiomatization M (which we could never recognize as the axiomatization of our mathematical intuition); instead, we should refer only to ‘provable in E’. I will therefore replace my earlier definition of weak virtual belief with the following:

$$W_E\text{‘}\varphi\text{’} \leftrightarrow_{df} P_E\text{‘}J_E\text{‘}\varphi\text{’’}.$$

Provability in E iterates just in case self evidence in E does; that is, just in case every self-evident sentence is self-evidently so.

The following considerations support the thesis that self-evidence iterates. The point of the notion of self-evidence is to explain the conclusiveness of mathematical proof. If self-evidence is not itself self-evident, then any account of the conclusiveness of proof faces an infinite regress. The set of sentences self-evident to mathematical intuition must be effectively decidable by mathematical intuition, if every proof is recognizable as such.[27]

If we assume that every instance of the schema (PJ) is provable in E,

(PJ) P_E‘φ’ $\rightarrow J_E$‘φ’,

which simply states that whatever is provable from self-evident axioms is ultimately justifiable (one does not even countenance the possibility of inconsistency among self-evident truths), and if my definition of ‘W’ is self-evident in E, then we can easily prove the following theorem schema:

(WW) W_E‘φ’ $\rightarrow W_E$‘W_E‘φ’’.[28]

[26] Flagg (1984).

[27] See Chapter 3, especially the discussion of Alonzo Church's argument, for this point.

[28] The proof goes as follows:

(1) W_E‘φ’,	Assumption
(2) P_E‘J_E‘φ’’ & $S_E(M)$ & P_E‘$S(M, \mathrm{E})$’,	(1), definition of ‘W’
(3) P_E‘P_E‘J_E‘φ’’’ & P_E‘P_E‘$S_E(M)$’’,	(2), iterability of P_E
(4) P_E‘W_E‘φ’’,	(2), (3), definition of ‘W’ in M_E
(5) P_E‘P_E‘W_E‘φ’’’,	(4), iterability of P_E
(6) P_E‘J_E‘W_E‘φ’’’,	(5), PJ in M_E
(7) W_E‘W_E‘φ’’	(2), (3), (6), definition of ‘W’

Given this notion of weak virtual belief, we can define a corresponding notion of mutual belief. Let epistemic states E_A and E_B be such that it is virtually believed in each of them that A is in state E_A, that B is in state E_B, and that *p*. Then if A is in E_A and B is in E_B, A and B are in a state of mutual belief that *p*. Clearly, both A and B virtually believe that *p*. Since weak virtual belief iterates, they also virtually believe that they both virtually believe that *p*, and so on.

Although the iterability constraint is met, we have not made much progress toward satisfying the feasibility constraint. Once again, Gödel's incompleteness result, together with Church's thesis, means that there exists no effective procedure (much less a computationally feasible one) for determining whether a given sentence is weakly virtually believed in a given epistemic state. If A is in state *E* and is queried about 'φ', A has no choice but to begin trying to construct a proof that 'φ' is ultimately justifiable in *E*, a process that may never terminate (if neither a proof nor a disproof exists). In game theory, and in social science generally, we are interested in virtual beliefs only to the extent that we can count on their influencing the human agent's actual decisions, should the issues addressed by those beliefs become relevant to the agent's deliberations. The principal defect of mutual belief as defined in terms of weak virtual belief is that a perfectly rational agent might have the virtual belief that *p*, know that the truth-value of '*p*' is relevant to his present deliberations, and yet reach a decision without having acquired an actual belief that *p*.

By way of illustration, suppose that *J*'φ' is provable in *E*, but A does not know whether it is either provable or disprovable in *R*. Agent A cannot postpone her decision indefinitely, so she cannot resolve herself to continue searching until she finds either a proof or a refutation of '*J*'φ''. She may therefore give up before discovering a proof of '*J*'φ'' and so may make his decision without having formed the actual belief that φ.

We need a stronger notion of virtual belief. Roughly, something is a strong virtual belief if it is a weak virtual belief and there exists an algorithm such that it is known that the algorithm terminates in polynomial time, and it is in fact the case that the algorithm will discover a proof of the belief's justifiability. An ideal reasoner, given adequate time and resources, can be counted on to acquire as actual beliefs before making his decision all of his strong virtual beliefs related to issues known to be relevant to the decision. The ideal reasoner runs no risk of perpetual indecision in searching for a proof of 'J'φ'', where 'φ' is a strong virtual belief, since he already knows that a particular algorithm terminates in polynomial time.

In order to make this notion of strong virtual belief more precise, we need to explain what it is for an algorithm to be 'known' to terminate in polynomial time. First, we need to elaborate the notion of an epistemic state as introduced earlier. Besides the set of data sentences, the assignment of ranks or weights to data sources, and an axiomatizable theory P_E of provable-in-E mathematical truths, we need to add a finite corpus C_E of mathematical knowledge: a finite set of sentences for each of which there is a proof in M_E that is actually known. For a sentence 'φ' to be strongly virtually believed, some sentence of the corpus must say, in effect, that a specified algorithm always terminates in polynomial time (in a period of time that is a polynomial function of the complexity of its input).

More formally, with 'V' representing strong virtual belief, C_E'Ψ' representing the presence of Ψ in C_E, POLY(A) representing the fact that a Turing machine whose code is A terminates in a period of time that is a polynomial function of its input, $T(M, A)$ being a relation representing the fact that the output of a Turing machine A for any input is (the code of) a theorem of M, and TUR(A, x) being a function representing the output of A for argument x:

V_E'φ' $\leftrightarrow_{df}$ $(\exists Z)$ $(\exists M)$(Z is the characteristic number of a Turing machine & M is the code of a recursive axiomatization of some branch of mathematics &
(i) C_E'POLY(Z)' &
(ii) C_E'$T(M < Z)$' &
(iii) C_E'$S_E(M)$' &
(iv) TUR(Z,'φ') = 'J_E'φ'').

This definition simply says that φ is a virtual belief in epistemic state E if there is an algorithm that is known (by virtue of some apodeictic mathematical proof) to be feasible and to generate only theorems of some self-evident-in-E theory ((i)–(iii)) and that will in fact succeed in finding a proof of the justifiability of accepting φ, given the data available in state E ((iv)).

Strong virtual belief clearly satisfies the feasibility constraint just discussed. An ideal reasoner with sufficient time and inclination can be counted on to discover that each of her strong virtual beliefs are justifiable in her actual epistemic state. Therefore, she can be counted on to make her decisions in light of the information contained by these beliefs.

The iterability condition is also met if we make certain assumptions about the reasoning about knowledge that is provable in E. Let us suppose that φ is a virtual belief of state E. We need to show that there is an algorithm Z' such that Z' satisfies conditions (i)–(iii) above and such that, given the input 'V_E'φ'', Z' can find a proof of the fact that accepting 'V_E'φ'' is justifiable in E.

The following procedure would constitute such a Z'. For simplicity's sake, let us assume that Z' responds only to inputs having the form 'V_E'ψ'', for some sentence 'ψ'. For all other inputs, Z' simply gives a tautology, like '0 = 0'. If the input is of the proper form, then Z' checks the corpus C_E, looking for all algorithms that satisfy conditions (i), (ii), and (iii). There will be some finite number of such algorithms (since C_E is finite). Suppose that Z is such an algorithm. Then, as a subroutine of Z', we run Z on the input 'ψ'. It is known (given CE) that each of these algorithms terminates in a length of time that is some polynomial function of the length of 'ψ'. Therefore, the total time required to run all such algorithms will also be a polynomial function of 'ψ', and so also of 'V_E'ψ'. If any of these algorithms yields as output 'J_E'ψ'', then Z' should yield the output 'J_E'V_E'ψ'''. Otherwise, Z' can simply yield '0 = 0'.

We have just sketched a proof establishing that Z' always terminates in polynomial time, that Z' yields only outputs that can be proved in M_E, and that, whenever 'ψ' is a virtual belief in E and Z' is given the input V_E'ψ', Z' yields the output 'J_E'V_E'ψ'''. If we assume that C_E contains this very proof (we can construct such a self-referential C_E by Gödel's technique), then virtual belief in E will iterate. We can also show, by analogous reasoning, that, for *compatible* epistemic states, mutual belief will also iterate. (Two epistemic states are *compatible* when they share the same mathematical corpus.)

At this point, it is vitally important to go back over the proof just sketched and make explicit the principles of reasoning that are being used. We need to formalize a proof in E of the fact that the algorithm Z' will always terminate in polynomial time and always yield sentences provable-in-E. Z' will always terminate in polynomial time just in case all of its possible subroutines always terminate in polynomial time. For each possible subroutine, there is in C_E a proof in E of the fact that it terminates in polynomial time. It must be self-evident in E that everything proved in C_E is really true. The most natural and plausible way to accomplish this is to make sure that all instances of the axiom schema (P*) are self-evident in E,

(P*) P_E'φ' $\rightarrow \varphi$,

which states that everything provable-in-E, and therefore everything actually proved in C_E, is really so. Given (P*), we can prove that every possible subroutine of Z' will terminate in polynomial time, and so, therefore, will Z' itself.

Suppose that it is the case that 'ψ' is a virtual belief in E. Then there exists an algorithm Z that meets the three conditions in the definition of strong virtual belief. If each of these conditions is met, then it can certainly be proved in E to have been met. It is quite straightforward, given a canonical description of C_E, to establish that C_E does in fact contain proofs of the sort needed to satisfy conditions (i) through (iii). Similarly, given a canonical specification of Z, it is trivial to prove that its output for 'ψ' is in fact 'J_E'ψ''. So, whenever it is the case that 'ψ' is a virtual belief in E, it can be proved in M_E that this is the case. Using the schema (PJ) introduced earlier, we can further deduce that accepting 'V_E'ψ'' is justifiable in E.

The algorithm Z' yields interesting, nontrivial output only when given as input a true sentence of the form 'V_E'ψ''. As we have seen, whenever such a sentence is true, it is provable in E that it is justifiable in E (which is just what Z' outputs). Thus, we have succeeded in showing that Z' yields only sentences provable in E.

There is therefore no reason why C_E could not contain proofs both of the fact that Z' always terminates in polynomial time and that it yields only sentences that are provable in E. Consequently, whenever 'ψ' is a virtual belief, so is 'V_E'ψ''. We can therefore successfully define mutual belief in terms of strong virtual belief:

A and B mutually believe that 'p' iff

(1) A is in state E_{A} and B is in state E_{B}, and

(2) $(\forall x)(C_{E\mathrm{A}}(x)$ iff $C_{E\mathrm{B}}(x))$,

(3) $V_{E\mathrm{A}}$'p' and $V_{E\mathrm{B}}$'p', and

(4) $V^*_{E\mathrm{A}}$'(1)' and $V^*_{E\mathrm{B}}$'(1)'.[29]

Since the virtual beliefs of a given epistemic state are feasibly computable, so are the mutual beliefs of a group, given the epistemic states of each of the members. Moreover, since virtual belief iterates, so does

[29] 'V^*' represents a special kind of virutal belief: a person in state E virtually believes $*_E$ a sentence of the form '$F(n) = m$' if and only you he can be counted on to compute in polynomial time which answer to the question '$F(n) = ?$' is ultimately justifiable in state E. Therefore, condition (4) stipulates that both A and B can be counted on to discover which epistemic states each is in. (Recall that an epistemic state consists of a finite apodeictic corpus, a finite set of data, and an assignment of weights to each datum.)

mutual belief. Finally, if a given sentence '*p*' is mutually believed by A and B, it follows that A virtually believes that B virtually believes that *p*, that B virtually believes that A virtually believes that B virtually believes that *p*, and so on. Suppose, for example, that A is queried thus: 'Does B virtually believe that *p*?' Given condition (4), A can compute which epistemic state B is in. Given this information, A can discover that B does in fact virtually believe that *p*.

However, how realistic an account of mutual belief does such a definition provide? Prima facie, it does seem unlikely that human agents have theorems of complexity theory stored in their brains, to which they make frequent recourse in reasoning about everyday situations.

Although this definition certainly involves some degree of idealization (primarily in the use of the sophisticated notion of 'polynomial time' in the analysis of feasibility), I maintain that it does reflect certain practically important distinctions among sorts of virtual belief and that it makes precise an intuitively sound pattern of inference. I have argued that our beliefs fall into two classes: our apodeictic beliefs, so luminously certain that the possibility of their being unsound (much less inconsistent) is never taken seriously as a practical possibility, and those tentative beliefs that we have deduced from data that we take to be plausible but by no means unassailable. We do take seriously the possibility that the data of mere plausibility is inconsistent: we do not hold that a human reasoner will, if he reasons perfectly, accept every sentence entailed by his data.

The distinction between apodeictic and tentative beliefs is thus a pragmatic one: the boundary of the distinction may therefore shift from one context to another; it is not fixed once and for all. Beliefs taken as absolutely certain and fixed in relation to one practical or theoretical problem may be treated as merely tentative in another context. In relation to each problem, some beliefs must be treated as apodeictic, so that what it is to solve the problem is well defined.

There is, moreover, an intermediate level of belief, between the apodeictic and the merely tentative: those sentences that are held, on the basis of apodeictic beliefs, to be entailed by the maximal coherent subset of the data. We can confidently predict that a human reasoner, if she reasons perfectly and if she receives no new relevant data, will in fact continue to accept such sentences. We cannot predict that she will accept every sentence whose justifiability, given her data, is deducible from her apodeictic beliefs: there is no effective procedure, much less a feasible one, for discovering which sentences have this property. She may, however, have a repertoire of computationally feasible deductive procedures to which she has recourse habitually. The feasibility of these computations may itself be one of her apodeictic beliefs, even if those beliefs came to be accepted as a mere hunch or as a result of trial-and-error learning or the natural selection of a certain brain hardware. (Apodeictic beliefs and tentative data were distinguished on the basis of their present doxastic status, not on the basis of their origins.)

It is intuitively clear that a finite composition of feasible algorithms is itself also feasible: so if each of a finite set of algorithms is known to be feasible, it is intuitively correct to infer that the composition of these algorithms is also feasible. If I know that the set of another's virtual beliefs is generated by a feasible computation, then I can include the computation of the virtual beliefs of a finite number of other reasoners within the computation of my own virtual beliefs, without losing, thereby, the known feasibility of the latter computation. It is this intuitively correct argument that makes mutual belief (with respect to strong virtual beliefs) possible.

The sort of idealization incorporated into this account is much more benign than a pseudoidealization like mathematical omniscience. It is reasonable to hypothesize that the mind (or brain, if you will) economizes its expenditure of time and of computational space by reliance on some theory of complexity, acquired by a combination of natural selection, analogy-guided guesswork, and trial-and-error learning. This theory need not be *elegantly* axiomatized, but it must have an axiomatic structure, since finitely many general principles will have to be applied to an indefinite number of particular cases. Indeed, it need not even be a sound theory, or even consistent, so long as it is fairly reliable in yielding the right answers in concrete application. (Of course, it may be both sound and elegantly axiomatized: this is a matter for empirical investigation.)

At this point, I would like to review the axiom schemata I used in showing that strong virtual belief iterates. In talking about the formalization of provability in M, I have been, of course, tacitly assuming the following schema:

(PK) P_E ('$\varphi \rightarrow \psi$') $\rightarrow$ [P_E ('φ') $\rightarrow$ P_E('ψ')].

I have also assumed that all of the axioms of logic are provable:

(PL) P_E'φ', where 'φ' is any axiom of logic,

I have also made use, in two crucial places, of the schema (PT):

(PT) P_E'φ' $\rightarrow$ φ.

Finally, I have assumed that each of these principles of provability in E are self-evident in E, which can be represented as follows:

(PN) P_E'φ', where 'φ' is an instance of (PMP), (L), or (P*).

Given schema (PT), any instances of the following will also be instances of (PN):

(PU) P_E'(P_E'φ' $\rightarrow$ φ)'.

4.5 PARADOX

As I discussed in the preceding chapter, David Kaplan and Richard Montague[30] proved, using Löb's theorem,[31] that any system containing schemata (PK), (PL), (PT), and (PU) is inconsistent (the paradox of the knower). Our attempt to construct a computational account of mutual belief has led us straight into the kind of epistemic logic Kaplan and Montague showed to be beset by contradiction.

In fact, any adequate computationalist account of mutual belief will be beset by this paradox. We have already established that an adequate account of mutual belief must satisfy the following schema:

(M4) M'φ' $\rightarrow$ M'M'φ''.

If it is reasonable to demand this, it is surely a fortiori reasonable to demand that, if 'φ' is mutually believed, it must *not* be mutually believed that 'φ' is *not* mutually believed:

(MJ) M'φ' $\rightarrow$ $\neg M$'$\neg M$'φ''.

Given our computationalist framework, it is possible to construct a sentence 'a' such that it is provable in arithmetic that $a \leftrightarrow \neg M$'a'. This sort of arithmetical fact is certainly eligible for being the object of mutual belief; for example, we can imagine a group going over a proof of the theorem together. Therefore, let us assume that 'M' represents the property of being mutually believed in such a group. We can now add the assumptions

(M1) M'a' $\rightarrow$ M'$\neg M$'a'',

(M2) M'$\neg M$'a'' $\rightarrow$ M'a'.

(M1) and (MJ) together entail that 'a' is not mutually believed. Suppose (M1) and (MJ) are themselves objects of mutual belief. Then it would be reasonable to suppose further that it could be a matter of mutual belief that

[30] Kaplan and Montague (1960).

[31] Löb (1955). See Chapter 3, this volume.

'a' is not mutually believed. But from (M2), we can then deduce that 'a' is mutually believed, contradicting our earlier conclusion.

Montague[32] and others, such as Richmond Thomason,[33] have taken such results as conclusive reason for abandoning the computationalist approach to the psychological attitudes. Students of semantics, confronted by the analogous paradox of the liar, have not so easily despaired of coping with paradox, nor so quickly resorted to simply evading it. Moreover, not only is it not necessary to abandon the computationalist framework in order to cope with the paradoxes, I have argued in Chapter 1 that abandoning the computationalist framework is also not sufficient by itself as a means of evading contradiction. An analogous paradox also besets the possible-worlds framework.

Kripke's "Outline of a Theory of Truth"[34] was the seminal paper in this area, uncovering the possibility of describing a language that succeeds, at least in part, in containing its own semantics. Asher and Kamp have applied the Kripkean approach to the paradox of the knower.[35] Since Kripke's paper, a number of lines of inquiry into the problem of the liar have been pursued; let me mention briefly the hierarchical/indexical theories of Charles Parsons and Burge, and of Barwise and Etchemendy.[36] The Parsons–Burge theory is an attempt to apply the Tarskian hierarchy of truth-predicates (each in a separate "language") to the analysis of the predicate 'is true' in natural language, despite the fact that 'true' in English is univocal (and, consequently, English cannot be divided into a hierarchy of object language and metalanguage). The theory's solution to this problem is to hypothesize that 'true' is an indexical predicate having a variable extension (an infinite hierarchy of extensions) that is a function of the context of use. Thus, instead of distinguishing syntactically between the members of a series of predicates (as Tarski recommends doing in formal languages), Parsons and Burge urge us to distinguish pragmatically between the members of a series of possible interpretations of a single, indexical predicate.

Barwise and Etchemendy likewise seek to dissolve the liar paradox by finding a heretofore unnoticed element of indexicality in natural language. They suppose that every proposition is implicitly relativized

[32] Montague (1963).
[33] Thomason (1980).
[34] Kripke (1975).
[35] Asher and Kamp (1986) and (1987).
[36] Parsons (1974a), Burge (1979), Barwise and Etchemendy (1987).

to some environmentally salient "situation". The two solutions agree in that the contradiction that apparently can be derived within the intuitive theory of truth is only an apparent contradiction. When we first conclude that the liar is untrue, and then later decide that it is true after all, our second thought only apparently denies what was affirmed by our first thought: there has been a subtle shift in the context of interpretation of the predicate 'true' or of the entire proposition 'The liar is true'. For example, Burge would characterize the situation as one in which the liar is not true_1 but is true_2 (where the subscripted numerals represent the implicit element of indexicality). Thus, our intuitive theory of truth is not inconsistent after all. None of the intuitively correct principles of truth need be given up (see Chapter 6 for a fuller discussion of this approach to the liar).

This same sort of solution can be applied to the paradox of the knower, as has been discussed by Anthony Anderson.[37] A paradoxical proposition, such as 'This cannot be known_1', cannot be known_1 but can be known_2. Similarly, 'This is not mutually believed_1' may be mutually believed_2. In Chapter 7, I will address in detail how such a solution will work.

[37] Anderson (1983).

PART II

Solutions

5

A critique of context-insensitive solutions to the liar paradox

I will discuss five families of proposals for dealing with the paradox of the liar. Each of these five has a counterpart that could be proposed as a solution to the paradox of the disprover (discussed in Part I). In some cases, the proposed solutions to the liar incur the very same advantages and disadvantages when applied to the disprover, in such cases, the disprover is of relatively little interest. In many cases, however, proposals that are quite plausible and feasible when applied to the liar suffer collapse or encounter major new difficulties when applied to the disprover; it is in these cases that the paradox of the disprover holds the most promise of new insights.

The five families of approaches to solving the liar as it appears in natural language are as follows:

(1) Insist that significant semantic self-reference is impossible.
(2) Maintain a dichotomy between the metalanguage in which the theory is cast and the natural language that is the object of study.
(3) Maintain a distinction between denying a sentence and asserting its negation.
(4) Weaken the axioms or the logic used to derive the contradiction.
(5) Treat sentence tokens, rather than sentence types, as the bearers of truth and falsity.

I do not include the Tarskian object language–metalanguage distinction as a proposed solution to the liar as it occurs in natural language. Tarski was interested only in developing a consistent and adequate theory of truth for formal languages. He believed that significant self-reference (the meaningful and potentially true application of the predicate 'true' within the language to sentences of the language itself) was possible in the case of natural language and, for that reason, that natural language was inconsistent. For this reason, Tarski's work does not fall within family (1). Similarly, since Tarski did not attempt to develop a theory of truth for a language in which significant self-reference is possible (like natural language), his work does not fall within family (2), either.

In this chapter I will discuss solutions belonging to the first four families, and in the next chapter I will compare several solutions belonging to family (5). The first four families of solutions do not fare well when applied to the paradox of the disprover developed in Chapter 3. This failure of generality raises serious doubts about the correctness of these solutions as applied to the liar. The solutions of family (5) the one I favor, handle the paradox of the disprover as felicitously as they do the paradox of the liar.

The first family of solutions to the liar includes redundancy theories of truth, which in effect treat 'it is true that' as a sentence-forming operator rather than as a predicate of sentences. Another example would be the treatment of 'true' as applied to propositions in Russellian ramified type theory, in which the ramification of the types makes it impossible to represent a proposition that says of itself that it is true or that it is false. Variables occurring within a proposition of a given type can range over propositions belonging only to lower levels of the ramified hierarchy. Thus, self-referential propositions are excluded.[1]

Both of these approaches have been applied to the case of the paradox of the knower. Richard Montague took the moral of the knower to be that knowledge (and necessity) must be represented by means of a sentence-forming operator and not as a predicate of sentences.[2] In his models of the intensional logic IL, he represented the objects of knowledge as sets of possible worlds, rather than anything having sentence-like structure. Just as sets of worlds cannot in any obvious way be self-referential, the objects of knowledge (and presumably of belief) cannot refer to themselves, thus blocking the construction of the paradoxical sentence. Similarly, Alonzo Church and Anthony Anderson have begun to develop a Russellian logic of knowledge and belief, in which ramified types prevent self-referential objects.

Both Montague and Richmond Thomason argued that the Kaplan–Montague paradox refutes any structuralist theory about the objects of the psychological attitudes. A structuralist theory about the objects of the attitudes takes them to be sentences, or sentence-like entities with quasi-syntactic structure, built up of parts, consisting either of Fregean

[1] I do not include Alonzo Church's work applying Russell's ramified type theory to 'true' as a predicate of sentences in any of these families of solutions to the liar in natural language (Church [1976]). Like Tarski, Church in that article was concerned with avoiding the paradox in formal, not natural, languages. I will consider applying something analgous to the hierarchical approach developed by Church to natural language in the next chapter.

[2] Montague (1963).

senses or of actual individuals (as in Russell–Kaplan individual propositions). Montague and Thomason argued that, since we want some of these psychological attitudes (such as knowledge and ideal belief) to satisfy the very principles that lead to the Kaplan–Montague paradox, we must avoid that paradox by representing the attitudes by means of statement operators rather than by means of predicates of sentences or of sentence-like entities. They draw the moral that the objects of the attitudes must be represented as relatively unstructured objects, like sets of possible worlds.

There are several well-known disadvantages of representing knowledge (and similarly provability) by means of an operator. First of all, if such an approach does not permit quantification over propositions, it makes it impossible to express things that are apparently expressible in natural language, such as Jane knows something Bill knows, John can prove something no one in the class can prove, and the like. But if quantification over propositions is permitted and we can add to the language a predicate that expresses the relation between a sentence and the proposition that it expresses, then we can define a predicate of sentences representing x knows/can prove the proposition expressed by sentence s. This relation is fully defined semantically, in the sense that its extension is fully determined in each model of this extended system, so it would seem natural to add a primitive binary predicate representing it to the language. Under suitable conditions, one can prove that the axioms governing the knowledge or provability operator also hold for this defined predicate of sentences, in which case the contradiction follows in exactly the same way as in the paradox of the knower.

The paradox of the disprover holds a strategically crucial position, between the other psychological-attitude paradoxes, like the paradox of the knower, and the Tarskian direct discourse version of the liar. As in the Tarskian version of the liar, there is no question of avoiding the paradox of the disprover by replacing the crucial predicate with a sentential operator. Provability is clearly a property of sentences or of some sort of entity with sentential structure (like an equivalence class of intensionally isomorphic sentences). It just does not make sense to ask whether a set of possible worlds is provable.

Subjective provability is close enough to the other psychological attitudes that whatever solution is used in the case of the paradox of the knower or the ideal believer should certainly by analogous to the solution used in the case of the paradox of the disprover. If retreating to operators cannot be used to avoid the paradox of the disprover, then it should not be used to avoid the other paradoxes.

Moreover, in Chapter 1, I constructed a version of the paradox of ultimate justifiability in modal epistemic logic (treating 'ultimate justifiability' as an operator, not a predicate). This version of the paradox shows that representing propositional attitudes by means of operators is not sufficient to avert paradox.

The second sort of theory in the first family (that of Russellian intensional logic) also suffers the disadvantage of making significant self-application impossible. I will argue in Chapter 6 that intensional logics adequate to the task of representing common sense reasoning about situations of mutual belief (or "common knowledge") must permit significant self-application by sentences of predicates like 'is provable'. The ramified type hierarchy is simply too restrictive to do the job.

The second major family of proposed solutions to the logical antinomies includes all solutions that maintain a dichotomy between the metalanguage in which the solution is expressed and the natural language to which the solution is to be applied. The most prominent member of this family is the theory of Kripke.[3] In all of Kripke's theory, as he put it, "the ghost of the Tarski hierarchy is still with us," because "there are assertions we can make about the object language which we cannot make in the object language."[4] This approach differs from Tarski's in that the truth-predicate of the object language is allowed to be applied meaningfully, and occasionally truthfully, to sentences of the object language itself. Tarski's negative result is avoided by allowing truth-value gaps or "gluts" for some sentences of the object language.

The principal drawback to this approach is that natural language does not seem to separate naturally into a hierarchy of metalanguages, as would be required. Kripke speaks of providing a semantics for "natural language in its pristine purity, before philosophers reflect on its semantics" or for "natural language at a stage before we reflect on the generation process associated with the concept of truth, the stage which continues in the daily life of nonphilosophical speakers."[5] Contra Kripke, it seems quite clear that, no matter how reflectively sophisticated we philosophers become, we are still speaking the same natural language we began with.

[3] Kripke (1975).
[4] Ibid., in Martin (1984), pp. 79–80.
[5] Kripke (1975), p. 80, n34.

Essentially the same point has been argued quite forcefully by Keith Donnellan[6] and Tyler Burge.[7] The truth-value-gap theorist tells us that the liar sentence is pathological, that is, that it lacks a truth value. This seems to entail that the liar is not true. But this is simply a restatement of the liar itself. If the object language and metalanguage are the same language, then the gap theorist has asserted something that logically entails something that, according to his own theory, is not true (because it lacks a truth-value). Kripke avoids this objection by simply refusing to identify object language and metalanguage.

A somewhat different approach belonging to this family is the theory developed by Gupta and Herzberger,[8] in which the truth-predicate of natural language lacks a stable or determinate extension. It is crucial to their solution that the predicate 'is stably/determinately true' not belong to the object language. Moreover, this solution implies an antirealist stance with respect to semantic facts that I do not favor. According to Gupta, the predicate 'true' lacks the sort of "rule of application" governing the extension of ordinary predicates, like 'square' or 'red'.[9] Instead, it has merely a "rule of revision" that specifies how to improve a given putative extension for the word. I very much prefer a solution in which 'true' has a rule of application. This preference is especially acute when I turn from truth to consider the concept of rational justifiability. If we think only about what is prima facie justifiable or justifiable at a given stage in a process of reflection, then the Gupta–Herzberger construction is a useful descriptive model of the fluctuations that occur as one moves from one stage to the next. However, if we instead consider what is ultimately, finally justifiable, given an initial set of data (or in the case of semantics, if we consider what is stably true), then the paradox returns unabated.

The idea for the third family of proposed solutions was developed by Terry Parsons.[10] Parsons's idea is to distinguish between denying a sentence and asserting its negation. This enables Parsons to maintain a truth gap theory of the paradoxes without falling into the trap of the extended liar, since he denies the sentence 'The liar is true' but refrains from asserting the sentence 'The liar is not true', because to assert it would commit him to asserting the liar sentence itself.

6 Donnellan (1970).
7 Burge (1979).
8 Herzberger (1982); Gupta (1982/84).
9 Gupta (1984); p. 212.
10 T. Parsons (1984).

Although this approach may seem to work well when limited to the case of the liar paradox, it completely fails to block a paradoxical result very close to the original version of the paradox of the disprover. According to Parsons's idea, "a theory cannot be identified with the class of sentences which it tells us to accept, as is normally done; the theory must independently specify the class of sentences to be rejected."[11] A logic of acceptance and rejection must tell us, given an initial set of accepted and a set of rejected sentences, what further sentences we must accept and what further sentences we must reject. Given the set of self-evidently acceptable sentences and the set of self-evidently rejectable sentences, let us call the sentences that logic requires us to accept "provable" (represented '$P(x)$') and the sentences that logic requires us to reject "refutable" (represented '$R(x)$').

Let us use the diagonal lemma to construct a sentence G that is provably equivalent to 'R'G''. Let '$\vdash^*$' express the illocutionary force of denial. Understand a sentence not preceded by '$\vdash^*$' to be asserted. To derive a contradiction, we then need the following axiom schemata and rules:

(A1) R's' $\rightarrow$ P'R's'', where 's' is a standard name,

(A2) $(x)[Px \rightarrow \sim R(x)]$,

(R1) From $\vdash (\varphi \rightarrow \sim \varphi)$, deduce $\vdash^* \varphi$,

(R2) From $\vdash^* \varphi$, deduce $\vdash R$('φ').

Schema (A1) states that, if a sentence is refutable, then it is provable that it is refutable (where the sentence is named by a standard name, understood to be a name whose reference is epistemically accessible). This is unproblematic, assuming that whatever is self-evidently acceptable or rejectable is self-evidently so.

The point of the notion of self-evidence is to explain the conclusiveness of mathematical proof. If self-evidence is not itself self-evident, then any account of the conclusiveness of proof (or of refutation) faces an infinite regress. The set of sentences self-evident to mathematical intuition must be effectively decidable by mathematical intuition, if every proof is recognizable as such (as I have argued in Chapter 3).

Schema (A2) expresses the consistency of our self-evident theory, that "one cannot be justified in both asserting and rejecting the same claim."[12] Rule (R1) enables us to move from accepting a *reductio ad absurdum* of a sentence to rejecting the sentence itself. It will be valid, given any reasonable three-valued truth table for the conditional. For

[11] Ibid., p. 141.
[12] Ibid.

example, consider the strong Kleene and the Lukasiewicz truth tables for the conditional:

Kleene:

$\varphi \rightarrow \Psi$	t	u	f
t	t	u	$\underline{f}$
u	t	$\underline{u}$	u
f	t	$\underline{t}$	t

Lukasiewicz:

$\varphi \rightarrow \Psi$	t	u	f
t	t	t	$\underline{f}$
u	t	$\underline{t}$	u
f	$\underline{t}$	t	t

Since we are considering the case in which 'Ψ' is '$\sim\varphi$', we need only look at the values on the diagonal that are underlined. According to the strong Kleene tables, the only case in which '$(\varphi \rightarrow \sim\varphi)$' is true($t$) is the case in which '$\varphi$' is false($f$). In such a case, it is correct to reject 'φ', and rule (R1) is valid. (Note that the same is true of the weak Kleene table.) According to the Lukasiewicz table, '$(\varphi \rightarrow \sim\varphi)$' is true in two cases: when 'φ' is false and when it is undefined(u). In both of those cases, it is correct to reject 'φ' and again rule (R1) is valid. (R2) simply enables us to infer the refutability of a sentence, given an actual refutation of it.

Let us introduce a standard name 'G', which we will give, by means of the appropriate baptismal process, the denotation '$R(G)$'. From these assumptions, a contradiction ensues:

(1) $R(G) \rightarrow P(\text{'}R(G)\text{'})$,	(A1)
(2) $P(\text{'}R(G)\text{'}) \rightarrow P(G)$,	(1), substitution of identicals
(3) $P(G) \rightarrow \sim R(G)$,	(A2)
(4) $R(G) \rightarrow \sim R(G)$,	(1)–(3)
(5) $\vdash^{*} R(G)$,	(4), (R1)
(6) $R(\text{'}R(G)\text{'})$,	(5), (R2)
(7) $R(G)$,	(6), substitution of identicals
(8) $\sim R(G)$.	(4), (7)

Because of the viciously circular character of G, Parsons will certainly want to reject it. But if we can infer from this that G is refutable, then we seem to be forced to accept G as well.

The fourth family of proposed solutions for the logical antinomies is that of weakening the principles or the logic (it is difficult to draw a sharp distinction between the two) used to derive the contradiction. There are two ways in which this can be done. The first is to so weaken the system that we can still derive 'not-true(L)', and therefore 'L' (the liar sentence) itself, but we can no longer derive 'true(L)'. The second way is to further weaken the system so that we can derive neither 'true(L)' nor 'not-true(L)'. The first of these is developed in a paper by

Solomon Feferman;[13] the second has been proposed by Martin.[14] Martin's approach is unassailable, except for the fact that it shrouds the whole matter of the liar in a veil of impenetrable mystery. This approach makes sense only as a last resort.

Feferman's proposal has the troubling feature of enabling us to derive sentences that, according to the theory, are not true. In the case of the paradox of the disprover, this defect becomes fatal, since the analogues of Feferman's axioms would enable us to prove sentences that we can also prove are not provable, an unsatisfactory result if there ever was one. In particular, we would be able to prove 'not provable(*D*)', from which we can prove '*D*' (the paradoxical "disprover" sentence) itself.

In the system $S'(\equiv)$ of Feferman's paper, which he refers to as a "type-free formal system in an extension of the classical predicate calculus,"[15] '$\equiv$' is an intensional operator that represents some sort of strong equivalence. The general strategy adopted is that of weakening the truth schema used to derive the contradiction by replacing the material biconditional with the intensional operator '$\equiv$'.

The axioms for '$\equiv$', as stated in Feferman's paper, are as follows:

(1) $\equiv$ is an equivalence relation.

(2) $\equiv$ is preserved by $\sim$, $\wedge$, $\equiv$, and $\forall$.

(3) (i) $(\varphi \equiv t) \leftrightarrow \varphi$, for φ atomic,
(ii) $(\varphi \equiv f) \leftrightarrow \sim\varphi$, for φ atomic in L_o, the nonsemantic segment of the language.

(4) (i) $((\sim\varphi) \equiv t) \leftrightarrow (\varphi \equiv f)$,
(ii) $((\sim\varphi) \equiv f) \leftrightarrow (\varphi \equiv t)$.

(5) (i) $((\varphi \wedge \Psi) \equiv t) \leftrightarrow (\varphi \equiv t \wedge \Psi \equiv t)$,
(ii) $((\varphi \wedge \Psi) \equiv f) \leftrightarrow (\varphi \equiv f \vee \Psi \equiv f)$.

(6) (i) $((\forall x\, \varphi) \equiv t) \leftrightarrow \forall x\, (\varphi \equiv t)$,
(ii) $((\forall x\, \varphi) \equiv f) \leftrightarrow \exists x\, (\varphi \equiv f)$.

(7) (i) $((\varphi \equiv \Psi) \equiv t) \leftrightarrow D\varphi \wedge D\Psi \wedge \varphi \equiv \Psi$,
(ii) $((\varphi \equiv \Psi) \equiv f) \leftrightarrow D\varphi \wedge D\Psi \wedge \sim (\varphi \equiv \Psi)$,
where '$D\varphi$' abbreviates '$(\varphi \equiv t) \vee (\varphi \equiv f)$'.

$(TA)_{\equiv}$ $T(`\varphi') \equiv \varphi$.

Feferman mentions a number of lemmas, provable in this system, including:

[13] Feferman (1982).

[14] D.A. Martin, paper presented at a seminar on the liar paradox, University of California, Los Angeles, October 14, 1985.

[15] Feferman (1982), pp. 267–8.

(v) $(\varphi \equiv f) \rightarrow \sim\varphi$, for all φ.[16]

Feferman's system has in effect four truth-values, as noted by Bunder:[17]

(0) $\varphi \wedge (\varphi \equiv t)$,

(1) $\varphi \wedge \sim(\varphi \equiv t)$,

(2) $\sim\varphi \wedge (\varphi \equiv f)$,

(3) $\sim\varphi \wedge \sim(\varphi \equiv f)$.

Values 0 and 2 are the classical values 'true' and 'false'. Sentences with value 1 are assertible but not true (or false), while sentences with value 3 are not false, but their negations are assertible. The truth table for Feferman's '≡' looks like this:

$\varphi \equiv \Psi$	0	1	2	3
0	0	3	2	3
1	3	1	3	1
2	2	3	0	1
3	3	1	3	1

The sentence '$\varphi \equiv \Psi$' is true (0) if both φ and Ψ have the same classical value; it is assertible whenever φ and Ψ are both true, both false, or both neither true nor false. Likewise, '$\varphi \equiv \Psi$' is false if φ and Ψ have different classical values; it is deniable whenever the two have different classical values or one has a classical value and the other does not.

I have to introduce nonsymmetric connective '⇒', in the spirit of Feferman's symmetric '≡'. The semantics of the connective will be give '$\varphi \Rightarrow \Psi$' the following meaning: the truth-value of φ is less than or equal to that of Ψ, using the ordering: false < neither true nor false < true. The truth table is the following:

$\varphi \Rightarrow \Psi$	0	1	2	3
0	0	3	2	3
1	1	1	3	1
2	0	1	0	1
3	1	1	3	1

We could then add the following axiom schemata:

(1*) ⇒ is a transitive and reflexive relation.

(2*) ⇒ is preserved by ~, ∧, ⇒, and ∀.

(3*) (i) (a) $(t \Rightarrow \varphi) \leftrightarrow \varphi$, for φ atomic or f,

(b) $\varphi \Rightarrow t$

(ii) (a) $\sim\varphi \leftrightarrow (\varphi \Rightarrow f)$, for φ an atomic $L_\circ$ formula,

(b) $f \Rightarrow \varphi$.

[16] Ibid., p. 268.

[17] Bunder (1982).

(4*) (i) $(t \Rightarrow \sim\varphi) \leftrightarrow (\varphi \Rightarrow f)$.
(ii) $((\sim\varphi) \Rightarrow f) \leftrightarrow (t \Rightarrow \varphi)$

We need the analogue of Feferman's Lemma (v):

(v*) $(\varphi \Rightarrow f) \rightarrow \sim\varphi$, for all φ.

Finally, we need a knowledge schema:

$(\mathrm{KA})_{\Rightarrow}$ $P(`\varphi') \Rightarrow \varphi$.

The system $S(\Rightarrow)$, so axiomatized, can be shown to be consistent by essentially the same proof used by Feferman for $S'(\equiv)$. First, we interpret the connectives by means of the strong Kleene truth tables, treating $\Rightarrow$ as equivalent to the material conditional. We then find a fixed-point model M^*. Finally, we construct a classical two-valued model M by means of the following truth definition:

(1) For φ atomic, $M \vdash \varphi \leftrightarrow [\varphi]_{M^*} = T$,
(2) $M \vdash \sim\varphi \leftrightarrow M \vdash \varphi$,
(3) $M \vdash (\varphi \wedge \Psi) \leftrightarrow (M \vdash \varphi \;\&\; M \vdash \Psi)$,
(4) $M \vdash \forall x\, \varphi \leftrightarrow$ for each $m \in M$, $M \vdash \varphi\,[m/x]$,
(5) $M \vdash (\varphi \Rightarrow \Psi) \leftrightarrow [\varphi]_{M^*} \leq [\Psi]_{M^*}$, where $F < I < T$.

It is straightforward to show that each of the axioms of $S(\Rightarrow)$ is validated in M.

We then construct the disprover sentence D such that

(1) $P(`\sim D') \Rightarrow P(\sim`P(`\sim D')')$	(1') (reflexivity), substitution of identicals

This can be done by baptizing a singular term τ referring to the sentence '$P(\mathrm{Neg}(\tau))$', where 'Neg' is the function that yields the negation of its argument. Line (1) then follows by the reflexivity of '$\Rightarrow$'. (Let '$\sim\varphi$' represent the name for the negation of φ.) From these, we can deduce the following:[18]

(2) $P(`\sim P(`\sim D')') \Rightarrow \sim P(`\sim D')$,	$(\mathrm{KA})_{\Rightarrow}$
(3) $P(`\sim D') \Rightarrow \sim P(`\sim D')$, (1), (2),	Axiom (1*) (transitivity)
(4) $P(`\sim D') \rightarrow (t \Rightarrow P(`\sim D'))$,	Axiom (3*)(i)(a)
(5) $(t \Rightarrow P(`\sim D')) \rightarrow (t \Rightarrow \sim P(`\sim D'))$,	(3), Axiom (1*) (transitivity)
(6) $(t \Rightarrow \sim P(`\sim D')) \rightarrow (P(`\sim D') \Rightarrow f)$,	Axiom (4*)(i)
(7) $P(`\sim D') \Rightarrow f) \rightarrow \sim P(`\sim D')$,	Lemma (v*)
(8) $\sim P(`\sim D')$.	(4)–(7), propositional logic

Thus, we have proved '$\sim P(`\sim D')$', which is the negation of D. We have proved '$\sim D$' and thereby have proved that '$\sim D$' is *unprovable*. This is unacceptable, since if we have actually proved a sentence, we should

[18] Feferman (1982), pp. 266–7.

surely be able to infer that it is provable. If we add to our system a rule of necessitation, from $\vdash\varphi$ to infes $\vdash P(`\varphi')$, we can derive an explicit contradiction:

(9) $P(`{\sim}P(`{\sim}D')')$, (8), necessitation
(10) $P(`{\sim}D')$. (9), substitution of identicals

A defender of Feferman's theory, applied to the knower paradox, might reply that the preceding proof depends on confusing two distinct notions of knowability. The first is knowability in the strict sense, a sense of knowledge that entails truth. For this sense of knowable or provable, every sentence of the form '$P(`\varphi') \Rightarrow \varphi$' is true, since $P(`\varphi')$ is always at least as true as φ (using the $f < u < t$ ordering). However, necessitation is not a valid rule for this interpretation of '*P*', since Feferman's approach permits ideal theories to have consequences that are not true (that are indeterminate, like the liar sentence). Hence, the fact that a sentence can be correctly deduced from the correct axioms does not entail that is knowable in this strict sense. Alternatively, if '*P*' is interpreted as meaning ideally assertible, then some sentences of the form '$P(`\varphi') \Rightarrow \varphi$' are false, since it may be true that φ is assertible even though φ itself is indeterminate. On neither interpretation can one have both the $(KA)_{\Rightarrow}$ axiom and necessitation, so the contradiction is blocked.

In response, I would grasp the first horn of the dilemma. It is true that necessitation will not always yield *true* sentences in the context of a correct proof, but this occurs within Feferman's system as well (e.g., the liar sentence is provable but not true). I need only claim that, if φ has been proved, it is *assertible* that φ is knowable in the strict sense. If φ has been proved, then it is either true or indeterminate. Therefore, $P(`\varphi')$, in the strict sense of knowable or provable, is either true or indeterminate. Moreover, it seems to me obvious that it is assertible in either case: what better grounds could there be for the claim that something is knowable than to produce a correct proof of it?

All of the solutions in the fifth family share an important characteristic: sentence tokens rather than sentence types are taken to be the fundamental truth bearers (and provability bearers). This idea was first developed independently by Ushenko[19] and Donnellan.[20] It has been worked out most fully by Charles Parsons, Burge, Gaifman, and Barwise and Etchemendy. This family will be taken up in detail in the next chapter.

[19] Ushenko (1957).
[20] Donnellan (1957).

Anil Gupta has objected to solutions in the fifth family on the grounds that they mislocate the theory of levels in pragmatics. Gupta's reason for thinking that the theory of levels belongs to semantics rather than to pragmatics seems to be that the levels of the various occurrences of 'true' in a language can be completely fixed given only a model for the language.[21] This seems to be quite different from the situation of ordinary indexicals and demonstratives, but is it really? Given a theory about how the reference of various indexicals and demonstratives are determined by various facts about the tokens in which they occur, couldn't we construct a model-theoretic account of the evaluation of sentence tokens that did not simply leave the denotations of indexicals to the "garbage dump of informal pragmatics"?

The commonality between ordinary indexicals and predicates like 'true' is that, in both cases, the evaluation of a token containing them depends on facts about the token other than just its linguistic type. In the case of 'here' and 'now', the evaluation depends on spatiotemporal facts about the token. In the case of 'true', the evaluation depends on facts about what other tokens apply semantic predicates to terms that denote the token in question.

If a language is enriched (if necessary) so as to be able to express any of the facts about tokens that might enter into determining the denotation of the tokens' indexicals, then, given a model of the indexical-free segment of the language whose domain includes the tokens being evaluated, we could generate a semantic evaluation of all of the tokens, including those whose types include indexical elements. For example, consider the indexical 'here'. English already has the capacity to express the necessary relation between tokens and places: 'is-located-at(x, y)'. Take any model of the indexical-free segment of English whose domain contains all of the tokens to be evaluated. We could then construct a function, HERE(x, M), that gives the denotation of the word 'here' as it occurs in token x relative to model M (where M is a model of the indexical-free segment of English and $x \in$ Domain of M). HERE (x, M) = y if and only if $\langle x, y \rangle$ belongs to the extension in M of the predicate 'is-located-at'.

The indexicality of 'true' differs from that of 'here' and 'now' in that the assignment of extensions of all the occurrences of 'true' is subject to holistic constraints. One cannot assign extensions to occurrences of 'true' one by one, as one can for 'here' and 'now'. Instead, the

21 Gupta (1982/84), p. 204.

correctness of each assignment depends on what other assignments have been made. Nonetheless, given a model *M*, whose domain contains all of the tokens to be evaluated and that assigns extensions to all the context-insensitive predicates and constants of a given language, we can describe a recursive procedure, depending only on *M*, for arriving at a semantic evaluation of sentence tokens whose types include occurrences of 'true'.

6

Three context-sensitive solutions to the liar paradox

Tyler Burge,[1] Haim Gaifman,[2] and the team of Jon Barwise and John Etchemendy[3] have all proposed interesting new solutions to the liar paradox in recent years. The three solutions bear a striking family resemblance. I will explore in this chapter the important similarities and differences among the three approaches. I will also show how Gaifman's theory can be extended in order to provide the sort of *formal pragmatics* that the other two solutions require. Finally, I will prove that only two levels of truth ('true_0' and 'true_1') are needed in the interpretation of natural language.

The so-called strengthened liar paradox provides an important motivation for all three theories. It is simply an objection to any theory about the paradoxes that tries to distinguish between falsehood and other kinds of failure to be true (having a truth-value gap, or failing to express a proposition). Consider the following liar sentence (A):

(A) Sentence (A) is not true.

The value-gap analyst describes such paradoxical sentences as being neither true nor false (perhaps because they "fail to express a proposition"). Sentence (B) is therefore a consequence of the value-gap position:

(B) Sentence (A) is not true (because gappy).

Sentence (B) is just sentence (A), so the value-gap theorist is forced to describe an integral part of her own theory as being neither true nor false, failing to express a proposition. Gaifman has described the liar paradox as a semantic "black hole," sucking proposed solutions into the void. Infinite descending chains constitute another kind of black hole – for example:

(1) Sentence (2) is not true,
(2) Sentence (3) is not true,
etc.

[1] Burge (1979).
[2] Gaifman (1988).
[3] Barwise and Etchemendy (1987).

Initially, we want to say that all of the sentences in the chain fail to be true because of the semantically pathological character of the chain. In particular, we want to say that sentence (1), like the other parts of the chain, is not true. But this claim can be labeled 'sentence (0)' and placed in its appropriate place in the chain. A negative semantic evaluation of the chain is merely part of a larger descending chain.

Burge's solution to the liar consists in postulating that the extension of the predicate 'true' varies according to the context of utterance, as does the extension of such 'indexical' expressions as 'here' and 'now'. Every occurrence of the predicate 'true' is contextually relativized to some level in a quasi-Tarskian hierarchy (a hierarchy, however, not of languages or predicates, but of extensions of a single context-sensitive predicate). In Burge's formulation, a level in this hierarchy corresponds to every ordinal number, although, as will be shown in Section 6.2, only two indices are needed. A particular utterance or assertion of a sentence token is true or false (at any given level) by virtue of the "Burgean proposition" it expresses, where a Burgean proposition consists of a sentence type of English together with an assignment of indices to each of the indexical elements of that sentence type (in particular, an assignment of ordinal numbers to each occurrence of 'true'). Burge treats natural English in use as implicitly a typed language, but a typed language of an unorthodox kind: the type levels are assigned contextually and do not depend solely on the intentions and knowledge of the speaker, and the types do not place restrictions on the well-formedness of sentences.

Burge analyzes the black hole phenomenon in the following way. Sentence (A) is interpreted as expressing the Burgean proposition that (A) is not $true_0$. Because of its circularity, sentence (A) is neither $true_0$ nor $false_0$: there is a $truth_0$-value gap. Since there is such a gap, it is *true* to say that (A) is not $true_0$. Therefore, we must be able to assert (C):

(C) Sentence (A) is true.

Sentence (C) is interpreted as expressing the proposition that (A) is $true_1$. Thus, we can assert both (A) and (C) without contradicting ourselves. Sentence (A) is both not $true_0$ and $true_1$. The paradox is solved by showing that the contradiction is only apparent. The infinite descending chain is handled in a similar fashion. Every sentence of the chain is both not $true_0$ and $true_1$.

In what they call "Austinian semantics" (after John Austin), Barwise and Etchemendy agree with Burge in postulating shifts in the extension of 'true' as used in natural language. According to them, sentences express Austinian propositions, which consist of three elements: a sentence type of English, an assignment of extensions to the indexical and demonstrative elements of that type, and a partial model of the world (a "situation") that the proposition is about. The truth-predicate is not itself indexical, but an occurrence of 'true' in a proposition is evaluated by means of a partial extension of the predicate in the relevant situation.

In this chapter, I want to focus on what Barwise and Etchemendy call the "denial liar", which is constructed in terms of one of two possible interpretations of negation. Corresponding to such statements of the liar are circular propositions such as l_s:

$$l_s = \sim \{s;\ \mathrm{true}(l_s)\}.$$

If s is an actual situation, as it must be for l_s to be actually expressible, then this liar proposition is in fact true: situation s cannot be a part of the world that makes it the case that l_s is true. Proposition l_s is true, relative to the world or to any sufficiently large part of it, but not relative to situation s. Similarly, each proposition in the infinitely descending chain will be true, but not true in the situation to which it is relativized.

Four differences between Burge's theory and Barwise and Etchemendy's are immediately apparent. First, Barwise and Etchemendy use Aczel's non-well-founded set theory to construct propositions that literally contain themselves, while Burge models paradoxicality by means of self-referential statements or assertions (i.e., statements that contain a term that designates the statements themselves). It is relatively easy to translate Burge's model into Barwise and Etchemendy's formalism, essentially by replacing names of propositions by the propositions themselves. Second, the situation parameter serves a function for Barwise and Etchemendy beyond introducing variability in the extension of 'true': the situation that a proposition is about fixes the universe of discourse over which the variables of quantification in the proposition are to range. In order to avoid the Burali–Forti paradox (in order to avoid occurrences of 'true' that must be assigned an ordinal number that *per impossible* must contain all ordinal numbers), Burge must follow Charles Parsons in attributing an element of context sensitivity to variables of quantification, as well as to 'true'. Therefore, a complete Burgean theory will more closely resemble Barwise and Etchemendy's. Third, a Burgean language is more expressive, since several occurrences of 'true' can be relativized to different ordinal levels in the very same proposition, while each

Austinian proposition has only one situation parameter. A relatively minor change in Barwise and Etchemendy's theory would eliminate this difference: namely, relativizing each proposition to a *parameter* (where a 'parameter' is either a situation or a finite sequence of parameters) instead of to a single situation whenever the proposition contains more than one occurrence of 'true'. Fourth, we will have to add to the Burgean language an 'inner' as well as an 'outer' form of negation, the inner form applying only to atomic formulas, corresponding to the dual of positive atomic propositions in Barwise and Etchemendy's system. All four of these changes will be explained in much more detail in the next section.

Gaifman's investigations began with an attempt to provide an algorithm for assigning Burge's ordinal levels to actual occurrences of 'true'. At some point, Gaifman abandoned this project and developed instead a simpler semantics in which Burgean propositions are entirely left out and concrete sentence tokens are directly evaluated. Gaifman insists that we distinguish between the self-referential token (A) and the non-self-referential (B), which is a token of the same type:

(A) (A) is not true.

(B) (A) is not true.

Gaifman's algorithm evaluates (A) as not true and (B) as true. Gaifman's theory, however, cannot resolve the problem of the infinite descending chain in a similarly elegant fashion; it remains a black hole for his theory.

Gaifman's principal contribution to this problem is his construction of an algorithm for evaluating a network of sentence tokens (or "pointers"). A collection of tokens constitutes a directed graph in which the nodes are sentence tokens and the directed edges represent the *calling* relation. One token calls another if the second is a logical component of the first (such as a conjunct or disjunct) or if the first is a token of an atomic sentence containing a term that denotes the second token. It is the location of a token in such a network that constitutes the context of the token that is relevant to assigning its Burgean levels or Austinian situation. In the final section of this chapter, I will describe an elaboration of Gaifman's algorithm that assigns Burgean levels to occurrences of 'true'. Such an extension of Gaifman's work offers two principal advantages. First, we can avail ourselves of the uniform resolution of both the loop case ((A) and (B)) and the descending-chain case made possible by Burge's (and by Barwise and Etchemendy's) theory. Second, we can then explain, as Gaifman cannot, how it is that different tokens of the same type can have (apparently) different semantic values. If (A) is not true and (B) is true, that must be either because (A) and (B) differ somehow in content, despite being tokens of the same type, or because the two occurrences of 'true' used in evaluating (A) and (B) differ in extension (or both).

6.1 A HOMOMORPHISM FROM BURGEAN INTO AUSTINIAN SEMANTICS

In order to simplify the problem by focusing exclusively on the kind of context sensitivity introduced by semantic expressions like 'true', I will assume that the Burgean and Austinian languages contain no set-theoretic expressions. The only facts about propositions that are representable in the language are semantic facts (truth and falsehood) and facts about what propositions are expressed by particular sentence tokens.

In order to formulate the homomorphism in standard set theory, I will assume that we begin with a *set* U of Burgean propositions and concrete objects that is 'referentially closed'. By the 'referential closure' of U, I mean that the universe of discourse of every proposition in U is a subset of U itself. Since every Burgean proposition has a set as its universe of discourse, every set of propositions can be extended to such a referentially closed set.

In order to be the object of a homomorphism from Burge's theory, the Austinian theory of propositions will have to be modified in several respects, as mentioned briefly in the preceding section. First, denial negation will have to be transformed into a genuine, iterable sentential connective. Second, we have to allow for the possibility of logically complex propositions being parameterized to a finite sequence of situations, instead of always to a single situation. Barwise and Etchemendy's definition 1,[4] a simultaneous definition of the classes of states of affairs (SOA), situations (SIT), atomic types (ATTYPE), and propositions (PROP), will have to be modified in the following way:

Preliminary Definitions. *Let X be a set of ordered pairs* $\{x; y\}$.

The closure $\Gamma(X)$ *of X is the smallest collection containing X and closed under*:

(1) *If* $Y \subset \Gamma(X)$, *and Z is a finite sequence of elements of Y, then* $[\wedge Z]$ *and* $[\vee Z]$ *are in* $\Gamma(X)$.

(2) *If* $Y \subset \Gamma(X)$ *is an infinite set, and for every* $y, y' \in Y$, $Par(y) = Par(y')$ *and y and y' are structurally isomorphic, then* $[\forall Y]$ *and* $[\exists Y)$ *are in* $\Gamma(X)$.

[4] Ibid., p. 123.

(3) *If* $z \in X$, *then* $[\sim z]$ *is in* $\Gamma(X)$.

Par $(x) = y$, *if* $x = \{y; z\}$,

$= r$, *if* $x = [\sim z]$ *and Par* $(z) = r$,

$= \langle r_0, r_1, \ldots, r_n \rangle$, if $x = [\wedge Z]$ or $x = [\vee Z]$, *Z is an n-ary sequence, and Par* $(Z_0) = r_0$, *Par* $(Z_1) = r_1, \ldots,$ *and Par* $(Z_n) = r_n$,

$= r$, *if* $x = [\forall Y]$ or $x = [\exists Y]$, *and Par* $(Y) = r$, *for some* $y \in Y$.

r is a subparameter of p iff either (i) *Par* $(p) = r$, *or* (ii) *r is a constituent of a subparameter of p.*

About (p) = *the union of the set of situations belonging to some subparameter of p.*

Definition. *Let* SOA, SIT, ATTYPE, *and* PROP *be the largest classes satisfying*

**Every* $\sigma \in$ SOA *is either of the form* $\langle H, a, c; i \rangle$ *(a typical nonsemantical atomic proposition) or* $\langle Tr, p; i \rangle$, *where H, Tr are distinct atoms, a and c are concrete individuals, i is either* 0 *or* 1, *and* $p \in$ PROP.

**Every* $s \in$ SIT *is a subset of* SOA.

**Every* $p \in$ PROP *belongs to* Γ(ATPROP).

**Every* $p \in$ ATPROP *is of the form* $\{s; \sigma\}$, *where* $s \in$ SIT *and* $\sigma \in$ SOA.

I can now introduce the following truth-definition for these modified Austinian propositions:

(1) The proposition $\{s; \sigma\}$ is true iff $\sigma \in s$.
(2) The proposition $[\sim p]$ is true iff p is not true.
(3) The proposition $[\wedge Z]$ is true iff every member of Z is true.
(4) The proposition $[\vee Z]$ is true iff some member of Z is true.
(5) The proposition $[\forall X]$ is true iff every member of X is true.
(6) The proposition $[\exists X]$ is true iff some member of X is true.

I will now describe how to construct a model s^* containing states of affairs involving concrete objects and expressible Austinian propositions, which is isomorphic to the given Burgean model M, with domain U of concrete objects and Burgean propositions. We will use only expressible Austinian propositions, that is, Austinian propositions whose parameters contain only actual situations, since nothing in a Burgean model corresponds to semantic evaluations of inexpressible propositions. Conversely, I can describe how, given any appropriately complete Austinian situation, a homomorphic Burgean model can be constructed, given the following assumption about actual situations: every actual situation is semantically well-founded. Semantic well-foundedness can be defined as follows:

Situation s is *semantically well founded* iff there exists an ordinal number α and a sequence of situations S: $s_0, \ldots, s_\beta, \ldots$ of order type α such that

(1) $s = \cup S$, and

(2) s_0 contains no semantic SOA's (such as $<Tr, p; 0>$ or $<Tr, p; 1>$),

(3) for every $\beta < \alpha$, if s_β contains $<Tr, p; 1>$, then for some $\gamma < \beta$:

(a) if $p = \{s', \sigma\}$, then $\sigma \in s' \cap s_\gamma$,

(b) if $p = {\sim}q$, then $<Tr, q; 0> \in s_\gamma$,

(c) if $p = [\wedge Z]$ or $[\forall Z]$, then for all z a member/constituent of Z, $<Tr, z; 1> \in s_\gamma$,

(d) if $p = [\vee Z]$ or $[\exists Z]$, then for some z, $<Tr, z; 1> \in s_\gamma$.

(4) for every $\beta < \alpha$, if $s\beta$ contains $<Tr, p; 0>$, then, for some $\gamma < \beta$:

(a) if $p = \{s', \sigma\}$, then either (i) $s' \subseteq s_\gamma$, or (ii) either σ or its dual $\in s_\gamma$,

(b) if $p = {\sim}q$, then $<Tr, q; 1> \in s_\gamma$,

etc.

Call such a series $s_0, \ldots, s\beta, \ldots$ a "foundation series" for s.

The assumption that all actual situations are semantically well founded embodies the intuition that truth is grounded, that semantic facts always supervene on nonsemantic facts. An important consequence of this assumption is that all expressible truth-teller propositions ('This proposition is true') are false. Such an assumption is built into Burge's semantic theory.

Definition. *For every situation s, $P(s)$ is the smallest set containing every p such that either $\langle Tr, p; i\rangle \in s$ or $\langle Tr, p; i\rangle \in Par(q)$ for some q in $P(s)$.*

Definition. *A situation s is fundamentally complete iff there exists a situation s_0 such that, for every nonsemantic* SOA *β, either β, or its dual belongs to s_0, and for all $p \in P(s)$, $s_0 = \{\beta \in Par(p{:}\ \beta$ is nonsemantic$\}$.*

The situation s_0 represents the totality of nonsemantic (concrete) facts about the actual world. In a fundamentally complete s, all propositions in $P(s)$ are parameterized only to situations that extend s_0.

A Burgean language simply lacks the resources for evaluating propositions relativized to situations that are not fundamentally complete. Since the absence of fundamental completeness plays no role in Barwise and Etchemendy's analysis of the liar, I will stipulate that all of the situations with which we are here concerned shall be fundamentally complete.

A Burgean model M consists of a domain U, an interpretation function V that assigns extensions to all of the constants and nonsemantic predicates of the language, and an infinite sequence of interpretations $[Tr_0]$, $[Tr_1]$, . . . , $[Tr_\alpha]$, ... Each interpretation $[Tr_\alpha]$ consists of disjoint sets $[Tr_\alpha]+$ and $[Tr_\alpha]-$, representing the extension and antiextension of 'true$_\alpha$', respectively. In a complete Burgean model, $[Tr_\alpha]+ \cup [Tr_\alpha]- = \{$the set of propositions in $U\}$, for every α. The hierarchy of extensions is cumulative, $[Tr_0]+ \subseteq Tr_1]+ \subseteq [Tr_2]+ \subseteq \ldots$ In complete models, for every proposition p in U, there is an α such that $p \in [Tr_\alpha]+$ or $\sim p \in [Tr_\alpha]+$.

I assume that model M is referentially closed (as already explained) and *logically saturated*: if a proposition p is in the universe of discourse of proposition $q \in U$, or if p is a logical component (disjunct, conjunct, negatee) or a quantificational instance of $q \in U$, then $p \in U$. Each Burgean proposition $[\varphi, f]$ consists of a sentence type φ of language $\mathcal{L}$ (including the predicate 'true') and an assignment f of ordinal numbers to each occurrence of 'true' in φ. The series of extensions of 'true' supervenes on the partial model (U, V).

I will define the construction of a transfinite series of models, M_0, $M_1, \ldots, M_\beta$, where M_β is the complete Burgean model determined by (U, V), and the ordinal β is the least upper bound of the ranges of all the functions of Burgean propositions in U. In M_0, $[Tr_0]+$ consists of the existension of 'true$_0$' reached at the minimal fixed point of Kripke's construction in "Outline of a Theory of Truth,"[5] using Kleene's strong truth tables and simultaneously constructing the extension and antiextension of 'true$_\alpha$', for every α. Following Kripke, construct a series of partial models $M_{0,0}$, $M_{0,1}, \ldots, M_{0,\delta}$. In $M_{0,0}$, the extension and antiextension $[Tr_\alpha]+$ and $[Tr_\alpha]-$ are both empty, for each α. All of the sentences that are verified (using the strong Kleene truth tables) by $M_{0,0}$ are added to the extension $[Tr_\alpha]+$ in model $M_{0,1}$, for all α; similarly, all the sentences that are falsified by $M_{0,0}$ are added to $[Tr_\alpha]-$ in $M_{1,1}$ for all α. This process is repeated until a minimal fixed point, $M_{0,\delta}$, is reached. The extension $[Tr_\alpha]+$ in M_0 is identical to the extension $[Tr_\alpha]+$ in this fixed-point model $M_{0,\delta}$, for all α. For $\alpha > 0$, the antiextension $[Tr_\alpha]-$ in M_0 is identical to $[Tr_\alpha]-$ in $M_{0,\delta}$. The antiextension $[Tr_0]-$, however, does *not* consist of the antiextension of 'true$_0$' at the minimal fixed point; instead, it consists of the complement of $[Tr_0]+$ relative to the set of propositions. Thus, after reaching Kripke's minimal fixed point, the interpretation of 'true$_0$', is closed

[5] Kripke (1975), reprinted in Martin (1984), pp. 53–82.

off, throwing every proposition not in $[Tr_0]+$ at the fixed point into $[Tr_0]-$.

The model M_1 results from applying Kripke's construction to reach a minimal fixed point for the interpretation of 'true$_1$'. Again, we start with a model $M_{1,0}$, which in this case is identical to M_0. In model $M_{1,1}$, for all $a > 0$, the extension $[Tr_a]+$ consists of all the sentences verified by $M_{1,0}$ and the anti extension $[Tr_a]-$ consists of all the sentences falsified by that model. The value of $[Tr_0]$ no longer changes: it is fixed permanently at the first stage. Model M_1 consists of closing off the interpretation of 'true$_1$' at the minimal fixed point of this construction. Subsequently, all higher models agree with M_1 with respect to the value of $[Tr_1]$. In each model M_a for successor ordinals a, the value of $[Tr_a]$ represent the result of closing off the interpretation of 'true $_a$' at the minimal fixed point of Kripske's construction, starting with model M_{a-1}. At limit ordinals λ, the model M_λ assigns, for every ordinal μ greater than or equal to λ, to the extension $[Tr_\mu]+$ the union of all the $[Tr_\lambda]+$'s, for $\gamma < \lambda$. For ordinals $\mu > \lambda$, $M\lambda$ assigns to the antiextension $[Tr_\mu]-$ the union of the $[Tr_\gamma]-$'s, for $\gamma < \lambda$. The antiextension $[Tr_\lambda]$'s, for $\gamma < \lambda$. The antiextension $[Tr_\lambda]-$ at M_λ is the complement, relative to the set of propositions in U, of $[Tr_\lambda]+$. We continue this process until reaching model M_β, at which point the set of ordinals appearing in propositions in U has been exhausted. Every proposition in U is either verified or falsified by M_β.

I will represent outer negation in the Burgean language by means of '~' and inner negation by **boldfacing** atomic formulas. For nonsemantic atomic formulas 'Hab' the truth definition for inner negation will be [**Hab**, f] is true if and only if $V(\text{Hab}) = 0$, where V may be a partial function. For outer negation, in contrast, the definition is [~Hab, f] is true if and only if $V(\text{Hab}) \neq 1$. In the case of atomic semantic formulas:

$$M_{a,\beta} \vdash [\boldsymbol{Tr}\ [\boldsymbol{\Psi}, \boldsymbol{g}], f] \text{ iff } Tr\ [\sim\Psi, g] \in [Tr_{f(0)}]+ \text{ at } M_{a,\beta},$$

$$M_{a,\beta} \vdash [\sim Tr\ [\Psi, g], f] \text{ iff } Tr\ [\Psi, g] \in [Tr_{f(0)}]- \text{ at } M_{a,\beta}.$$

Given the same D and V, we can construct an isomorphic Austinian model in the following way. There is a situation (a set of states of affairs) corresponding to the interpretation of V. Call this situation s_0. By adding to s_0 all of the semantic facts contained in M_0, we obtain situation s_1. Similarly, corresponding to each model Ma, there is a situation s_{a+1}. Finally, corresponding to the complete model $M(=M_\beta)$, there is a situation s $(= s_{\beta+1})$. Situation s would be an Austinian model, except for the fact that it contains semantic facts about Burgean propositions, not Austinian ones. In order to rectify this, replace the Burgean parameters in the propositions in U with Austinian parameters, resulting in a new (but wholly isomorphic) situation s^*. Simply replace each ordinal number a in the range of the function of a Burgean proposition with the situation s^*_{a+1} and each constant c in a Burgean formula with the Austinian proposition $(c^M)^*$, where s^*_{a+1} comes from s_{a+1} and $(c^M)^*$ comes from c^M by the same transformation. Such a situation exists, by Aczel's antifoundation axiom. To show this, construct a system of directed graphs representing the denotational and compositional relations among Burgean propositions. This system has a unique "decoration" (assignment of sets to nodes).[6] It is important that statements of identity between propositions be excluded from the language, since this is obviously a point at which the two theories disagree.

Theorem 1. *Situation s^* is isomorphic to M.*

We can define the isomorphism τ by recursion:

$\tau\,[Hab, f] = \{s_0, <H, a, b; 1>\}$,

$\tau\,[\mathbf{Hab}, f] = \{s_0, <H, a, b; 0>\}$,

$\tau\,[\sim\varphi, f] = \sim\tau\,[\varphi, f]$,

$\tau\,\{z_1 \wedge z_2 \wedge \ldots z_n, f\,] = [\wedge <\tau\,[z_1, f_1], \tau\,[z_2, f_2], \ldots, \tau\,[z_n, f_n]>]$,

where, for each occurrence x of 'Tr' in z_i, $f(x) = f_i(x)$,

$\tau\,[\forall X, f\,] = [\forall\,\{\tau\,[x, f\,] : x \in X\}]$,

$\tau\,[Tr\,[\varphi, f\,], g] = \{s_{g(0)+1}, \langle Tr, \tau\,[\varphi, f\,]; 1\rangle\}$,

$\tau\,[\mathbf{Tr}\,[\varphi, f\,], g] = \{s_{g(0)+1}, \langle Tr, \tau\,[\varphi, f\,]; 0\rangle\}$,

$\forall x$ *(x is not a proposition* $\rightarrow \tau\,(x) = x$).

τ is obviously a one-to-one function. The interpretations of nonsemantic predicates are isomorphic:

$$V(\text{'}H\text{'}, \langle x, y\rangle) = 1 \text{ iff } \langle H, \tau(x), \tau(y); 1\rangle \in s_0,$$
$$V(\text{'}H\text{'}, \langle x, y\rangle) = 0 \text{ iff } \langle H, \tau(x), \tau(y); 0\rangle \in s_0.$$

Thus, it remains to be shown that the interpretations of 'true' in M and s* are isomorphic, that is, that

$$[\varphi, f\,] \in [Tr_a]+ \text{ iff } \langle Tr, \tau\,[\varphi, f\,]; 1\rangle \in s^*_{a+1}, \text{ and}$$
$$[\varphi, f\,] \in [Tr_a]- \text{ iff } \langle Tr, \tau\,[\varphi, f\,]; 0\rangle \in s^*_{a+1}.$$

By the construction of the Burgean model, the interpretation of Tr_a becomes fixed beginning at model M_a. Consequently, the definition of s^* guarantees the truth of the two biconditionals.

6 Aczel (1988), p. 13.

Similarly, we can, given any semantically well-founded possible Austinian situation s that contains no s-inexpressible propositions, construct an isomorphic Burgean model M. First, we must extend s to a "Burgean" situation s'.

Definition. *A possible situation s is Kleene closed relative to set P iff for every proposition* $p \in P$:

(1) *If* $p = \{s', [\sigma]\}$ & $\sigma \in s' \cap s$, *then* $\langle Tr, p; 1\rangle \in s$.

(2) *If* $p = \{s', [\sigma]\}$ & $\sigma \notin s'$ & *either* σ *or the dual of* $\sigma \in s$, *then* $\langle Tr, p; 0\rangle \in s$.

(3) *If* $p = \sim q$ & $\langle Tr, q; 1\rangle \in s$, *then* $\langle Tr, p; 0\rangle \in s$.

(4) *If* $p = \sim q$ & $\langle Tr, q; 0\rangle \in s$, *then* $\langle Tr, p; 1\rangle \in s$.

(5) *If* ($p = [\wedge X]$ or $p = [\forall X]$) & $(\exists x \in X)$ $(\langle Tr, x; 0\rangle \in s)$, *then* $\langle Tr, p; 0\rangle \in s$.

(6) *If* ($p = [\wedge X]$ or $p = [\forall X]$) & $(\exists x \in X)$ $(\langle Tr, x; 1\rangle \in s)$, *then* $\langle Tr, p; 1\rangle \in s$.

(7) *If* ($p = [\wedge X]$ or $p = [\forall X]$) & $(\exists x \in X)$ $(\langle Tr, x; 1\rangle \in s)$, *then* $\langle Tr, p; 1\rangle \in s$.

(8) *If* ($p = [\wedge X]$ or $p = [\forall X]$) & $(\exists x \in X)$ $(\langle Tr, x; 0\rangle \in s)$, *then* $\langle Tr, p; 0\rangle \in s$.

Let the Kleene closure of situation s relative to P ('$\kappa_P(s)$') *be the smallest Kleene-closed situation extending s.*

Definition. *A possible situation s is the closing off of situation s'* [$s = \rho_p(s')$] *relative to set P if, s is the smallest situation such that, for all propositions,* $p \in P$:

If $p = \{s'', \langle Tr, q; i\rangle\}$, $s'' \subseteq s'$ *and* $\langle Tr, q; i\rangle \notin s''$, *then* $\langle Tr, p; 0\rangle \in s$.

Definition. *A situation s is Burgean iff there exists a sequence of situations* $S = \langle s_0, s_1, \ldots . \rangle$ *and a set P such that*

(1) s_0 *contains no semantical* SOA*'s, and* s_0 *is complete with respect to nonsemantic facts,*

(2) $s_1 = \kappa_P(s_0)$,

(3) *for all successor ordinals a,* $s_{a+1} = \kappa_P(\rho_P(s_a))$,

(4) *for all limit ordinals* λ, $s_{\lambda+1} = \cup_{a<\lambda} s_a$, *and*

(5) $s = \cup S$.

Definition. *A sequence S satisfying conditions* (1) *through* (5) *for some set P is a Burgean basis of situation s.*

Clearly every Burgean situation s has a unique Burgean basis. (Let s_0 be the maximal subsituation containing no semantic SOA's, and let P be $P(s)$.)

Theorem 2. *Every fundamentally complete situation s actual in a semantically well-founded model A and such that P(s) contains no* $\mathcal{A}$-*inexpressible propositions can be extended to a Burgean situation* s^* *actual in* $\mathcal{A}$.

Proof. (See Appendix B).

Every Burgean situation s meeting the conditions of Theorem 2 is homomorphic to some Burgean model M. A homomorphism μ can be defined recursively ('$\mu_1(x)$' represents to first constituent of $\mu(x)$; '$\mu_2(x)$' represents the second constituent):

$$\mu\{s', \langle H, a, b; 1\rangle\} = [\text{Hab}, \emptyset],$$
$$\mu\{s', \langle H, a, b; 0\rangle\} = [\textbf{Hab}, \emptyset],$$
$$\mu(\sim p) = [\neg\mu_1(p), \mu_2(p)],$$
$$\mu[\wedge Z] = [\mu_1(z_1)\wedge \ldots \wedge\mu_1[z_n], \mu_2[Z]\}, \mu_2\,[Z][m]$$
$$= \mu_2\,[z_i]\,[m - t_i], \text{ where } t_i \text{ is the number of occurrences of } `Tr' \text{ in } \{z_1, \ldots, z_i - 1\},$$
$$\text{and } m - t_i \in \text{dom } \mu_2[z_1],$$
$$\mu\{\forall Y\} = \{\mu_1[y]\colon\ z \in Y\}, \mu_2(Y)],$$
$$\mu_2[Y][m] = x \text{ iff } \mu_2[y][m] = x \text{ for some } y \in Y,$$
$$\mu\{s', \langle Tr,\ p;\ 0\rangle\} = (\boldsymbol{Tr}(\boldsymbol{\mu}(\boldsymbol{p})), \eta(s', p)],$$
$$\mu\{s', \langle Tr,\ p;\ 1\rangle\} = (Tr(\mu(p)), \eta(s', p)], \text{ where, if } \langle Tr, p; i\rangle \in s',$$
$$\text{then } \eta(s', p) = \inf\{a\colon s' \subseteq s_{a+1}\} \text{ (the outer measure of } s'),$$
$$\text{and, if } \langle Tr,\ p;\ i\rangle \notin s', \text{ then } \eta(s', p)$$
$$= \min\{\sup\{a\colon \langle Tr, p; i\rangle \notin s_{a+1} \;\&\; \text{the dual of } \langle Tr,\ p;\ i\rangle \notin s_{a+1}\}, \inf\{a\colon\ s' \subseteq s_{a+1}\}\},$$
$$\forall x(x \text{ is not a proposition} \rightarrow \mu(x) = x).$$

Since s is semantically well founded, I can introduce a partial well ordering on the propositions that are semantically evaluated in s: $p < p'$ if and only if p is evaluated at an earlier level than p' in every semantic foundation series for s. This partial well ordering can be mirrored in Burgean propositions: $p <^* p'$ in model M if and only if $\exists a(p \in [Tr_a]+/-\ \&\ \ p' \ \notin\ [Tr_a]+/-)$.

Lemma 1. *For all* $s'' \subset s, r < \{s'', \langle Tr, r; j\rangle\}$ *iff either* $\langle Tr, r; j\rangle$ *or its dual belong to* s''.

Proof. See Appendix B.

Lemma 2. $\langle Tr, p; i\rangle \in s_{\eta(s',p)+1}$ *iff* $\langle Tr, p; i\rangle \in s'$.

Proof. See Appendix B.

Theorem 3. μ *is a homomorphism of s into the Burgean model M based on the interpretation function V that agrees with* s_0.

Proof. See Appendix B.

The genuine differences between Burge's and Barwise and Etchemendy's theories fall into two groups. First, the two theories posit different identity criteria for propositions (qua objects of thought and semantic evaluation). In Burge's theory, a single interpreted language $\langle \mathcal{L}, M \rangle$ can have several distinct liar propositions, even after fixing the intended level of 'true', each containing a different constant of $\mathcal{L}$. In situation theory, in contrast, for a fixed situation s there is only one (denial) liar proposition: $p = \{s, \sim\langle Tr, p; 1\rangle\}$. Which theory is more adequate depends on whether some form of representation analogous to proper names (constants) is needed in modeling de re beliefs.

Second, the Burgean theory is inherently more restrictive in three ways (i) It excludes the evaluation of inexpressible propositions, (ii) It excludes the possibility of situations that are not semantically well-founded, and (iii) it excludes the evaluation of propositions relativized to situations that are not fundamentally complete. I cannot see that anything of interest is lost by the first restriction, and I believe that the possibility of semantically non-well-founded situations is precluded by the very essence of truth. Thus, it is the third difference that is crucial. If the situation theorist can make the case for the necessity of situational parameters in nonsemantic propositions, then perhaps the most uniform treatment of propositions would handle the semantic paradoxes in essentially Barwise and Etchemendy's way. Otherwise, there is no need to go beyond the far simpler and more economical theory of Burge. Moreover, there is some disanalogy between situational parameters introduced on the basis of perception and other causal interactions with the environmental and the semantically enriched situational parameters used to resolve the paradox of the liar.

Is the richer structure of the Austinian propositions needed in an account of beliefs and other attitudes toward semantic propositions, even if they are not needed in pure semantic theory itself? They would be needed only if there were reason to discriminate the objects of thought more finely than Burge's theory allows. In the next section I will develop an account, based on work by Burge and Gaifman, in which ordinal parameters are assigned by the interpreter to situated objects of thought, guided by certain interpretive principles such as a principle of charity. There arises no need to assign to propositions more finely individuated parameters such as Austinian situations.

6.2 EXTENDING GAIFMAN'S FORMAL PRAGMATICS

In this section, I sketch an extension of Gaifman's pointer-semantics algorithm that enables us, given a set of tokens and certain facts about those tokens, to determine what Burgean propositions they express.

Let us suppose that we have a language $\mathcal{L}$, containing 'true' but (for simplicity's sake) not containing any set theoretic expressions (like 'ϵ' or abstraction operators). Let us also suppose that we have an intended model for $\mathcal{L}$ – {true}, $\langle U,V \rangle$. As we have already seen, such a partial model of $\mathcal{L}$ can be extended to a complete Burgean model $\langle U, V, [Tr_0], [Tr_1], \ldots, [Tr_\beta] \rangle$. Let us further suppose that we have a set K of tokens, a subset of the universe U. Each token is a token of exactly one sentence of $\mathcal{L}$. We are to imagine that there are only two atomic expressions in $\mathcal{L}$ that can be true of propositions: the semantic predicate 'true(x)' and the relational predicate 'x is expressed by token y'. Tokens of $\mathcal{L}$ also contain demonstratives, some of which demonstrate concrete objects and some of which demonstrate propositions through a token. (By a demonstration of a proposition through a token, I mean the use of a demonstrative in an utterance whose value is proposition p and to which is associated a unique token k that expresses p. I am supposing that we cannot point out a proposition directly, that such a demonstration succeeds only if there is a unique token of the intended proposition that is associated in the appropriate way with the demonstration.)

Thus, we have a function TYP: $K \rightarrow \mathcal{L}$, which assigns a type to each token. Moreover, there is a function D such that, for each propositional demonstrative 'that$_1$' and each token k whose type $T(k)$ contains 'that$_1$', $D(k, \text{that}_1)$ is the unique token (in K) associated with the demonstration, or the unique concrete object in U demonstrated. Finally, there is a function S: $K \rightarrow \wp(U)$, which assigns to each token in K its universe of discourse. (I will not in this chapter tackle the difficult problem of investigating how this function is determined.)

We shall also assume that K is logically saturated: (i) that every token associated by D with a demonstrative in a token in K is in K, (ii) every token in the universe of discourse of a token in K is also in K, and (iii) there are tokens in K corresponding to the logical parts and the quantificational instances of each token in K. Each token is a part or instance of at most one other token in K. Let the function Neg: $K \rightarrow K$ be the partial function that assigns to each negation in K its principal component. Let Dis^n: $K \rightarrow K$ and Con^n: $K \rightarrow K$ be the partial functions that assign to each finite disjunction and each conjunction (respectively) in K its nth component. Finally, let EI: $K \rightarrow \wp(K)$ and UI: $K \rightarrow \wp(K)$ be the partial functions that assign to each existential and each universal generalization (respectively) in K the set of its instances.

Given these assumptions, we can reinterpret $\mathcal{L}$ as a language whose variables and constants take only tokens in K and other concrete objects as values. That is, we can construct a new model for $\mathcal{L}$, $M^* = \langle U^*, V, [Tr_0]^*, [Tr_1]^*, \ldots \rangle$, in which $K \subseteq U^* \subseteq U$, U^* contains only tokens and other concrete objects. Let each demonstrative 'that$_1$' in each token k be assigned the token $D(k, \text{that}_i)$ as its value. Let the expression 'proposition x is expressed by token y' be interpreted as the identity relation. Given a function B that assigns propositions to tokens in K by assigning the appropriate objects in U^* to each demonstrative and ordinal numbers to occurrences of 'true', and the Burgean model $M = \langle U^* \cup \text{ran}(B), V, [Tr_0], [Tr_1], \ldots, [Tr_\beta] \rangle$, we can assign members of K to the extensions and antiextensions of true$_0$, true$_1$, and so fourth, on the basis of the rule

$$k \in [Tr_a]^{*M^*} \text{ iff } B(k) \in [Tr_a]^M.$$

Thus, corresponding to U^*, V, and B, there is a complete model M^* of the language $\mathcal{L}$, in which 'true' is interpreted as applying to tokens rather than to propositions. We can use this fact to construct an ideal proposition-assigning function B, given only U^* and V. In fact, all that we need to construct is a function B_1 that assigns ordinal numbers to occurrences of 'true' in tokens in K. From B_1, together with D and S, we can easily define the desired function B. Let B_1 be a function from $\omega \times K$ into the ordinals, such that '$B_1(n, k) = a$' represents assigning the ordinal number a to the nth occurrence of 'true' in k.

Following Gaifman, we can now define the *calling* relation among tokens.

Definitions.

(1) *k calls k′ directly iff either* (a) *k′ is a logical component or instance of k, or* (b) TYP(k) = '$F(c)$' *and* $V(c) = k'$, or (3) TYP(k) = '$F(that_1)$' *and* $D(k, that_1) = k'$ *(where 'F' is any atomic predicate of* $\mathcal{L}$*, including 'true').*

(2) *A calling path from k to k′ is a sequence* $k_1, \ldots, k_n$*, with* $n > 1$, $k = k$, $k' = k_n$*, such that every* k_i *calls* k_{i+1} *directly.*

(3) *k calls k′ iff there is a calling path from k to k′.*

Corresponding to U^* and V there is a *directed graph* representing the calling connections among tokens in K. As we shall see, two kinds of structure of special importance in such graphs are loops and infinitely descending chains.

Definitions.

(1) *A set of tokens is a loop iff* $S \neq \emptyset$*, and for all k, k′ in S, there is a calling path from k to k′.*

(2) *A set of tokens is an infinitely descending chain iff S contains no self-contained loops (loops none of whose tokens call any token in S outside themselves) and every token k in S directly calls another token in S.*

I will now describe how to define the function B_1 and the interpretations $[Tr_0]^*$, $[Tr_1]^*$, and so on. In order to construct the correct interpretations for 'true', I will describe an evaluation algorithm that constructs B_1, the series $[T_0]$, $[T_1]$, . . . , and the series $[F_0]$, $[F_1]$, . . . Repeated application of the rules will eventually reach a fixed point, at which we can let $[Tr_a]^{*+} = \cup\{[T_\beta]: \beta \leq a\}$ and let $[Tr_a]^{*-} = K - [Tr_a]^{*+}$, for each a less than or equal to the fixed point. (For brevity's sake I will omit the rules for finite disjunctions and existential generalizations.) A loop or descending chain S is *closed in the set of unevaluated tokens* at a given stage of the process if and only if no token S calls a token outside S that has not yet been assigned to $[T_a]$ or $[F_a]$, for any a. A chain S is a *maximal descending chain closed in the set of unevaluated tokens* if and only if it is closed in that set and is not a proper subset of any other such chain.

In order to evaluate tokens containing universal generalizations, I have to distinguish between two kinds of occurrences of 'true' in such tokens, which I will label "even" and "odd". The nth occurrence of 'true' in token k is even if and only if it occurs in k within the scope of an even number of negations and conditional antecedents; otherwise, it is odd.

(A1) Rule for nonsemantic tokens:

If $\text{TYP}(k) \in \mathcal{L} - \{\text{true}\}$, then $k \in [T_0]$ iff $V(\text{TYP}(k)) = T$.
If $\text{TYP}(k) \in \mathcal{L} - \{\text{true}\}$, then $k \in [F_0]$ iff $V(\text{TYP}(k)) = F$.

(A2) Rule for negation:

If $\text{TYP}(k) = {\sim}\varphi$ and $\text{Neg}(k) = k'$, then
(a) If $k' \in [T_a]$, then $k \in [F_a]$.
(b) If $k' \in [F_a]$, then $k \in [T_a]$.

(A3) Rules for finite conjunctions:

(a) If $\text{TYP}(k) = [\wedge\Phi]$ and $\text{Con}^i(k) = k'$ and $k' \in [F_a]$, then $k \in [F_a]$.
(b) If $\text{TYP}(k) = [\wedge\Phi]$ and, for every k' such that $\text{Con}^i(k) = k'$ for some i, $k' \in [T_a]$, then $k \in [T_a]$.

(A4) Rules for universal generalizations:

(a) If $\text{TYP} = [\forall\Phi]$ and $k' \in UI(k)$ and $k' \in [F_a]$, then $k \in [F_a]$.
(b) If $\text{TYP} = [\forall\Phi]$ and, for every $k' \in UI(k)$ and, $k' \in [T_a]$, then $k \in [T_a]$.

(A5) Rules for atomic semantic tokens:

(a) If TYP(k) = 'true(c)' and $V(c) = k'$, or TYP(k) = true(that$_1$) and $D(k, \text{that}_1) = k'$, and $k' \in [T_\alpha]$, then $k \in [T_\alpha]$.

(b) If TYP(k) = 'true(c)' and $V(c) = k'$, or TYP(k) = true(that$_1$) and $D(k, \text{that}_1) = k'$, and $k' \in [F_\alpha]$, then $k \in [F_\alpha]$.

(A6) Rule for loops and descending chains:

If S is a loop or maximal descending chain closed in the set of unevaluated tokens, and none of the preceding rules applies to any token in S, then, for every atomic semantic token k that is either in S or directly calls a token in s, $k \in [F_1]$.

(A7) Monotonicity rule:

If token k belongs to $[T_\alpha]$ (or to $[F_\alpha]$), then it belongs to $[T_\beta]$ (or to $[F_\beta]$) for every $\beta > \alpha$.

Rule (A4) ensures that universal generalizations with false$_\alpha$ instances are evaluated as false$_\alpha$, and that generalizations all of whose instances are true$_\alpha$ are evaluated as true$_\alpha$.

Propositions

I. Starting with the empty valuation $[T_0] = [F_0] = \cdots = [T_\alpha] = [F_\alpha] = \cdots = \phi$, repeated application of the preceding rules reaches a fixed point at which every token in K belongs either to $[T_i]$ or to $[F_i]$ for $i = 0$ or $i = 1$.

Proof. An immediate consequence of rule (A6).

IIA. If a token is assigned the value $T(F)$ by Gaifman's rules, then the same token is assigned to $[T_i]([F_i])$ by the preceding rules, for $i = 0$ or $i = 1$.

IIB. If a token is assigned the value GAP by Gaifman's rules, then it is assigned to neither $[T_0]$ nor $[F_0]$ by the preceding rules.

Proof. The standard rules (for nonsemantic atomic propositions, for negation, disjunction, and grounded semantic evaluations) are identical with respect to the assignment of T or F. I have assumed that the basic interpretation function V is total for $\mathcal{L} - \{\text{true}\}$, so Gaifman's simple gap rule does not apply. Thus, it remains to be established that the preceding rules agree in the relevant sense with the following two rules:

(1) *The jump rule*. If TYP(k) = 'true(c)', $V(c) = k'$, $k' \in$ GAP, and $k \notin$ GAP, then $k \in F$. If we assume that V is total, gaps can result only from closed loops and infinitely descending chains that cannot be given grounded evaluations. Gaifman's jump rule applies only when k' belongs to a closed loop, and rule (A6) dictates that k, which

directly calls a member of a closed loop, be given the value F_1.

(2) *The give-up rule.* If the set of unevaluated tokens is not empty and none of the preceding rules applies to any of its members, then every unevaluated $k \in$ GAP. Since this rule can never lead to any new assignment of T or F, it poses no threat to part IIA of the proposition. The give-up rule applies only to tokens in ungrounded infinitely descending chains. Rule (A6) assigns all semantic atomic tokens in such chains to F_1, so no token of the chain can be assigned to T_0 or F_0, as can easily be verified by surveying rules (A1)through (A6).

In addition to assigning tokens to the extension and antiextension of the various levels of 'true', it is essential that there be concordant assignments of level indices to the occurrences of 'true' in the tokens themselves. The following three rules, (B1) through (B3), define an assignment that is total, which includes assignments of levels to all occurrences of 'true' (Proposition III). Moreover, as is stated in Proposition IV, the assignment defined by (B1) through (B3) agrees with the interpretation defined by (A1) through (A7).

(B1) Rule for negations and conjunctions:

(a) If $\text{Neg}(k) = k'$, then $B_1(k, n) = B_1(k', n)$.

(b) If $k' = \text{Con}^i(k)$, and there are j occurrences of 'true' in $\text{Con}^1(k)$. . .$\text{Con}^{i-1}(k)$ and no more than n occurrences of 'true' in k', then $B_1(k, j + n) = B_1(k', n)$.

(B2) Rule for universal generalizations:

(a) If $\text{TYP}(k) = [\forall\Phi]$ and $k \in [F_a]$ for some a, then

(i) if $\langle k, n\rangle$ is even, then $B_1(k, n) = \min\{\beta\text{: } (\exists k' \in UI(k))(k' \in [F_\gamma]$ for some γ & $B(k', n) = \beta)\}$,

(ii) if $\langle k, n\rangle$ is odd, then $B_1(k, n) = \max\{\beta\text{: } (\exists k' \in UI(k))(k' \in [F_\gamma]$ for some γ & $B(k', n) = \beta)\}$.

(b) If $\text{TYP}(k) = [\forall\ \Phi\ ]$ and $k \in [T_a]$ for some a, then

(i) if $\langle k, n\rangle$ is even, then $B_1(k, n) = \max\{\beta\text{: } (\exists k' \in UI(k))(B(k', n) = \beta)\}$,

(ii) if $\langle k, n\rangle$ is odd, then $B_1(k, n) = \min\{\beta\text{: } (\exists k' \in UI(k))(B(k', n) = \beta)\}$.

(B3) Rule for atomic semantic tokens:

(a) If k was assigned to $[F_1]$ by rule (A6), then $B_1(k, 1) = 0$;

(b) Otherwise, if $\text{TYP}(k) =$ 'true(c)' and $V(c) = k'$, or $\text{TYP}(k) =$ true(that_1) and $D(k, \text{that}_1) = k'$, then $B_1(k, 1) = \min\{\alpha\text{: } k' \in [T_a] \vee k' \in [F_a]\}$.

If the language contains as primitive the biconditional or other ambivalent connective, then the definition of 'odd' and 'even' will have to be more elaborate; moreover, some indeterminacy of interpretation will be unavoidable. Alternatively, we might discover that the biconditional is, in natural language and the language of thought, always an elliptical conjunction.

Propositions

III. Starting with a total evaluation fixed point (as in Proposition I) and an empty level-assignment function B_1, repeated application of the preceding rules reaches a fixed point that is total for occurrences of 'true' in tokens in K and whose range is $\{0, 1\}$.

Proof. By induction on logical complexity of types.

Proposition III implies that, in natural language, as interpreted by this algorithm, it is impossible to express "higher-order" liars, like λ_1 : λ_1 is not true$_1$. Only two Tarskian "languages" are needed: a Kripkean object "language" and a "metalanguage." All viciously circular tokens are interpreted as belonging to the object language. In interpreting natural language, we are not forced to attribute higher and higher indices to the occurrences of 'true'; only two indices are required. (Unfortunately, as will be discussed in the next chapter, this result does not carry over to languages with doxastic predicates.)

IV. Each token k is assigned a b-proposition by B_1, which, for all a, is true$_a$ iff $k \in [T_a]$ (and likewise for falsity$_a$).

Proof. (by induction on complexity of types). The result is obvious for negations and conjunctions. The definitions of 'even' and 'odd', occurrences, together with rule (B2), guarantee that the b-proposition assigned to a universal generalization is true$_a$ iff all of the generalization's instances belong to $[T_a]$ and false$_a$ iff at least one of its instances belongs to $[F_a]$. The result is obvious for atomic semantic tokens not affected by rule (A6). In the case of tokens assigned to $[F_1]$ by (A6), it is clear that no token in a closed loop or descending chain belongs to either $[T_0]$ or $[F_0]$. Consequently, if a token assigned to $[F_1]$ by (A6), is assigned the index 0, it will indeed be false$_1$.

These rules have been constructed in such a way as to mimic Gaifman's evaluations. I do not think these rules are optimal, however. Consider, for example, the simple liar sentence (L):

(L) Sentence (L) is not true.

The token (L) constitutes, all by itself, a closed loop. Consequently, we interpret (L) as saying that (L) is not $true_0$, and the principal component of (L)('(L) is $true_0$') is $false_1$. Therefore, (L) is $true_1$. Let us try to express this positive reevaluation of (L):

(N) sentence (L) is true.

But if we interpret (N) according to the preceding rules, we must interpret it as saying that (L) is $true_0$. Since this is wrong, we have interpreted (N) in such a way as to make it $false_1$. (N) was produced by a fully reflective thinker in full possession of the facts. We should interpret it as saying something true.

In order to avoid this result, we must recognize a distinction between two kinds of occurrences of semantic predicates in tokens in *K*: "positive" and "negative." In order to discover whether a given occurrence of a semantic predicate in a token belonging to *K* is positive or negative, we must first find the *maximal* token to that the given token is related. A maximal token is a token that is neither an instance nor a logical component of a larger token in *K*. These maximal tokens can be identified with the tokens that people actually assert or accept.

An occurrence of 'true' in a maximal token is *negative* if the corresponding occurrence in the prenex-disjunctive normal form of the sentence type of the token is negated. Otherwise, the occurrence of 'true' in the maximal token is *positive*. An occurrence of 'true' in a nonmaximal token is positive if and only if the corresponding occurrence in the related maximal token is positive, and similarly for negative occurrences. Being charitable to the asserter/accepter of a maximal token is compatible with always interpreting positive occurrences so as to raise its level until it becomes true.

Charity entails a more selective level raising of the negative occurrences, since the token being evaluated by the negative occurrence might be $untrue_\alpha$ but $true_{\alpha+1}$. Raising the level assigned to such a negative occurrence from i to $i + 1$ might make the maximal token false. We must modify the rules for atomic semantic tokens in the following way.

First, we must distinguish two kinds of loops and chains: pure and impure. A pure loop either contains only positive semantic tokens or contains only negative ones. A pure chain S is a chain that can be divided into two sets S_1 and S_2 such that S_1 is an infinitely descending chain containing only positive or only negative semantic tokens, S_2 is not a descending chain, and no token in S_1 calls any token in S_2. Call the atomic semantic tokens in S_1 the *anchored* tokens of S.

(A6) Rules for loops and descending chains:

(a) If S is a pure loop or maximal descending chain closed in the set of unevaluated tokens, and none of the preceding rules applies to any token in S, then for every anchored atomic semantic token k that is in S, $k \in [F_1]$.

(b) If S is an impure loop or maximal descending chain closed in the set of unevaluated tokens, and none of the preceding rules applies to any token in S, then for every negative atomic semantic token k that is in S, $k \in [F_1]$.

Now we can state the new rule for assigning indices to atomic semantic tokens.

(B3) Rule for atomic semantic tokens:

(a) If k was assigned to $[F_1]$ by rule (A6), then $B_1(k, 1) = 0$.

(b) Otherwise, if TYP(k) = 'true(c)', and $V(c) = k'$, or TYP(k) = true(that$_1$) and $D(k, \text{that}_1) = k'$,

(i) if k is *positive*, then $B_1(k, 1) = \min\{a: k' \in [T_a] \vee k' \in [F_a]\}$.

(ii) if k is negative and $k' \in [F_a]$ for some a, then $B_1(k, 1) = \inf\{\alpha: k' \in [F_a]\}$,

(iii) if k is negative and $k' \in [T_a]$ for some a, then $B_1(k, 1) = 0$.

Propositions I through IV can be reproduced for the new set of rules: the resulting construction will also reach a complete evaluation of the tokens in K, which assigns levels to all of the occurrences of 'true'. By the modified rules, token (N) (since it is positive) will be assigned the proposition '(L) is true$_1$' and so will be evaluated as itself true$_1$.

Gaifman's theory, so modified, is still not optimal. In particular, it does not yet satisfy Burge's principle of minimality or beauty, that is, it systematically assigns indices that are unnecessarily high. To illustrate this, let us consider the following case:

A: Whatever B says is true.

B: $2 + 2 = 4$.

C: This is not true.

Let us suppose that C's utterance is within the domain of quantification of A's remark. I will use lowercase letters to refer to each speaker's statement (e.g., A says a). There are at least three instances of the generalization made by A:

(a1) If B says a, then a is true,

(a2) If B says b, then b is true,

(a3) If B says c, then c is true.

The antecedents of (a1) and (a3) are false, so the level of 'true' in *a* should, intuitively speaking, be independent of the levels at which *a* or *c* is true or false. The occurrence of 'true' in *a* should be 0, since the only thing B says is *b*, and *b* is true_0. My modification of Gaifman's algorithm, however, assigns an index of 1 to 'true' in *a*, since *c* is true_1 (and untrue_0), so the index of 'true' in (a3) must be 1. The index of 'true' in *a* is the supremum of the indices of its instances, so its index must also be 1.

The simplest way to solve this problem is to place a ceiling on the indices of conjunctions and universal generalizations. Where X is a set of propositions, let $\text{Minimax}_B(X)$ be the minimum of all the ordinals that are maximal indices in some member of X, under interpretation function B. I will then modify rules (B1) and (B2) in the following way.

(B1) Rule for negations and conjunctions:

(a) If $\text{Neg}(k) = k'$, then $B_1(k, n) = B_1(k', n)$ [unchanged].

(b) If $k' = \text{Con}^i(k)$, and there are j occurrences of 'true' in $\text{Con}^1(k) \ldots \text{Con}^{i-1}(k)$ and no more than n occurrences of 'true' in k', then $B_1(k, j + n) = \min[B_1(k', n), \text{Minimax}_{B1}(\{k': k' = \text{Con}^j(k) \text{ for some } j \wedge k' \in [F_\gamma] \text{ for some } \gamma\})\}$.

(B2) Rule for universal generalizations:

(a) If $\text{TYP}(k) = [\forall\Phi]$ and $k \in [F_a]$ for some a, then

(i) if $\langle k, n\rangle$ is even, then $B_1(k, n) = \min\{\min\{\beta: (\exists k' \in UI(k))(k' \in [F_\gamma] \text{ for some } \gamma \;\&\; B(k', n) = \beta)\}, \text{Minimax}_{B_1}(\{k' \in UI(k): k' \in [F_\gamma] \text{ for some } \gamma\})\}$,

(ii) if $\langle k, n\rangle$ is odd, then $B_1(k, n) = \min\{\max\{\beta: (\exists k' \in UI(k))(k' \in [F_\gamma] \text{ for some } \gamma \;\&\; B(k', n) = \beta)\}, \text{Minimax}_{B_1}(\{k' \in UI(k): k' \in [F_\gamma] \text{ for some } \gamma\})\}$.

(b) If $\text{TYP}(k) = [\forall\Phi]$ and $k \in [T_a]$ for some a, then

(i) if $\langle k, n\rangle$ is even, then $B_1(k, n) = \max\{\beta: (\exists k' \in UI(k))(B(k', n) = \beta)\}$,

(ii) if $\langle k, n\rangle$ is odd, then $B_1(k, n) = \min\{\beta: (\exists k' \in UI(k))(B(k', n) = \beta)\}$.

[Unchanged.]

6.3 ILLUSTRATIONS

I will now illustrate the answers that this theory gives to several of he puzzles about truth that appear in the recent literature. First, let us consider Burge's situation *C*.[7] In this situation, the following sentence is written on the board in room 9 at noon 8/13/76:

[7] Burge (1979), p. 94.

($\mathscr{A}$) There is no sentence token written on the board in room 9 at noon 8/13/76 that is true.

A closed loop, consisting of ($\mathscr{A}$) and the instance resulting from replacing the variable by a name for ($\mathscr{A}$), results that is closed in the set of unevaluated tokens and to which no rule applies except rule (A6) (the rule for loops and chains). Thus, the index of 'true' in the instance is fixed at 0, and consequently the index of 'true' in ($\mathscr{A}$) is likewise 0. ($\mathscr{A}$) is therefore untrue$_0$ but true$_1$. If someone else produces a different token of the same sentence at a different time and place (call this token "$\mathscr{B}$"), then $\mathscr{B}$ will not be part of a closed loop, but the function B will also assign to the occurrence of 'true' in $\mathscr{B}$ the level 0, since the occurrence of 'true' in ($\mathscr{B}$) is negative, and ($\mathscr{A}$) is true$_1$.

A second example is that of Kripke's Dean and Nixon puzzle.[8] Dean and Nixon make the following statements:

Dean: All Nixon's utterances about Watergate are untrue.

Nixon: Everything Dean utters about Watergate is untrue.

We are to take it as obvious that both statements are "about Watergate" in the relevant sense. There are several possible cases; we will examine the one that differs in the most interesting way from the preceding case. Suppose first of all that Dean uttered something else about Watergate that comes out true$_0$. Then Nixon's statement is false$_0$. Consequently, 0 is the minimax level for Nixon's utterance, and B assigns 0 as the index of 'true' to it. Dean's token will be assigned a level α high enough to be appropriate for the other statements made by Nixon (assuming that the rest of them are false and that there are no other loops). Dean's statement would then be true$_\alpha$

Another example to consider is a situation constructed by Burge:[9]

(iii) Mitchell is innocent and (iv) is not true,

(iv) (iii) is not true.

We are to assume that the first conjunct of (iii) is false$_0$. (iii) is false$_0$ (because one of its conjuncts is false$_0$, and so (iv) is true$_0$. The second conjunct of (iii) (let us call it "(iiib)") is false$_0$. All occurrences of 'true' are assigned the index 0.

Next let us look at some more intricate examples produced by Tyler Burge in "Tangles, Loops and Chains."[10] The first consists of the case of the policeman and the prisoner:

[8] Kripke (1975), p. 60.

[9] Burge (1979), p. 111–12.

[10] Burge (1981).

Policeman: (1) Anything the prisoner utters is untrue.
Prisoner: (2) Something the policeman utters is true.

The interesting case is that in which neither has said or will say anything else. The two statements form an impure loop. According to the theory presented earlier, the negative element, statement (1), is assigned level 0 by rule (B3)(a). Moreover, (1) is evaluated as true$_1$, since the atomic semantic token that is a part of the relevant instance of (1) is evaluated as false$_1$ (by rule (A6)). B will assign level 1 to the occurrence in (2), since level 1 is the lowest level at which (2) is true. Therefore, statement (1) is indeed true$_1$, since (2) is untrue$_0$. Statement (2) is true$_1$, because, as we have seen, statement (1) is true$_1$.

Burge handles this case somewhat differently. He argues that, by the principle of justice, both occurrences of 'true' should receive the same level assignment. The issue turns on whether there is any reason for treating the two tokens differently. I think that there probably is: the fact that one denies truth of the other, while the other affirms truth of the first implies that by treating them differently we can make both true$_1$. On Burge's view, statement (1) is indeed true$_1$, for the reason just given, but statement (2) is false$_1$, because it says that (1) is true$_0$, whereas (1) is in fact untrue$_0$ because unrooted$_0$. Perhaps it could be argued that my version is inappropriately charitable to the prisoner. If so, a minor change in the theory can bring it into concordance with Burge's intuitions.

The other examples from Burge's article that I will consider consist of infinite descending chains. For example:

(1) (2) is true,
(2) (3) is true,
(3) (4) is true
etc.

The graph of the situation is that of a purely positive descending chain. All of the tokens are therefore anchored tokens. The occurrences of 'true' in each of the tokens is therefore assigned level 0 by *B*, and all the tokens are false$_1$.

A similar example is that of a negative descending chain.

(1) (2) is not true,
(2) (3) is not true,
etc.

They constitute a purely negative descending chain. Therefore, each token is anchored. *B* therefore assigns level 0 to each occurrence of 'true'. Each is $untrue_0$, and therefore $true_1$.

A more complicated example is the following chain, labeled (II) by Burge:[11]

(1) (2) is true or 2 + 2 = 4,
(2) (3) is true or 2 + 2 = 4,
etc.

Let us call the first conjunct of (1) "(la)" and its second disjunct "(1b)," and similarly for the other statements. Under assignment *B*, each statement is $true_0$, because its second disjunct is $true_0$. *B* gives 0 to all occurrences of 'true', and all the tokens are $true_0$.

Burge's chain (III) is even more complex:

(1) The first disjunct of (2) is true or 2 + 2 = 4,
(2) The first disjunct of (3) is true or 2 + 2 = 4,
etc.

Under assignment *B*, (1), (2), (3), and so on are all $true_0$, because their second disjuncts are all $true_0$. The series of first disjuncts therefore constitutes a purely positive descending chain. All of the constituent atomic semantic tokens are anchored. Therefore, *B* will assign level 0 to all occurrences of 'true'. The first disjuncts are all $untrue_0$, and therefore all are $false_1$.

Finally, I would like to look at some loops and chains involving quantification. First, let us consider a case raised by D.A. Martin:[12]

(1) Snow is white,
(2) (1) is true,
(3) $\sim (\forall x) \sim (x$ is true and $[x = 2$ or $x = 3])$.

We must represent the negata of the two crucial instances of the universal generalization negated in (3):

(3a) (2) is true and [(2) = (2) or (2) = (3)],
(3b) (3) is true and [(3) = (2) or (3) = (3)].

Under *B*, (2) is $true_0$, since it asserts the truth of (1), which is in fact $true_0$. (3a) is therefore also $true_0$. The negation of (3a) is $false_0$, so the universal generalization in (3) is also $false_0$. Thus, (3) itself is $true_0$. Token (3b) is therefore also $true_0$. There is here no need to resort to rule (A6), and all occurrences of 'true' are assigned a 0.

11 Ibid., p. 363.
12 D.A. Martin, paper presented at a seminar on the liar paradox, University of California, Los Angeles, October 14, 1985.

7

Applying context-sensitive solutions to doxic paradox

In applying the context-sensitive solutions to paradoxes involving rational belief and strategy, there are several choices to be made. First, there is a choice concerning the objects of belief, specifically, whether real things are involved directly in these objects of belief or only indirectly (via some representations of those things). This distinction corresponds to one that logicians have traditionally made between de re and de dicto treatments of belief. On a de re account, if one thinks that Mt. Blanc is snowy, then the object of one's belief is something that contains the mountain itself as well as, perhaps, the property of snowiness. As a consequence of this ontological claim, the de re theorist must hold that two names that designate the same object must be intersubstitutable in belief contexts salve veritate (i.e., without effect on the truth-value of the report). In contrast, on a de dicto account, if one thinks that Mt. Blanc is snowy, one's thought contains, not Mt. Blanc itself, but some representation or mode of presentation of that mountain. If different proper names of a thing correspond to different representations of that object, then they will not, on the de dicto account, be intersubstitutable salve veritate in belief contexts.

If the de re theorist insists that the objects of belief consist of sets of possible worlds (as in modal doxic logic) or constructions of objects and properties in traditional, well-founded set theory (as in theories that follow the lead of Betrand Russell), then the sort of circularity that produces self-referential liar-like paradoxes can be averted. However, as I argued in Part I, this is neither necessary nor desirable. In contrast, if the de re theorist constructs thoughts in non-well-founded set theory, then the issue of de dicto versus de re treatments of belief has little relevance to the solution of doxic paradox. Nonetheless, a choice between the two must be made, since the details of the construction of a solution will depend on which choice is made. My own sympathies lie with the de dicto approach, but the de re approach results in a number of technical simplifications, so I will presuppose it in what follows.

The second major choice to be made is this: should the context of a given token of thought consist entirely of actual situations (including facts about other actual tokens), or should it include some merely possible situations (including facts about merely possible tokens), namely, those situations that are compatible with the beliefs of the agent? This first alternative I will call the "situated" approach, and the second I will call the "nonsituated" approach. In the nonsituated approach, the content of a thought token depends only on the other thoughts tokened in the same mind and on the abstract space of possibilities compatible with those tokens, taken collectively. The actual environment of the agent makes no special contribution. On the situated approach, in contrast, the paradoxicality of a given token may depend on facts about the agent's environment (such as thoughts of other agents) about which the agent is unaware or even misinformed. The first approach accords well with the maxim of methodological solipsism propounded by Jerry Fodor, while the second suggests a more ecological approach to the psychological attitudes.

Again for the sake of simplicity, I will adopt the situated approach in what follows. Once again, the difference between the two approaches does not correspond to a significant difference in the general outlines of the solution, although it is essential in formulating the definitions to make one choice or the other. If the nonsituated approach is adopted, the network of tokens that must be evaluated extends beyond the actual world into those possible worlds compatible with the beliefs of real or envisaged agents. On the situated approach, the network is limited to actual tokens of actual agents.

7.1 THE SOLUTIONS ILLUSTRATED

We will assume there is given a set of agents or "cognitive individuals." Corresponding to each cognitive individual is a collection of possible belief tokens. For simplicity's sake, we can stipulate that there is exactly one possible token for each sentence type in some "language of thought." The collection of possible tokens of individual *a* thus constitutes a kind of language unique to the given individual *a*, the language $\mathcal{L}_a$. Logically complex members of $\mathcal{L}_a$ contain subtokens. Each subtoken belongs to a unique node of a unique maximal token in $\mathcal{L}_a$. The extended set of tokens consisting of $\mathcal{L}_a$ plus all of its subtokens I will call "$\mathcal{L}_a$*."

In the last two sections of this chapter, I develop solutions to the doxic paradoxes that mirror the solutions to the liar paradox of Gaifman and of Barwise and Etchemendy. In the case of the Gaifman solution, a calling relation between tokens is defined. One thought token k calls another token k' if the evaluation of k depends on the evaluation of k'. This can occur in any one of three ways. First of all, k may be of the type $[Jak']$, that is, k may be a token of a thought to the effect that token k' is justifiable. Second, k and k' may both be tokens in the same individual's mind, and the justifiability of k may depend on how token k' is evaluated. Third, k' may be a subtoken of k.

As described by this calling relation, the thought tokens of a given model form a directed network. A Gaifman-like construction is completed by adding rules for the extension of a given evaluation function. As in the case of the liar paradox, Gaifman's evaluation function is three-valued, assigning the values T, F and GAP to the tokens in the network. Paradoxes arise from the existence of closed loops and infinitely descending chains in this network. The solution to the paradox is achieved by means of rules that assign GAP to tokens in such loops and chains.

Let us apply this solution construction to some of the doxastic paradoxes discussed in earlier chapters. First of all, let us consider the self-referential paradox of the disprover. In its simplest version, we have a token k in $\mathcal{L}_a$ whose type is $[\neg Jak]$. Token k clearly calls itself. Moreover, it forms a closed loop to which no other rule applies. Consequently, by the closed-loop rule, k is assigned the value GAP. A distinct token k' in language $\mathcal{L}_b$ whose type is $[\neg Jak]$ will not be part of this closed loop and will consequently be evaluated as T by the jump rule.

The Rowena–Columna story and the iterated reputation games have the same doxastic structure. Columna has a token k that is assigned some weight as a datum in her epistemic state E_c and that is of the type $p \leftrightarrow \neg Jrk'$, where p stands for the proposition that taking the \$100 is optimal, r is a discourse referent anchored to Rowena, and k' designates a token in Rowena's language whose type is Jck (where c is a discourse referent anchored to Columna). The situation can be pictured thus:

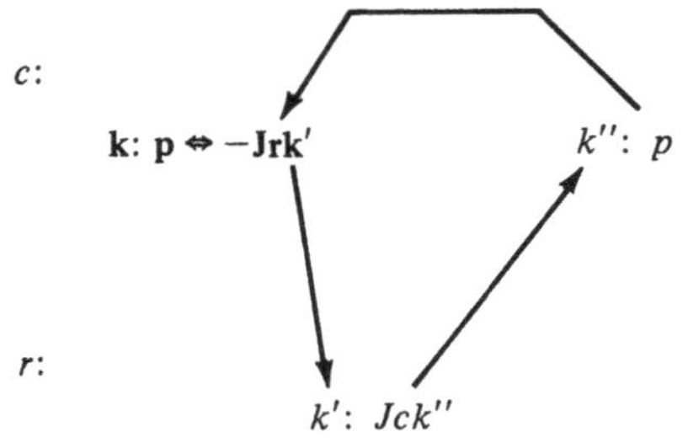

The tokens on the top of the diagram are in $\mathcal{L}_c$, and the token at the bottom is in $\mathcal{L}_r$. Token k is in boldface to indicate that it is assigned some weight as a data sentence in the epistemic situation of the competitor. Call the subtoken of k whose type is [Jrk'] "k_1." k_1 calls k', and k' calls k'' (both by clause (1) of the calling definition). Token k'' calls k_1 by clause (2) of that definition, as can be shown by the following argument. Let k^* be a token in $\mathcal{L}_c$ of the type [$\neg Jrk'$]. Let V be a valuation that assigns T to k^* and F to k_1. Let V' agree with V except in assigning GAP to k_1. Relative to $\langle E_c, V\rangle$, tokens k^* and k are justifiably believed, and token k'' is deduced from them. Relative to $\langle E_c, V'\rangle$, belief in k is blocked, since k inherits the GAP evaluation from k_1. Consequently, k'' is justifiably believed relative to $\langle E_c,V\rangle$ but not relative to $\langle E_c,V'\rangle$, so k'' calls k_1.

Since k_1, k', and k'' form a closed loop, they are all assigned GAP. Consequently, token k inherits the GAP value from k_1, and Columna is blocked from justifiably believing the biconditional and from inferring that p from the fact that Rowena is unable to believe justifiably that Jck''. A detached observer, in contrast, can recognize the truth of the biconditional as well as the facts that Columna cannot justifiably believe that p and that Rowena cannot justifiably believe that Columna can believe k''. Therefore, the detached observer, given the same data, can do what Columna is unable to do: deduce the truth of p.

This solution to the doxic paradoxes can be implemented in the case of the chain-store paradox discussed in Chapter 2 by means of the following graph of tokens:

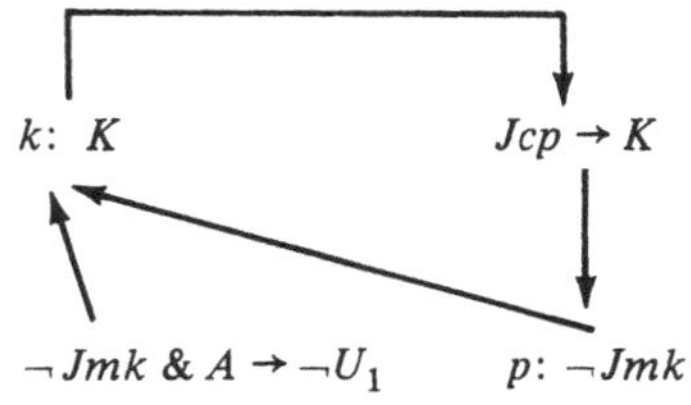

On the top line are tokens that are potential beliefs of the monopolist, and on the bottom line are potential beliefs of the competitor. Once again, '*K*' abbreviates the subjunctive conditional: if the monopolist were to retaliate, the competitor would stay out. The monopolist is inclined to accept the token whose type is [$Jck \rightarrow K$], and the competitor is inclined to accept the token whose type is [$\neg Jmk$ & $A \rightarrow \neg U_1$].The directed edges of the graph are of two kinds: (i) an atomic token or token of the form [*Jxy*] points to the token *y*, and (ii) a token *x* points to a subtoken *y* of another token belonging to the same agent when the acceptability of *x* depends on the evaluation of *y*. The edge connecting token *k* with the antecedent subtoken [*Jcp*] of the token to *k*'s right is of this second kind.

The tokens *p* and *k* and the subtoken of type [*Jcp*] form a closed loop, so on Gaifman's construction they all receive the value GAP. Thus, the monopolist is blocked from accepting the subjunctive conditional *K*, and the competitor is blocked from recognizing that the monopolist does not accept *K*. Both monopolist and competitor are afflicted with situation-generated blindspots. Neither can predict what the other would do, even given full information about the other's data and utility function.

In Section 7.3, I construct a solution to the doxic paradoxes in the style of Barwise and Etchemendy's work on the liar (specifically, their "Austinian" theory of propositions). In this theory, atomic propositions are always about some limited situation in the world. This hidden situation parameter, which context contributes to concrete thought tokens, enables the theory to avert a contradiction in analyzing paradoxical tokens. For example, instead of having a proposition of the form ~[*Jap*], that is, that proposition *p* is not justifiable for *a*, in the Austinian theory there will always be a specific situation built in the propositions, for instance, ⟨*s*, ⟨*J*, *a*, *p*; 0⟩⟩ (i.e., that the unjustifiability of proposition p for a is a fact contained by situation s) or $\sim\langle s, \langle J, a, p; 1\rangle\rangle$ (i.e., that the justifiability of proposition p for a is not a fact contained in situation s). In this Austinian theory, there is an important distinction between internal negation (represented by indexing an atomic fact with '0' rather than '1') and external negation (represented by appending an entire proposition with the operator '~'). These new restrictions on the formation of propositions necessitates a rewriting of doxic logic. The following schemata shall be postulated for any situation s and s', any agent x, and any Austinian proposition p:

(J1) $\langle s, \langle J, x, \sim\langle s', \langle J, x, p; 1\rangle\rangle; 1\rangle\rangle \rightarrow \sim\langle s', \langle J, x, p; 1\rangle\rangle$,
(J2) $\langle s, \langle J, x, p; 1\rangle\rangle$, where p is a logical axiom,
(J3) $\langle s, \langle J, x, (p \rightarrow q); 1\rangle\rangle \rightarrow (\langle s, \langle J, x, p; 1\rangle\rangle \rightarrow \langle s, \langle J, x, q; 1\rangle\rangle)$,
(J4) $\langle s, \langle J, x, p; 1\rangle\rangle$, where p is an instance of (J1)–(J3).

These schemata are simply the natural analogues of those introduced in Chapter 1. Now, consider the apparently paradoxical proposition p, asserting that its own justifiability is not a fact contained in some situation s:

$$p = \sim\langle s, \langle J, i, p; 1\rangle\rangle.$$

Suppose s is actual, and p is false. Then $\langle J, i, p; 1\rangle \in s$. By the definition of p, $\langle J, i, \sim\langle s, \langle J, i, p; 1\rangle\rangle; 1\rangle \in s$. By axiom (J1), $\langle J, i, p; 1\rangle \notin s$. This is a contradiction. So if s is actual, p is true. Thus, if s is an actual situation, it must not contain the justifiability of p. If agent i is aware of the relevant facts, then p may indeed be justifiable for i, but this fact will be contained only in situations that contain a more comprehensive view of the matter than that represented by s itself.

Next, let us consider a doxic paradox that does not involve self-reference, such as the one generated by the Rowena–Columna story in Chapter 1. Let 'c' represent Columna, and let 'p' represent the proposition that taking the $100 is Columna's optimal choice. The following Austinian propositions are analogues of the assumptions (A1) and (A2) needed in Chapter 1 to generate the paradox:

(A1a) $\langle s, \langle J, c, (p \rightarrow \sim\langle s, \langle J, c, p; 1\rangle\rangle); 1\rangle\rangle$,
(A1b) $\langle s, \langle J, c, (\sim\langle s, \langle J, c, p; 1\rangle\rangle \rightarrow p); 1\rangle\rangle$,
(A2) $\langle s, \langle J, c, \langle s, \langle J, c, (p \rightarrow \langle s, \langle J, c, p; 0\rangle\rangle); 1\rangle\rangle; 1\rangle\rangle$.

These assumptions assert that there is some situation s such that the justifiability for c of the biconditional '$p \leftrightarrow \sim\langle s, \langle J, c, p; 1\rangle\rangle$' is a fact contained in s and that the justifiability for c of this very proposition (namely, that s contains the justifiability for c of this biconditional) is also contained in s. Given these three assumptions, we can still derive a contradiction as follows:

(1) $\langle s, \langle Ji, (p \rightarrow \sim\langle s, \langle J, i, p; 1\rangle\rangle); 1\rangle\rangle$,	(A1a)
(2) $\langle s, \langle J, i, p; 1\rangle\rangle \rightarrow \langle s, \langle J, i, \sim\langle s, \langle J, i, p; 1\rangle\rangle; 1\rangle\rangle$,	(1), (J3)
(3) $\langle s, \langle J, i, \sim\langle s, \langle J, i, p; 1\rangle\rangle; 1\rangle\rangle \rightarrow \sim\langle s, \langle J, i, p; 1\rangle\rangle$,	(J1)
(4) $\sim\langle s, \langle J, i, p; 1\rangle\rangle$,	(2), (3)
(5) $\langle s, \langle J, i, \sim\langle s, \langle J, i, p; 1\rangle\rangle; 1\rangle\rangle$,	(A2), (J4), (J2), (J3) (see lines (1)–(4))
(6) $\langle s, \langle J, i, (\sim\langle s, \langle J, i, p; 1\rangle\rangle \rightarrow p); 1\rangle\rangle$,	(A1b)
(7) $\langle s, \langle J, i, \sim\langle s, \langle J, i, p; 1\rangle\rangle; 1\rangle\rangle \rightarrow \langle s, \langle J, i, p; 1\rangle\rangle$,	(6), (J3)
(8) $\langle s, \langle J, i, p 1\rangle\rangle$.	(5), (7)

Thus, it is a consequence of doxic logic that at least one of (A1a), (A1b), and (A2) must be false.

Ideally, we would like to have a principled explanation of why (A2) must be false for any situation s of which (A1a) and (A1b) are true. In order to do this, we must have some account of how the relevant situations become attached to concrete tokens of thought, which themselves make no explicit mention of such situations. This account should explain how the context of a thought token determines the situation parameters that are to be assigned to it, resulting in a well-formed Austinian proposition as the object of thought mediated by that token. In the last section of this chapter, I construct such an account that fulfills certain desiderata of symmetry, economy, and charity. Here I will discuss the application of this construction to the Rowena–Columna paradox.

The network of tokens corresponding to the assumptions (A1a), (A1b), and (A2) may be pictured thus:

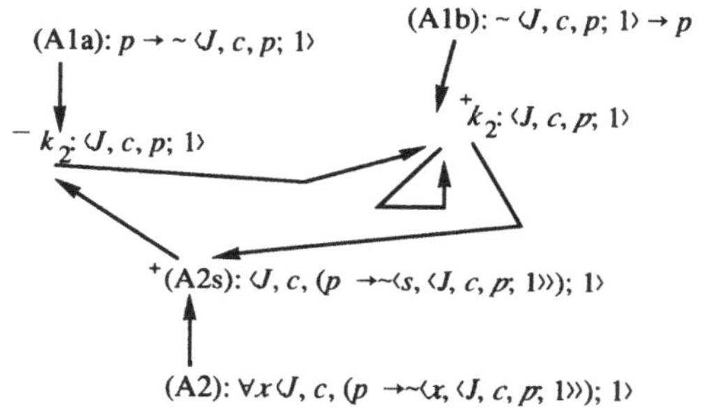

The arrows on the graph represent instances of the calling relation between tokens. One token calls another when the interpretation of the first is dependent on the interpretation of the second. Following the principle of charity leads to distinguishing between positive and negative atomic doxic subtokens. A subtoken is positive if it occurs within an even number of negations in the normal form of the thought of which it is a part; otherwise, a token is negative. A given thought is more likely to be interpreted as having a true proposition as its object if positive tokens are assigned larger, more comprehensive situations and negative tokens are assigned smaller, more limited ones.

The graph contains a closed loop consisting of tokens k_1(a subtoken of (A1a)), k_2 (a subtoken of (A1b)), and (A2s) (a subtoken that is an instance of the universally quantified token (A2)). Among the atomic doxic tokens in this loop, only k_1 is negative, so it is immediately assigned the minimal situation s_0 as its parameter. Token (A1a) inherits this assignment, with the result that token (A1a) is interpreted as expressing the proposition '$(p \rightarrow {\sim}\langle s_0, \langle J, c, p; 1\rangle\rangle)$'. This assignment breaks the closed loop, but another closed loop remains, this one consisting of token k_2 alone. Thus, k_2 must also be assigned the minimal situation s_0, and consequently (A1b) is interpreted as expressing '$({\sim}\langle s_0, \langle J, c, p; 1\rangle\rangle \rightarrow p)$'. At this point, all of the closed loops in the graph have been eliminated. Token (A2s_0) (one of the instances of (A2)) can therefore be assigned the richer, more comprehensive situation s_1 as its parameter. Thus, (A2s_0) can be interpreted as expressing the proposition '$\langle s_1, \langle J, c, (p \rightarrow {\sim}\langle s_0, \langle J, c, p; 1\rangle\rangle); 1\rangle$'. In summary, the following three propositions correctly describe the situation:

(A1a) $p \rightarrow {\sim}\langle s_0, \langle J, c, p; 1\rangle\rangle$,
(A1b) ${\sim}\langle s_0, \langle J, c, p; 1\rangle\rangle \rightarrow p$,
(A2s_0) $\langle s_1, \langle J, c, (p \rightarrow {\sim}\langle J, c, p; 1\rangle\rangle); 1\rangle$.

When doxic logic is applied to these propositions, we do not get a contradiction. Instead, we can derive ${\sim}\langle s_0, \langle J, c, p; 1\rangle\rangle$ and $\langle s_1, \langle J, c, p; 1\rangle\rangle$, that is, that the justifiability for Columna of p is a fact contained by situation s_1 but not by s_0. In other words, we interpret Columna as believing that taking the $100 is optimal if and only if the justifiability of her thinking so is not a fact contained in the limited situation s_0. An analysis of the situation reveals that the justifiability of her thinking so cannot be contained in s_0. However, it is quite possible for Columna to recognize that this is so and thereby to conclude that taking the $100 is optimal. The fact that it is justifiable for her so to conclude will be contained, not in s_0, but in some more comprehensive situation s_1.

A similar analysis can be provided for the chain-store paradox. The upshot of such an analysis would be that certain true propositions about the situation are cognitively inaccessible to the monopolist and the competitor. The context sensitivity of Austinian propositions containing the relation *justifiably believes* explains why the situation is a blindspot for the participants: they simply are not in a position to grasp certain true propositions (at least, not given the limitations of natural, nonramified language). Let p represent the subjunctive conditional: if the monopolist retaliates, the competitor will stay out. Let q represent the indicative conditional: if the monopolist retaliates and $<J, m, p; 0>$ (p is unjustifiable for the monopolist m), then the monopolist's utility function is U_2 (a function that produces retaliation even without deterrence). The relevant part of the network of thought tokens can be pictured thus, with the top three tokens in the monopolist's mind and the bottom three in the competitor's:

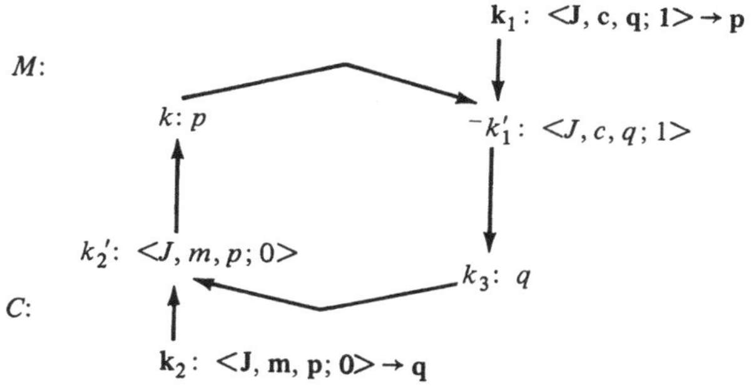

Tokens k_1 and k_2 are in boldface to represent the fact that these tokens are assigned some weight as data in the epistemic situations of the monopolist and the competitor, respectively. Tokens k_1 and k_2, each call their own atomic doxic subtokens, k_1' and k_2'. Each of these two subtokens calls the other, since the justifiability of p for the monopolist depends on the interpretation of k_1', and the justifiability of q for the competitor depends on the interpretation of k_2'. Tokens k_1' and k_2' are both negative, since each occurs in the antecedent of a conditional (internal negation does not count). Since both are negative and belong to a closed loop, both are assigned the limited situation s_0. This limited situation s_0 contains neither the fact that p is unjustifiable for the monopolist, nor the fact that q is justifiable for the competitor.

Therefore, the monopolist cannot correctly conclude that p, and the competitor cannot conclude that q.

The unjustifiability of both of these propositions is recorded, however, in the richer situation s_1. If the competitor could grasp the proposition $\langle s_1, \langle J, m, p; 0\rangle\rangle$, she could conclude that q was true, and she would then be deterred by an act of retaliation on the monopolist's part. The proposition, however, is inaccessible to her, because of the network in which the relevant token, k_2, is enmeshed.[1]

By a similar analysis, we can show that the alternative conditionals 'If m were to retaliate, c would play IN' and 'If the monopolist retaliates, then his utility function is U_1' are also unavailable as justifiable conclusions to the two players. If we were using subjective probabilities to characterize the mental states of the two players, we would have to use *interval-valued* probability functions, with the probability intervals assigned to these conditionals spanning the crucial points. In order to derive a solution to the game, we would first have to settle the question of how the players reach decisions under such nonstandard conditions. In the Conclusion, I will take up the question of how rational agents might be expected to cope with these perspectival blindspots, and I will suggest that solving this problem will shed light on the relation between the rational agent model, on the one hand, and social theory proper (the study of rules, practices, and institutions), on the other.

A further research problem that remains is how reasoning in paradox-infested waters can be implemented. We need to learn both how human beings actually implement such reasoning and how it might best be implemented in artificial intelligence programs. There are two prominent directions. One is to incorporate reasoning about situation parameters explicitly. The other is to leave the parameters implicit and localize the superficial inconsistency that results through some sort of paraconsistent logic. For some problems, most promising of all is the option of combining both approaches through a system of nonmonotonic reasoning.

In the case of mutual belief as modeled by strong virtual belief, the kind of two-level approach postulated by a solution in the style of Barwise and Etchemendy (or of Parsons and Burge) is especially

[1] A more complete analysis would examine the rational subjective probabilities of the two players, rather than look only at belief and absence of belief. This would introduce a bit of additional complexity, but it would not substantially alter the results reached here.

attractive and natural. Modeling the computation of the virtual beliefs of other reasoners is best described as a two-step process. At the first level, I begin to infer the virtual beliefs (with respect to some list of issues) of the other reasoner, but I find myself stymied by the fact that the other reasoner is also trying to compute my virtual beliefs. Part of the input required by my computation is the output of that very computation. Obviously, I cannot produce in this way a complete description of the other's virtual beliefs. I can, however, determine some things that definitely are and others that definitely are not among his virtual beliefs (and likewise, some that are and some that definitely are not among my own virtual beliefs in the present situation). I can use these beliefs to turn the vicious circle into a virtuous spiral. The more I know about my own virtual beliefs, the more I know about the other's, and vice versa.

Eventually, this inductive, boot-strapping procedure reaches a fixed point. At that point, I may be uncertain about what the other's (and my own) virtual beliefs are on certain subjects in which I am interested. I can recognize that I have reached a fixed point, so it would appear that anything that is not yet recognized as a virtual belief of the other cannot be among his virtual beliefs. But suppose that I have not yet been able to establish whether or not '*p*' is among the other's virtual beliefs (relative to his epistemic state *E*), but I do know that '$\neg V_E$ '*p*' $\rightarrow$ *p*' is virtually believed by him. I know that we both recognize that '*p*' is not among his established virtual beliefs at the fixed point, so apparently we both virtually believe that '$\neg V_E$'*p*''. Since he virtually believes the conditional '$\neg V_E$ '*p*' $\rightarrow$ *p*', and since virtual belief is closed under modus ponens, it seems that he does virtually believe '*p*' after all, which undermines the inference just completed. We now enter a cycle in which '*p*' goes in and out of the set of the other's virtual beliefs, unless we recognize that virtual belief must be relativized to a level of reflection.

Given a theory of the contextual relativization of doxic predicates to Tarskian levels, the reasoning process resolves itself in the following way. At the fixed point, we recognized that '*p*', and all other tokens involved in closed loops and descending chains are not virtually believed$_1$. Everything that I and other reasoners infer from this recognition is virtually believed$_2$. In particular, '*p*' itself is virtually believed$_2$, on the basis of the inference just described.

Using the information gained by "closing off"[2] the interpretation of 'virtual belief$_1$' at the first fixed point, I can use the virtuous spiral process already described to infer more and more about both my own and the other's virtual beliefs$_2$. Eventually, this process exhausts all of the tokens in the network. Whatever is believed$_2$ or not believed$_2$ by anyone is a matter of mutual belief$_2$ for all.

7.2 APPLYING GAIFMAN'S CONSTRUCTION TO DOXIC PARADOX

In order to apply a Gaifman-like construction to doxic paradox, I must redefine the calling relation between tokens. First, I must define a fully interpreted epistemic state $\langle E, V\rangle$. Suppose E is the epistemic state of cognitive individual a. Then V assigns one of the values T, F, or GAP to each atomic doxic subtoken (a subtoken of the form $[Jb\varphi]$) in the set $\mathcal{L}_a$. Moreover, V assigns T, F, or GAP to other tokens in $\mathcal{L}_a$ whenever the values follow by Kleene's strong truth table from other values assigned by V, that is:

(1) If $V(\varphi) = T$, then $V({\sim}\varphi) = F$.
If $V(\varphi) = F$, then $V({\sim}\varphi) = T$.
If $V(\varphi) =$ GAP, then $V({\sim}\varphi) =$ GAP.

(2) If $V(\varphi) = T$ and $V(\psi) = T$, then $V(\varphi \,\&\, \psi) = T$.
If $V(\varphi) = F$ or $V(\varphi) = F$, then $V(\varphi \,\&\, \psi) = F$.
If $V(\varphi) =$ GAP and $V(\Psi) = T$ or GAP,
or vice versa, then $V(\varphi \,\&\, \Psi) =$ GAP.

(3) If for every instance φ' of $\forall x\varphi$, $V(\varphi') = T$, then $V(\forall x\varphi) = T$.
If for some instance φ' of $\forall x\varphi$, $V(\varphi') = F$, then $V(\forall x\varphi) = F$.
If for every instance φ' of $\forall x\varphi$, $V(\varphi') = T$ or $=$ GAP, and for some instance φ'', $V(\varphi'') =$ GAP, then $V(\forall x\varphi) =$ GAP.

The fully interpreted epistemic state $\langle E,V\rangle$ can be identified with the epistemic state that results from making two sorts of changes in E: (i) whenever φ is a maximal token and $V(\varphi) = T$, add φ as a datum with maximal weight; and (ii) whenever φ is a datum in E and $V(\varphi)$ is equal to F or GAP, then remove φ from the data set. A proposition is justifiable relative to an epistemic state $\langle E,V\rangle$ if and only if it is a logical consequence of the intersection of the maximal coherent subsets of the data sentences of $\langle E,V\rangle$ (see Chapters 1 and 4).

The valuation V must meet certain conditions in order to be even prima facie acceptable. Assume $\varphi, \psi \in \mathcal{L}_a$.

(1) If $V(\varphi) = T$, and token ψ is of the type $[Ja\varphi]$, then $V(\psi) \neq F$.

[2] Kripke (1975), p. 715.

If $V(\varphi) = F$, and token ψ is of the type $[Ja\varphi]$, then $V(\psi) \neq T$.

(2) If $V(\varphi) = T$, and ψ is of the same type as φ, then $V(\psi) \neq F$.

If $V(\varphi) = F$, and ψ is of the same type as φ, then $V(\psi) \neq T$.

$\langle E, v\rangle$ is a partially interpreted epistemic state just in case there is an acceptable valuation V such that $v \subseteq V$. A proposition is justifiable in state $\langle E, v\rangle$ if and only if it is justifiable in every fully interpreted epistemic state $\langle E, V\rangle$ such that $v \subseteq V$. A token in $\mathcal{L}_a$ is justifiable in state $\langle E, v\rangle$ if and only if its type is justifiable in $\langle E, v\rangle$ and it has not been assigned the value GAP. Such a token is unjustifiable in state $\langle E, v\rangle$ if and only if either the negation of its type is justifiable in $\langle E, v\rangle$ or it is assigned either $\mathcal{F}$ or GAP.

Let G be a graph of cognitive individuals. Let $\mathcal{F}$ be a function that assigns to each cognitive individual a an acceptable partial valuation function v_a. I am now in a position to define the calling relation between tokens in the languages of the individuals in G.

Definition. *k calls k' directly (given $\mathcal{F}$) iff*

(1) *$k \in \mathcal{L}_a{}^*$, $k' \in \mathcal{L}_b$, and $Typ(k) = [Jbk^\urcorner]$, or*

(2) *$k \in \mathcal{L}_a$, $k' \in \mathcal{L}_a{}^*$, $k \neq k'$, k' is not a subtoken of k, and there exist valuation functions V and V' extending $\mathcal{F}(a)$ such that*

  (a) *V and V' differ only in that one assigns GAP and the other assigns a standard value* (T or F) *to k', and*

  (b) *the proposition expressed by k is justifiable in $\langle E_a, V\rangle$ iff it is not justifiable in $\langle E_a, V'\rangle$,*

  or

(3) *$k \in \mathcal{L}_a{}^*$, k is a conjunction, k' is one of its conjuncts, and there is no conjunct of k to which $\mathcal{F}(a)$ assigns F, or*

(4) *k is the negation of k', or*

(5) *$k \in \mathcal{L}_a{}^*$, k is a universal generalization, k' is one of its instances, and there is no instance of k to which $\mathcal{F}(a)$ assigns F.*

Token k calls token k' if and only if there is a finite sequence *of* tokens $k_0, k_1, \ldots, k_n$ such that $k_0 = k$, $k_n = k'$, and for each i, k_i calls k_{i+1}.

The valuation construction begins with the class $\mathcal{F}_0$, which assigns the empty valuation function $\emptyset$ to every cognitive individual in the graph G. Given a class $\mathcal{F}_a$, we construct the class $\mathcal{F}_{a+1}$ by simultaneously applying the following rule:

(I) For every cognitive individual c, $\mathcal{F}_{a+1}(c)$ is the smallest acceptable valuation function satisfying the following three conditions:

  (1) Jump rule.

(a) If $k \in \mathcal{L}_a^*$, $\mathcal{F}_a(c)(k)$ is undefined, TYP$(k) = [Jbk^*]$, $k^* \in \mathcal{L}_b$, and k^* is justifiable in the state $\langle E_b, \mathcal{F}_a(b)\rangle$, then $\mathcal{F}_{a+1}(c)(k) = T$.

(b) If $k \in \mathcal{L}_a^*$, $\mathcal{F}_a(c)(k)$ is undefined, TYP$(k) = [Jbk^*]$, $k^* \in \mathcal{L}_b$, and k^* is unjustifiable in the state $\langle E_b, \mathcal{F}_a(b)\rangle$, then $\mathcal{F}_{a+1}(c)(k) = F$.

(2) Closed-loop rule. If S is a loop closed in the set of unevaluated tokens, and the Jump rule does not apply to any member of S, then $\mathcal{F}_{a+1}(c)(k) =$ GAP for every individual c and token $k \in S \cap \mathcal{L}_a^*$.

(3) Give-up rule. If the set of unevaluated tokens is not empty and no preceding rule applies to any of them, then $\mathcal{F}_{a+1}(c)(k) =$ GAP for every such $k \in \mathcal{L}_a^*$.

(II) Limit ordinal rule. For every limit ordinal λ, $\mathcal{F}_\lambda(c)$ is the smallest acceptable valuation function such that, for every $a < \lambda$, $\mathcal{F}_a(c) \subseteq \mathcal{F}_\lambda(c)$.

Unlike the Gaifman algorithm for truth given in the preceding chapter, the construction for justifiable belief is not unaffected by changing the order in which the rules are applied. The crucial difference lies in clause (2) of the new calling relation, which had no counterpart in the definition of the calling relation in the preceding chapter. In the case of belief, but not in the case of truth, the very existence of a calling relation between two tokens can be affected by the evaluation of a third token, since this evaluation can change in relevant ways the epistemic state of a conceptual individual. A change in the epistemic state of an individual affects the existence of calling relations through clause (2) of the definition. Consequently, it is important to specify, as I have done, that all possible applications of the jump and closed-loop rules be made before the epistemic states of any of the individuals are updated.

7.3 APPLYING SITUATION THEORY TO DOXIC PARADOX

In this section I will use a formal "language" of propositions, modeled after those used by Barwise and Etchemendy in *The Liar*, as modified by myself in Chapter 6. I will introduce three properties: 'I', for the interpretation of a token by a proposition, 'J', for the rational justifiability of belief in a proposition by a person, and 'Ep'; for the relation between an agent and his epistemic state. '$\langle I, i, k, p;\ 1\rangle$' shall express the atomic fact that sentence *k* in individual *i*'s language of thought expresses the proposition *p*. '⟨*J*, *i*, *p*; 1⟩' shall express the atomic fact that belief in proposition *p* is rationally justifiable for individual *i*. '⟨*Ep*, *i*,*e*; 1⟩' shall express the fact that *e* is *i*'s epistemic state.

Definition 1. *Let X and Y be any two classes.*

The closure Γ(X, Y) of X and Y is the smallest collection containing X and closed under the following:

(1) *If Z is a finite sequence of elements of Γ(X, Y), then* [∧Z] *is in Γ(X, Y).*
(2) *If p* ∈ *Γ(X, Y), and v* ∈ *Y, then* [∀*v*: *p*[*v*/*d*]] ∈ *Γ(X, Y).*
(3) *If z* ∈ *Γ(X, Y), then* [~*z*] *is in Γ(X, Y).*

I will assume, for simplicity's sake, that there is a single language of thought *L*. I will further assume that the structure of the sentences in this language mirrors that of propositions sans parameters. A *situated subsentence* is simply a part of some sentence in *L*, together with that part's location within that sentence. Formally, I will represent a subsentence as a finite sequence, the first of which is a sentence and the rest of which are sentences, each of which is an immediate constituent of its predecessor. The last constituent, the *face* of the subsentence, represents the grammatical form of the subsentence proper. The first constituent, the *base* of the subsentence, represents the ultimate cognitive context of that subsentence.

Definition 2. *Let* SOA, SIT, ATPROP, PROP, *V*, *L*, *and L+ be the largest classes satisfying*:

**Every σ* ∈ SOA *is of the form* ⟨*H*, *a*, *b*; *t*⟩ *(a typical nonsemantic atomic proposition)*, ⟨*Ep*, *i*, *e*, *t*⟩ ⟨*J*, *a*, *p*; *t*⟩ *or* ⟨I, *a*, *k*, *p*; *t*⟩, *where H*, *Ep*, *J and I are distinct atoms, a and b are concrete individuals or members of V*, *k* ∈ *L+*, *p* ∈ PROP, *and t is either* 0 *or* 1.

**Every s* ∈ SIT *is a subset of* SOA.

**Every p* ∈ PROP *belongs to Γ(* ATPROP,*V)*.

**Every p* ∈ ATPROP *is of the form* <*s*, *σ*>, *where s* ∈ SIT *and σ* ∈ SOA.

**Every v* ∈ *V is of the form* <*n*, *A*>, *where n is a natural number and A is a subset of U* (*the set of concrete individuals*), SIT, SOA, PROP, *V*, *L* , *or L+*.

**Every φ* ∈ *L belongs to Γ(*SOA, *V)*.

**Every k* ∈ *L+ is a finite sequence* <φ_0, . . . , φ_n> *such that* (i) *each* φ_i

belongs to $\mathcal{L}$*, and* (2) *for each i such that* $0 \leq i \leq n-1$*, either*
(a) $\varphi_i = {\sim}\varphi_{i+1}$,
(b) $\varphi_i = [\wedge Z]$ *and* φ_{i+1} *is a constituent of , or*
(c) $\varphi_i = [\forall v: \psi[c/d]]$, $\varphi_{i+1} = \psi\,[c/d]$, $v = <n, A>$*, and* $c \in A$.

For each set of concrete individuals, propositions, SOAS, situations, and sentences, there shall be denumerably many arbitrary individuals. Each arbitrary individual has such a set as its unique range of significance.

I can now introduce the following truth-definition for these propositions.

Definition 3. Truth-definition. *Let g be a function whose domain is a set of arbitrary individuals and whose range is a set of concrete individuals, propositions,* SOAS*, and situations such that, for each* $x \in D(g)$*,* $g(x) = x^3$ *or* $g(x)$ *is in the range of significance of x. Let* σ/g *be the result of replacing every occurrence of an individual d in the domain of g with* $g(d)$.

(1) *The proposition* $<s, \sigma>$ *is true relative to g iff* $\sigma/g \in s$.
(2) *The proposition* $[{\sim}p]$ *is true relative to g iff p is not true relative to g.*
(3) *The proposition* $[\wedge Z]$ *is true relative to g iff every member of Z is true relative to g.*
(4) *The proposition* $[\forall v: q\,[v/d]$ *is true relative to g iff for every member c of the range of v,* $q[c/d]$ *is true relative to g.*
(5) *p is true iff there is a g such that p is true relative to g.*

I will introduce a system of deduction for these propositions. First, I will define the conditions in which an individual occurs in a proposition. Then, I will define the relation of a proposition p's following deductively from a set of propositions Γ. Finally, I will define the relation of one set of propositions being a deductive consequence of another. This notion of deductive consequence is needed in order to require that the rational agent's beliefs be deductively closed. Since each Austinian proposition is either necessarily true or necessarily false, it is not immediately obvious what a useful notion of deductive consequence would be like. We could stipulate that two propositions $<s, \sigma>$ and $<s', \sigma>$ are logically independent whenever $s \neq s'$. Instead, I have stipulated that $<s, \sigma>$ entails $<s', \sigma>$ whenever $s \subseteq s'$.

Definition 4. *Individual c occurs in proposition p iff*
(1) $p = <s, \sigma>$ *and c is a constituent of* σ,
(2) $p = {\sim}\, q$ *and c occurs in q,*

(3) $p = [\wedge Z]$ *and* c *occurs in some constituent of the sequence* Z,
(4) $p = [\forall v\colon q]$ *and either* $c = v$ *or* c *does not occur in* q.

Definition 5. $\Gamma \vdash p$ *iff one of the following conditions holds*:

(1a) $[\forall v\colon q[v/d]] \in \Gamma$, $v = \langle n, A\rangle$, $c \in A$, and $p = q[c/d]$, *∀ Exploitation*

(2) $[\forall v\colon q[v/d]] \in \Gamma$, $v = \langle n, A\rangle$, $v' = \langle m, B\rangle$, $B \subset A$, and $p = q[v'/d]$, *∀E to arbitrary individual*

(3) p *is a tautology*, *Tautology*

(4) $p = \langle s, \sigma\rangle$, $q = \langle s', \sigma\rangle$, $q \in \Gamma$, *and* $s' \subseteq s$, *Parameter increasing*

(5) $p = q[v'/d]$, $\sim[\forall v\colon q[v/d]] \in \Gamma$, $v = \langle n, A\rangle$, $v' = \langle m, B\rangle$, $A \subseteq B$, *and* v' *does not occur in* Γ, *∃ Exploitation*

(6) $p = \sim[\forall v\colon q[v/d]]$, $v = \langle n, A\rangle$, $\sim q[c/d] \in \Gamma$, *and* $c \in A$, *∃ Introduction*

(7) $p = \sim[\forall v\colon q[v/d]]$, $v = \langle n, A\rangle$, $v' = \langle m, B\rangle$, $B \subseteq A$, *and* $\sim q\,[v'/d] \in \Gamma$, *∃I from arbitrary individual*

(8) $p = \sim\langle s, \sigma\rangle$, $q = \langle s, \sigma'\rangle$, σ' *is the dual of* σ, *and* $q \in \Gamma$, *Internal–external negation*

(9) Γ' *is a consequence of* Γ *and* $\Gamma' \vdash p$. *Transitivity*

Definition 6. *A set* Γ' *of propositions is an immediate consequence of a set* Γ *iff one of the following holds*:
(1) *There is a* p *such that* $\Gamma \vdash p$ *and* $\Gamma' = \Gamma \cup \{p\}$. *Monotonicity*
(2) *For every* $p \in Y$, $\Gamma \vdash p$, *and* $\Gamma' = \Gamma \cup [\forall Y]\}$. *∀ Introduction*
(3) $\Gamma \cup \{p\} \vdash q$, *and* $\Gamma' = \Gamma \cup \{\sim[\wedge\langle p, \sim q\rangle]\}$. *Conditional proof*

Definition 7. *A set* Γ' *of propositions is a consequence of a set* Γ *iff there is a finite chain* $\Gamma_0, \ldots, \Gamma_n$ *such that* $\Gamma_0 = \Gamma$, $\Gamma_n = \Gamma'$, *and for each* $i < n$, Γ_{i+1} *is an immediate consequence of* Γ_i.
A set Γ *of propositions is inconsistent iff there is a proposition* p *such that* $\{p, \sim p\}$ *is a subset of a consequence of* Γ. *Otherwise,* Γ *is consistent.*

Definition 8. $\mathcal{A}$ *is a model iff* $\mathcal{A}$ *is a class of* SOAS *such that, for every* σ, *either* σ *or its dual belongs to* $\mathcal{A}$, *but not both.*

I will assume that, for each SOA σ, for each situation s in model $\mathcal{A}$ (i.e., s is a subset of $\mathcal{A}$) and for each model $\mathcal{A}'$, there is a counterpart $C(\mathcal{A}'$,

$s, \mathcal{A}, \sigma)$ of s in $\mathcal{A}'$. $C(\mathcal{A}', s, \mathcal{A}, \sigma)$ is always a subset of $\mathcal{A}'$. Moreover, the counterpart function is subset-preserving: if $s \subseteq s' \subseteq \mathcal{A}$, then $C(\mathcal{A}', s, \mathcal{A}, \sigma) \subseteq C(A', s', \mathcal{A}, \sigma) \subseteq \mathcal{A}'$, for every model $\mathcal{A}'$.

Definition 9. *Let g be a function whose domain is a subset of V such that, for every* $v \in D(g)$, *if* $v = \langle n, A \rangle$, *then* $g(v) \in A$.

A proposition *p* is *true in A relative to A' and g* (given counterpart function *C*) if and only if.
(1) *if* $p = \langle s, \sigma \rangle$, *then* $\sigma/g \in C(A', s, A, \sigma/g)$,
(2) *if* $p = {\sim}q$, *then q is not true in* $\mathcal{A}$ *relative to* $\mathcal{A}$ *and g*,
(3) *if* $p = [\wedge Z]$, *then every q in Z is true in* $\mathcal{A}$ *relative to* $\mathcal{A}'$ *and g*,
(4) *if* $p = [\forall v\!: q[v/d]]$ *and* $v = \langle n, A \rangle$, *then for every* $c \in \mathcal{A}$, $q[c/d]$ *is true in* $\mathcal{A}$ *relative to* $\mathcal{A}'$ *and g*.

A *set P of propositions is true in* $\mathcal{A}$ *relative to* $\mathcal{A}'$ if and only if there exists a *g* such that every member of *P* is true in $\mathcal{A}$ relative to $\mathcal{A}'$ and *g*.[3]

Definition 10. $\Gamma \vdash \Gamma'$ *iff* Γ *and* Γ' *are sets of propositions, and for every A, A' and C such that there is a g such that every member of* Γ *is true in A relative to A' and given C, there is an h such that every member of* Γ *and of* Γ' *is true in A relative to A' and h given C.*

An Ur-model shall be a situation that contains no doxic SOAS (those involving '*I*' or '*J*') and that are maximal and consistent with respect to nondoxic SOAS. I will assume that we have a fixed, denumerable set of concrete individuals, *U*.

Definition 11. *An Ur-model M is a situation that is such that*
(1) *it contains no doxic SOAS,*
(2) *for every pair of individuals a and b in U, every cognitive individual i, and every epistemic situation e, exactly one of each of the following pair of SOAS belongs to M*: $\langle H, a, b; 0 \rangle$ or $\langle H, a, b; 1 \rangle$, $\langle Ep, i, e; 0 \rangle$ or $\langle Ep, i, e; 1 \rangle$, *and*
(3) *if* $\langle Ep, a, e; 1 \rangle \in s$ *and* $\langle Ep, a, e'; 1 \rangle \in s$, *then* $e = e'$.

An *Ur-situation* is a situation which is a subset of some Ur-model.

Definition 12. *Situated subsentence k and proposition p are structurally isomorphic iff*
(1) $Face(k) = \varphi$, *φ is atomic and* $p = \langle s, \varphi \rangle$ *for some situation s*,
(2) $Face(k) = {\sim}\psi$, $p = {\sim}q$, *and* $k^\wedge\langle\psi\rangle$ *and q are isomorphic*,

[3] When $g(x) = x$, the proposition is interpreted as being about the variable *x*, as in <<Variable, *x*>, *s*> (this corresponds to the mention of a variable in standard formal languages). When $g(x)$ is some member of the range of *x*'s significance, the proposition is being interpreted as parametric, as about some unspecified member of this range (this corresponds to the use of a variable).

(3) *Face*$(k) = [\wedge Z], p = [\wedge Q]$, *Z and Q are finite sequences of the same length, and for each i*, $k^\wedge\langle Z_i\rangle$ *and* Q_i *are isomorphic, or*

(4) *Face*$(k) = [\forall v\colon \psi[v/b]]$, $p = [\forall v\colon q\ [v/b]]$, *and* $k^\wedge\langle\psi\rangle$ *and q are isomorphic.*

Definition 13. *A situated subsentence k is positive iff its face occurs within the scope of an even number of external negations (~) in its base sentence. k is negative iff its face occurs within an odd number of external negations.*

Definition 14. *The relation ≤ is defined on* PROP X PROP *by the following recursion*:

(1) $\langle s, \sigma\rangle \leq \langle s', \sigma\rangle$ *iff* $s' \subset s$,

(2) $\sim p \leq \sim q$ *iff* $q \leq p$,

(3) $[\wedge Z] \leq [\wedge Z]$ *iff Z and Z' are of length n, and for every* $i < n$, $z_i \leq z'_i$,

(4) $[\forall v\colon p[v/c]] \leq [\forall v'\colon q[v/c]]$ *iff* $v = v'$ & $p \leq q$.

Definition 15. *A situation s is possible iff*

(I) *Consistency*

(1) *There is no* SOA σ *such that both* σ *and its dual belong to s.*

(II) *Uniqueness of functional outputs*

(2) *If* $\langle I, i, k, p; 1\rangle \in s$ *and* $\langle I, i, k, q; 1\rangle \in s$, *then* $p = q$.

(3) *If* $\langle Ep, i, e; 1\rangle \in s$ *and* $\langle Ep, i, e'; 1\rangle \in s$, *then* $e = e'$.

(III) *Interpretation of negations*

(4) *If* $k = k'^\wedge\langle\varphi\rangle$, *Face*$(k') = \sim\varphi$, *and* $\langle I, i, k, p; 1\rangle \in s$, *then* $\langle I, i, k', \sim p; 1\rangle \in s$.

(5) *If* $k = k'^\wedge\langle\varphi\rangle$, *Face*$(k') = \sim\varphi$, *and* $\langle I, i, k, p; 0\rangle \in s$, *then* $\langle I, i, k', \sim p; 0\rangle \in s$.

(IV) *Interpretation of conjunctions*

(6) *If Face*$(k) = [\wedge Z]$, *Z is an n-ary sequence* $\langle\varphi_0, \ldots, \varphi_{n-1}\rangle$, *and for every* $m < n$, $\langle I, i, k^\wedge\langle\varphi_m\rangle, p_m; 1\rangle \in s$ *for some* p_m, *then* $\langle I, i, k, q; 1\rangle \in s$, *where* $q = [\wedge\langle p0, \ldots, p_m\rangle]$.

(7) *If Face*$(k) = [\wedge Z]$, *Z is an n-ary sequence* $\langle\varphi_0, \ldots, \varphi_{n-1}\rangle$, *and for some* $m < n$, $\langle I, a, k^\wedge\langle\varphi_m\rangle, p_m; 0\rangle \in s$ *for some* p_m, *then* $\langle I, i, k, q; 0\rangle \in s$, *where* $q = [\wedge Q]$ *and* p_m *is the mth component of Q.*

(V) *Interpretation of generalizations*

(8) *If Face*$(k) = [\forall v\colon \varphi[v/d]]$, *k is positive*, $v = \langle n, A\rangle$, *and for every* $c \in A$, $\langle I, i, k^\wedge\langle\varphi\ [c/d]\rangle, p_c; 1\rangle \in s$ *for some* p_c, *then* $\langle I, i, k, q; 1\rangle \in s$ *and* $\langle I, i, k, q'; 0\rangle \notin s$ *for all* $q' \neq q$, *where* $q = [\forall v$:

p[*v*/*d*]], *and p is a* ≤*-maximal proposition such that, for all c* ∈ *A*, *p*[*c*/*a*] ≤ p_c.

(9) *If Face*(*k*) = [∀v: φ[*v*/*d*]], *k is negative*, *v* = <*n*, *A*>, *and for every c* ∈ *A*, <*I*, *i*, *k*^<φ[*c*/*d*]>, p_c; 1> ∈ *s for some* p_c, *then* < *I*, *i* ,*k*, *q*; 1> ∈ *s and* <*I*, *i*, *k*, *q*'; 0> ∉ *s for all q'* ≠ *q*, *where q* = [∀v: *p*[*v*/*d*]], *and p is a* ≤*-maximal proposition such that, for all c* ∈ *A*, p_c ≤ *p*.

(10) *If Face*(*k*) = [∀v: φ[*v*/*d*]], *k is positive*, *v* = <*n*, *A*>, *and for some c* ∈ *A*, <*I*, *i*, *k*^<φ[*c*/*d*]>, *p*; 0> ∈ *s for every p such that q*[*c*/*d*] ≤ *p*, *then* <*I*, *i*, *k*, [∀v: *q*[*v*/*d*]]; 0> ∈ *s*.

(11) *If Face*(*k*) = [∀v: φ[v/d]], *k is negative*, *v* = <*n*, *A*>, *and for some c* ∈ *A*, <*I*, *i*, *k*^<φ[*c*/*d*]>, *p*; 0> ∈ *s for every p such that p* ≤ *q* [*c*/*d*], *then* <*I*, *i*, *k*, [∀v: *q*[*v*/*d*]]; 0> ∈ *s*.

(VI) *Structural isomorphism*

(12) *If k and p are not structurally isomorphic, then* <*I*, *i*, *k*, *p*; 0> ∈ *s*.

(VII) *Accessibility of objects of belief*

(13) *If* <*J*, *i*, *p*; *t*> ∈ *s and* <*s*', σ> *is a subproposition of p, then* *s*' ⊆ *s*.

(14) *If* <*I*, *i*, *k*, *p*; *t*> ∈ *s and* <*s*', σ> *is a subproposition of p, then* *s*' ⊆ *s*.

Situation theory introduces situation parameters for a variety of reasons; dealing with liar-like paradoxes is only one of them. I will assume that initially every atomic subsentence in the thought language of every cognitive individual has been assigned some Ur-situation as a preliminary parameter. The task of this chapter is to describe how to extend these preliminary parameters by adding appropriate doxic SOAS. I will assume that there is a *preliminary parameter function B* such that, for every cognitive individual *i* and every atomic situated subsentence *k*, *B*(*i*, *k*) is an Ur-situation such that *B*(*i*, *k*) ⊂ *M*.

We can represent a *thought token* by an ordered pair <*i*, *k*>, where *i* is a cognitive individual and *k* is a situated subsentence. The process of interpreting such tokens begins with an Ur-model *M* and a preliminary parameter function *B* and produces a new situation in which the appropriate facts about the interpretation of tokens are registered. I will describe an operation that is monotonic in the sense that, when applied to a situation *s* and a function *B*, it always results in a situation that extends *s*.

Epistemic states can be defined as partial functions that assign epistemic weights of some kind to sentences in $\mathcal{L}$. The exact nature of these epistemic weights I will leave undefined. What is important is that such an epistemic state induces a weak preference ordering on the set of subsets of $\mathcal{L}$.

Now, I must define when a proposition p is justifiable for a cognitive individual i. If M is an Ur-model, let $E_M(i)$ be the epistemic situation e such that $<Ep, i, e; 1> \in M$. A possible situation s is a *total context* for individual i if and only if s extends M and, for every situated subsentence k in $\mathcal{L}^*$, there is exactly one proposition p such that $<J, i, k, p; 1> \in s$. As an epistemic situation, $E_s(i)$ is a partial function that assigns epistemic weights to sentences in $\mathcal{L}$. Let $D_s(i)$ be the set of data sentences in $E_s(i)$, that is, $D_s(i)$ is the range of $E_s(i)$.

Definition 16. *The priveleged subset of $D_s(i)$ in total context s is that subset $K(i, s)$ of $D_s(i)$ having the greatest epistemic weight that satisfies the following condition. The set $P = \{p: \exists\varphi(<J, i, <K(i, s), \varphi>, p; 1> \in s)\} \cup \{p: \exists Q(p = <s, <J, i, Q; 1>> \; \& \; p \text{ is true})\} \cup \{p: p \text{ is a doxic axiom and } p \text{ is expressible in } s\}$ is deductively consistent.*

The set $\{p: \exists\varphi(<J, i, <K(i, s), \varphi>, p; 1> \in s)\} \cup \{p: p \text{ is a doxic axiom and } p \text{ is expressible in } s\}$ is called the propositional basis of $E(i)/s$.

Definition 17. *A proposition p is justifiable for i in such a total context s iff p is a member of the last member of a finite chain C of sets such that*
(1) *the first member C_0 is the propositional basis of $E(i)/s$,*
(2) *Each C_{a+1} is derivable from C_a.*

A proposition p is justifiable for cognitive individual i in situation s iff p is justifiable for i in every total context extending s.

A sentence k is justifiable for i in s iff for every s' which is a total context for a such that s' extends s, the proposition p such that $<J, i, k, p; 1> \in s'$ is justifiable for i in s'.

A sentence k is unjustifiable for i in s iff for every s' that is a total context for a such that s' extends s, the proposition p such that $<J, i, k, p; 1> \in s$ is not justifiable for i in *s'*.

Correlating tokens and situations

In the construction to follow, I will detail how, given a network of concrete thought tokens and basic, nondoxic parameters, the doxic situational parameters are to be assigned to each token. The first issue to be decided is: shall we include merely possible tokens in doxically accessible worlds in the network, or shall we limit the network to the actual world? If we take the first alternative, the interpretation of a cognitive individual's thoughts will be entirely independent of her actual environment and will depend only on features internal to the world as it appears to her. On the second alternative, facts about the actual world will make an ineliminable contribution to the content of a cognitive individual's thoughts. Since the second alternative seems more consonant with the spirit of situation theory, I will pursue it here.

The interpretation of tokens will be guided by three principles: the principles of symmetry, of charity, and of interest, in that order.[4] My first priority will be to avoid arbitrary violations of various symmetries within the network. Second, I will try to interpret each maximal token (representing a separate thought or belief) so as to make it true, if possible. Third, I will try to interpret each token so as to assign it as rich a content as possible (maximizing its interest, for us and the individual herself). In order to make sense of the charity requirement, we must define the truth-value of a token in a situation.

Definition 18. *The truth-value of token* $\langle i, k\rangle$ *in situation s (given B) is partially defined by recursion*:

(1) *If k is an atomic, nondoxic situated subsentence, then* $\langle i, k\rangle$ *has value 1 in s iff* $k \in B(i, k)$. *Otherwise,* $\langle i, k\rangle$ *has value* 0 *in s.*

(2) *If k is an atomic, doxic situated subsentence, then* $\langle i, k\rangle$ *has value 1 in s iff there is a true proposition* $\langle s', \sigma\rangle$ *such that* $\langle I, i, k, \langle s', \sigma\rangle; 1\rangle \in s$, *and* $\langle i, k\rangle$ *has value* 0 *in s iff there is a false proposition* $\langle s', \sigma\rangle$ *such that* $\langle I, i, k, \langle s', \sigma\rangle; 1\rangle \in s$.

(3) *If* $k' = k^\frown\langle\varphi\rangle$, *and Face(k)* $= \sim\varphi$, *then* $\langle i, k\rangle$ *has value* 1 *in s iff* $\langle i, k'\rangle$ *has value* 0 *in s, and* $\langle i, k\rangle$ *has value* 0 *in s iff* $\langle i, k'\rangle$ *has value* 1 *in s.*

(4) *If Face(k)* $= [\wedge Z]$, *Z is an n-ary sequence* $\langle\varphi_0, \ldots, \varphi_{n-1}\rangle$, *and for all* $m < n$, $\langle i, k^\frown\langle\varphi_m\rangle\rangle$ *has value* 1 *in s, then* $\langle i, k\rangle$ *has value 1 in s. If Face(k)*$= [\wedge Z]$, *Z is an n-ary sequence* $\langle\varphi_0, \ldots, \varphi_{n-1}\rangle$, *and for some* $m < n$, $\langle i, k^\frown\langle\varphi_m\rangle\rangle$ *has value* 0 *in s, then* $\langle i, k\rangle$ *has value* 0 *in s.*

(5) *If Face(k)* $= [\forall v{:}\varphi[v/a]]$, $v = \langle n, A\rangle$, *and for all* $c \in A$, $\langle i, k^\frown\langle\varphi[c/a]\rangle\rangle$ *has value* 1 *in s, then* $\langle i, k\rangle$ *has value* 1 in *s. If Face(k)* $= [\forall v{:}\varphi[v/a]]$, $v = \langle n, A\rangle$, *and for some* $c \in A$, $\langle i, k^\frown\langle\varphi[c/a]\rangle\rangle$ *has value* 0 *in s then* $\langle i, k\rangle$ *has value* 0 *in s.*

[4]See Burge (1979). His three principles were symmetry, charity, and minimality.

Definition 19. *Token <i, k> is open in situation s iff <i, k> does not have a value in s, and either*
(1) *k is a sentence* (a 1-*ary sequence*), *or*
(2) *k is an immediate constituent of k′, and <i, k′> is open in s.*

The calling relation will turn the set of concrete tokens into a directed network by incorporating information on which tokens depend on which for their interpretation.

Definition 20. The calling relation. *Token <i, k> immediately calls token <j, k′>* in situation *s* iff one of the following conditions holds:

(1) (a) *<i, k>* is open in situation *s*,
(b) Face(*k*) = *<J, j, p; t>*,
(c) *there are total contexts c and c′ extending s such that c and c′ agree on all atomic subsentences except for k′, and p is justifiable for j relative to c iff p is not justifiable for j relative to c′.*

(2) *<i, k> is open in s, and Face(k) = <I, j, k′, p; t>.*

(3) *i = j, Face(k′) is an atomic doxic token, and k′ is a subsentence of k.*

A *token <i, k> calls token <j, k′> iff there is a finite calling path from <i, k>* to *<j, k′>.*

I now need to define two monotonic operations on doxic trees. The first operation, represented by τ, adds information to the model about the doxic facts that have been determined at a given stage in the construction.

Definition 21. The *doxic closure $\tau(s)$ of situation s* is the minimal possible situation *s′* extending *s* such that

(1) *If p is justifiable for i in s, then <J, i, p; 1> $\in$ s′. If p is unjustifiable for i in s, then <J, i, p; 0> $\in$ s′.*

(2) *If* (a) *Face(k) = <J, j, p; t> and* (b) *<J, j, p; t +/–1> $\in$ s, then <I, i, k, <s′, <J, j, p; t>>; 1> $\in$ s′.*

(3) *If* (a) *Face(k) = <I, k′, p; t> and* (b) *<I, j, k, p; t +/–1> $\in$ s, then <I, i, k, <s′, <I, j, k′, p; t>>; 1> $\in$ s′.*

(4) *If* (a) *Face(k) is an atomic, doxic sentence and* (b) *<i, k> is not open in s, then <I, i, k, <s′, Face(k)>; 1> $\in$ s′.*

(5) *If Face(k) is an atomic, nondoxic situated subsentence, then <I, a, k, <B(i, k), Face(k)>; 1> $\in$ s′.*

Paradoxical tokens belong to loops or infinitely descending chains in the directed network associated with the calling relation. In order to interpret such tokens properly, the notion of a closed chain must be defined and several varieties of such chains distinguished.

Definition 22. *A set of tokens is a loop iff $S \neq \phi$, and for all k, k′ in S, there is a calling path from k to k′. A maximal loop is a loop that is not a proper subset of any loop.*
A set of tokens is an infinitely descending chain iff every token k in S immediately calls another token in S. A proper chain contains no loops. A maximal proper chain is a proper chain that is not a proper subset of any proper chain.

Definition 23. *An occurrence of 'J' or 'I' in a sentence is negative if the corresponding occurrence in the prenex-disjunctive normal form of the sentence is externally negated* (by ~). *Otherwise, the occurrence of 'J' or 'I' in the sentence is positive.*
An occurrence of 'J' or 'I' in a subsentence is positive iff the corresponding occurrence in the related sentence is positive, and similarly for negative occurrences. An atomic doxic token <i, k> is positive or negative as the occurrence of 'J' or 'I' in k is.

Definition 24. *A pure loop contains only positive atomic tokens or only negative ones.*
A partly pure chain S is a chain that can be divided into two sets S_1 and S_2 such that S_1 is an infinitely descending chain containing only positive or only negative atomic doxastic tokens and no token in S_1 calls any token in S_2. In this case, any maximal such S_1 is called a pure part of S.

Definition 25. *The foundationalization $\varphi(s)$ of a situation s relative to τ-fixed point s_0 is the minimal situation s′ extending s that meets the following four conditions:*

(1) *If S is a pure loop or chain, <i, k> belongs to a pure part of S, and Face(k) = <J, j, p; t>, then <I, i, k, <s_0, <J, j, p; t>>; 1> ∈ s′.*
(2) *If S is a pure chain containing no atomic J-tokens, <i, k> belongs to a pure part of S, and Face(k) = <I, j,,k′, p; t>, then <I, i, k, <s_0, <I, j, k, p; t>>; 1> ∈ s′.*
(3) *If S is an impure loop or chain, <i, k> is a negative token, <i, k> ∈ S, and Face(k) = <J, j, p; t>, then <I, i, k, <s_0, <J, j, p; t>>; 1> ∈ s′.*
(4) *If S is an impure loop or chain and S contains no atomic J-tokens, <i, k> is a negative token, <i, k> ∈ S, and Face(k) = <I, j, k′, p; t>, then <I, i, k, <s_0, <I, c, k′, p; t>>; 1> ∈ s′.*

The embellishment of a doxic network proceeds as follows. First, the monotonic operation τ is repeatedly applied (with limits taken at limit ordinals) until the minimal fixed point s_0 is reached. Then the foundationalizing operation φ is repeatedly applied, resulting in a fixed point s^*. Finally, a closure operation τ^* is again applied repeatedly, until a new fixed point s_1 is reached.

Definition 26. *The final doxic closure* $\tau^*(s)$ *of situation s (given* τ*-fixed point* s_0*) is the minimal situation s′ extending s such that*

(1) *If p is justifiable for i in s, then* $\langle J, i, p; 1\rangle \in s'$. *If p is unjustifiable for i in s, then* $\langle J, i, p; 0\rangle \in s'$.

(2) (a) *If* $Face(k) = \langle J, j, p; t\rangle$,
(b) *if there is no q such that* $\langle I, i, k, q; 1\rangle \in s$, *and*
(c) *if either* (i) *k is positive and either* $\langle J, j, p; t +/- 1\rangle \in s$ *or* $\langle J, j, p; t\rangle \in s$, *or* (ii) *k is negative and* $\langle J, j, p; t +/- 1\rangle \in s$,
then $\langle I, i, k, \langle s', \langle J, j, p; t\rangle\rangle; 1\rangle \in s'$.

(2′) (a) *If* $Face(k) = \langle J, j, p; t\rangle$,
(b) *if there is no q such that* $\langle I, i, k, q; 1\rangle \in s$, *and*
(c) *if k is negative and* $\langle J, j, p; t\rangle \in s$,
then $\langle I, i, k, \langle s_0, \langle J, j, p; t\rangle\rangle; 1\rangle \in s'$.

(3) (a) *If* $Face(k) = \langle I, j, k', p; t\rangle$,
(b) *if there is no q such that* $\langle I, i, k, q; 1\rangle \in s^*$, *and*
(c) *if either* (i) *k is positive and either* $\langle I, j, k', p; t +/- 1\rangle \in s$ *or* $\langle I, j, k', p; t\rangle \in s$, *or* (ii) *k is negative and* $\langle I, j, k', p; t+/-1\rangle \in s$,
then $\langle I, i, k, \langle s', \langle I, j, k', p; t\rangle\rangle; 1\rangle \in s'$.

(3′) (a) *If* $Face(k) = \langle J, j, k', p; t\rangle$,
(b) *if there is no q such that* $\langle I, i, k, q; 1\rangle \in s^*$, *and*
(c) *if k is negative and* $\langle I, j, k', p; t\rangle \in s$,
then $\langle J, i, k, \langle s_0, \langle I, j, k', p; t\rangle\rangle; 1\rangle \in s'$.

(4) (a) *If Face(k) is an atomic doxic sentence, and*
(b) $\langle i, k\rangle$ *is not open in s, and*
(c) *there is no q such that* $\langle I, i, k, q; 1\rangle \in s$,
then
(i) *if k is positive,* $\langle I, i, k, \langle s_0, Face(k); 1\rangle \in s'$, *and*
(ii) *if k is negative,* $\langle I, i, k < s', Face(k); 1\rangle \in s'$.

Propositions

I. If there is no q such that $\langle I, i, k, q; 1\rangle \in \tau(s)$ $[\tau^*(s)]$, then $\langle i, k\rangle$ calls some token (relative to s). And conversely, if $\langle i, k\rangle$ is an atomic doxic token.

Proof. This follows immediately from the definitions of τ, τ^* and the calling relation.

II. If <j, k'> is called by <i, k> relative to s, then there is no q such that <I, j, k', q; 1> $\in s$.

Proof.This follows immediately from the definition of the calling relation.

III. If s is a fixed point with respect to φ, then s contains no loops or descending chains.

Proof. The definition of the calling relation ensures that every loop or chain contains some uninterpreted atomic doxic tokens, and only uninterpreted atomic doxic tokens. The loop or chain must be either pure or impure, and in either case, an application of φ would result in the interpretation of some uninterpreted tokens. Hence, s cannot be a fixed point with respect to φ.

IV. If s^* is a fixed point with respect to φ given s_0, and s_1 is a fixed point with respect to τ^* that extends s^*, then for every cognitive individual i and every subsentence k, there is a q such that <I, i, k, q; 1> $\in s_1$.

Proof. Since s^* is a φ-fixed point, by Proposition II, it contains no loops or chains. Suppose for contradiction that k is uninterpreted in s_1. By Proposition I, k calls some token k' relative to s_1. By Proposition II, token k' must be uninterpreted in s_1. By induction, there must be a closed loop or chain in s. But since s_1 extends a φ-fixed point without introducing any new tokens, there can be no such closed loops or chains.

The existence of these fixed point depends crucially on the fact that all quantification is bounded, since each variable contains a set as its range of significance. If absolutely unbounded quantification is permitted, then it is impossible to define an interpretation function for a network of tokens (which may itself be a proper class) that can be guaranteed to be total. Therefore, the believer in unbounded quantification must either suppose that all tokens are interpreted but some receive their interpretation in a mysterious way beyond all formal definition, or she must suppose that some perfectly respectable tokens are not interpreted at all. The latter choice would be especially unfortunate, since it would cut out the ground beneath the context-sensitive approach to the liar paradox. One of the essential motivations for this approach is the avoidance of saying of perfectly respectable tokens, such as empirical liar paradoxes, that they do not express propositions at all.

But if all propositions are about limited, merely partial situations, how can any truly general propositions be expressed, including those that make up my own theory of the rational agent and the resolution of the logical antinomies? This question I take up in Appendix C, where I discuss a kind of generality, which I call "schematic generality," that escapes the restrictions discussed here.

Conclusion

I have shown that the careful investigation of such phenomena as mutual belief and strategic rationality leads inexorably to the confrontation of liar-like paradoxes. Affliction by such paradoxes is independent of the postulation of objects of belief with the kind of syntactic structure that makes self-reference (in the style of Gödel) possible. Hence, the paradoxes cannot be taken as providing good reason for rejecting such a postulate. Moreover, I have shown that a syntactic, computational theory of mental attitudes is compatible with a very attractive way of resolving the paradoxes: the context-sensitive solutions discussed in Chapters 6 and 7.

These results have significant implications for the philosophy of mind. One very attractive strategy for the philosophical materialist is to identify mental states and processes with computational states and processes. A mental process, for example, is identified with the internal processing of some representational structure. The phenomenon of liar-like paradoxes poses a prima facie challenge to such a strategy, since syntactically structured representations in the brain would permit the kind of pernicious self-reference that has traditionally been taken to be essential to the paradoxes. The challenge has now been effectively met.

Another striking implication of the context-dependent approach to the paradoxes is the inherent limitation on the comprehensiveness of thought that this context dependency imposes. Each individual thought is necessarily about some partial, limited part of the world: a truly comprehensive perspective (commonly referred to as a "God's-eye view") is impossible. At the same time, this limitedness can to some extent be overcome by means of the schematic representations discussed in Appendix C.

By applying this context-sensitive solution theory to the paradoxes of rational credibility that appear in the analysis of games of reputation, I been able to locate and to explain certain "cognitive blindspots" inherent in these games. As a result of these cognitive blindspots, players in these games are unable to predict how the other players might act, despite the fact that all the information relevant to determine how they will act is a matter of common knowledge, in public view.

With respect to the field of game theory, the arguments presented here give support to the view that the concept of Nash equilibrium solution is too narrow (Bernheim [1984], Brandenburger and Dekel [1984], Pearce [1984], Aumann [1987]). However, these arguments also suggest that the most popular candidate for replacing Nash equilibrium, namely, rationalizability or, equivalently, the correlated equilibrium, is also too narrow. The paradox-generated cognitive blindspots undermine any basis for confidence that the players will choose mutually coherent strategies (as in a Nash or correlated equilibrium), even under optimal conditions of mutual knowledge. At the same time, by exploiting the details of the doxic logics developed here, it should be possible to define a more satisfactory solution.

The cognitive blindspots postulated by the context-dependent solution theory have a wider set of implications, implications concerning the relation between institutionalist social theory and the rational agent model, and, in ethics, the relation between deontic, rule-based ethical theories and consequentialism. Traditionally, theories based on the rational agent model (including much of mainstream economics) and theories that describe social reality in terms of rules, practices, and institutions (what we might call "social science proper") have been taken to be hostile competitors or, at least, as unrelated and incommensurable approaches. The understanding of paradox-generated cognitive blindspots holds some promise of achieving a reconciliation of these two approaches by explaining how the phenomenon of rule following can emerge in a society of utility-maximizing rational agents.

In the paradoxical games of reputation of Chapter 2, the players are unable, as a result of these cognitive blindspots, to predict how another player might act, even given some particular utility function for that player. Consequently, the players are also unable to learn anything about the others' utilities from their actually observed behavior. Thus, the essence of reputation does not consist in conveying information (or misinformation) about one's actual state of mind to others via one's observable behavior. Instead, players afflicted by these cognitive blindspots must "learn" from the observed behaviors of others in a way quite different from the standard Bayesian model of hypothesis confirmation.

My conjecture is that rational agents must engage in some sort of as-if reasoning: they must (for want of a better alternative) operate on the basis of deliberate misrepresentations of the situation that, unlike the accurate representation, are not afflicted by cognitive blindspots. For example, they might pretend that there are two possibilities for the monopolist's utility function, one according to which retaliation is not costly at all and another according to which retaliation is so costly as to be prohibited even if it did deter. They must do this in order to avoid being disabled by blindspots, despite the fact that they know perfectly well that the monopolist's utility function is of neither of these two kinds! An interesting question which arises here is: what sort of properties make such fictional hypotheses salient choices for this purpose?

By using this sort of as-if modeling of the situation, the players will be able to "learn" (in some attenuated sense) from the observed behavior of others. For example, if the monopolist does in fact retaliate, they will take this as "confirming" the "hypothesis" that his utility function is such as to make retaliation optimal, even without deterrent effects. In this sense, the monopolist can be characterized as following a rule (namely, the rule of always retaliating against market entries) that is distinct from the rule of always maximizing one's actual utility. Moreover, if the monopolist recognizes that the other players will engage in this sort of as-if modeling of the situation, then it can be reasonable for him to conform to this rule, in order to increase the quasi-probability of the appropriate fiction. At this point, there is a fairly rich sense in which the monopolist is following a rule distinct from the rule of individual utility maximization. The monopolist is not merely employing a convenient rule of thumb: he is conforming to a salient regularity because such conformity is itself an integral part of his plan.

A similar line of reasoning could be used to explain the possibility of various kinds of "indirect" consequentialisms, such as rule-utilitarianism, and to explain why such indirect forms of consequentialism do not simply collapse into their direct counterparts. It has been argued, for example, that it would be simply inconsistent for a utilitarian to follow any rule other than **maximize utility**! An analysis in terms of paradox-driven cognitive blindspots could be used to show that this argument is simply wrongheaded: in the pursuit of a valuable reputation, it would be possible for a consistent utilitarian to follow (in a strict sense) rules other than that of utility maximization.

Appendix A Applying probability to mathematical sentences

In order to apply subjective probability measures to necessarily true or false mathematical statements, I suggest that we use Hintikka's distributive normal forms and the related idea of the depth of a formula.[1] We are to imagine the implications of intuitive mathematics as unfolding in an infinite series of stages. At stage n, all sentences of depth n or less and of length $f(n)$ or less (where f is some monotonically increasing one-place function) are checked for self-evidence. There are only finitely many such sentences, and we have seen that there must exist an effective procedure for deciding whether a given sentence is self-evident. Sentences that are found to be self-evident at stage n are called "n-self-evident sentences." All of the n-self-evident sentences are then transformed into Hintikka's distributive normal form at depth n. (There is an effective procedure for this transformation.) A sentence in distributive normal form at depth d is expressed as a finite disjunction of constituents of depth d.

There are only a finite number of constituents of depth n. They are mutually exclusive and jointly exhaustive of logical possibility. Those constituents of depth n that are not trivially inconsistent and that occur in the distributive normal form of all of the n-self-evident sentences are to be called the "n-possible constituents." The n-possible constituents describe states of the mathematical world that cannot be shown by means of any effective procedure to be mathematically impossible, given the state of development of intuitive mathematics at the nth stage. Some of these n-possible constituents are internally inconsistent (but not trivially inconsistent), some are inconsistent with the n-self-evident sentences, some are inconsistent with other self-evident sentences, and some are really consistent with the whole of intuitive mathematics; however, at stage n it is impossible to tell which are which.

At each stage n of the process, there are only finitely many n-possible constituents. Suppose that there are k such constituents. Then it seems

[1] Hintikka (1973).

natural to assign a probability (relative to stage n) to each n-possible constituent of $1/k$. The probability$_n$ of any sentence in the language of depth n or less can be determined by counting the number of n-possible constituents in its distributive normal form and multiplying by $1/k$.

If a sentence has a probability$_n$ of 1, then it has a probability$_{n+m}$ of 1, for every $m > 0$. Similarly, if a sentence has a probability$_n$ of 0, it has a probability$_{n+m}$ of 0. A sentence can receive a probability$_n$ of 1 or 0 only by having been shown, at stage n, to be a logical consequence of, or to be logically inconsistent with, some set of self-evident sentences. Once established, such facts are not lost at later stages. Probabilities between 0 and 1 can fluctuate, however.

A sentence is provable if and only if it has a probability$_n$ of 1 for some n. A sentence is self-evident only if it is given a probability$_n$ of 1, where n is the first stage at which the sentence is considered. (Its depth or length prevented its consideration at earlier stages.) The issue addressed in Section 3.1 about the self-evidence of P^* concerned whether the following conditional should be given a probability of 1 when and only when its consequent has been proved, or whether it should be given a probability of 1 at an earlier stage (i.e., it should always be considered self-evident):

(P*) P'φ' $\rightarrow \varphi$.

Let us select some stage n such that the depth of '(P'φ' $\rightarrow \varphi$)' is less than n and its length is less than $f(n)$. Let us also suppose that 'φ' does not have a probability$_n$ of 1. (If it does, it does not matter whether we consider this instance of (P*) to be self-evident: the disputed cases are those in which 'φ' has not been proved before the question of the self-evidence of '(P'φ' $\rightarrow \varphi$)' arises.)

There are then two cases: either there is some m such that 'φ' has probability$_{n+m}$ of 1, or there is not. If there is such an m, then it is to one's disadvantage to place on '(P'φ' $\rightarrow \varphi$)' a probability$_n$ of less than 1, since one would then be vulnerable to a Dutch book. Anyone who could foresee that 'φ' (and, therefore '(P'φ' $\rightarrow \varphi$)' will get a probability$_{n+m}$ of 1, will be willing to take very long odds at stage n, foreseeing that the mathematical reasoner will at stage $n + m$ be willing to suffer a net loss in order to be released from her previous bet. Alternatively, if there is no such m, then 'φ' is not provable and 'P'φ'' is not true. In this case, '(P'φ' $\rightarrow \varphi$)' is true, and again it is to one's disadvantage to place on it at stage n any probability but 1. Therefore, an ideally rational mathematician will give to instances of (P*) a probability of 1 as soon as he considers them; that is, he or she will treat them as self-evident.

Appendix B Proofs of Theorems 2 and 3 from Chapter 6

Theorem 2. *Every fundamentally complete situation s actual in a semantically well-founded model $\mathcal{A}$ and such that P(s) contains no $\mathcal{A}$-inexpressible propositions can be extended to a Burgean situation s* actual in $\mathcal{A}$.*

Proof. Let s_0 be the maximal subsituation of s containing no semantic SOAS, and let P be the smallest set of propositions p such that $\langle Tr, p; i\rangle \in s$ or $\langle Tr, p: i\rangle \in \text{Par}(q)$ for some $q \in P$. Consider the unique Burgean series S based on s_0 and P, $S = \{s_0, s_1, \ldots, s_a, \ldots\}$. Claim: $s \subseteq \cup S$. Since s is semantically well founded, there is a foundation series $S' = \{s_0, s_{1'}, s_{2'}, \ldots\}$ such that $s \subseteq \cup S'$. It is sufficient to show that, for all a, there is a γ such that $s'_a \subseteq s_\gamma$. Assume for a reductio that a is the least ordinal such that, for all γ, $\sim s'_a \subseteq s_\gamma$. Clearly, $a > 0$. By inductive hypothesis, for all $\delta < a$, there exists an ϵ such that $s'_\delta \subseteq s_\epsilon$. Let ζ be the supremum of all such ϵ, that is, for all $\delta < a$, $s'_\delta \subseteq s_\zeta$.

a is either a limit ordinal or a successor. If a is a limit ordinal, then it immediately follows that $s'_a \subseteq s_\zeta$, contradicting the hypothesis. So a is a successor, and $s'_{a-1} \subseteq s_\zeta$. Every nonsemantic SOA in $s'_a - s'_{a-1}$ belongs to s_0. Suppose that $\langle Tr, p; i\rangle \in s'_{a1}$. We can show that $\langle Tr, p; i\rangle \in s_{\zeta+1}$ by induction on the complexity of p.

(1) $p = \{s^*, \sigma\}$ and σ is nonsemantic.

(a) Suppose $\langle Tr, p; 1\rangle \in s_a$. By the fundamental completeness of $s, \sigma \in s_0$. Since $s_0 \subseteq s_\zeta$, $\langle Tr, p; 1\rangle \in s_\zeta$, by Kleene closure, clause(1).

(b) Suppose $\langle Tr, p; 0\rangle \in s_a$. By fundamental completeness, $s_0 \subseteq s^*$ and s_0 is complete with respect to nonsemantic soas. Therefore, the dual of σ belongs to s_ζ, and by Kleene closure, clause (2), $\langle Tr, p; 0\rangle \in s_\zeta$.

(2) $p = \{s^*, \langle Tr, q; j\rangle\}$.

(a) Suppose $\langle Tr, p; 1\rangle$ s_a. By semantic well-foundedness, $\langle Tr, q; j\rangle \in s^* \cap s_{a-1}$. So $\langle Tr, q; j\rangle \in s^* \cap s_\zeta$. By Kleene closure, clause (1), $\langle Tr, p; 1\rangle \in s_\zeta$.

(b) Suppose $\langle Tr, p; 0\rangle \in s_a$. By semantic well-foundedness, there are two cases:

(i) $\langle Tr, q; j\rangle$ or its dual $\in s_{a-1}$. By induction, $\langle Tr, q; j\rangle$ or its dual $\in s_\zeta$. By Kleene closure, clause (2), $\langle Tr, p; 0\rangle \in s_\zeta$.

(ii) $s^* \subseteq s_{a-1}$, and $\langle Tr, q; j\rangle \notin s^*$. By the definition of closing off, $\langle Tr, p; 0\rangle \in s_{\zeta+1}$.

(3) $p = \sim q$. By semantic well-foundedness, the dual of $\langle Tr, q; i\rangle \in s_{a-1}$. By Kleene closure, clauses (3) and (4), $\langle Tr, p; i\rangle \in s_\zeta$.
Etc.

Therefore, $s \subseteq \cup S$. Let $s^* = \cup S$. This completes the proof of Theorem 1.

Lemma 1. *For all $s'' \subseteq s, r < \{s'', \langle Tr, r; j\rangle\}$ iff either $\langle Tr, r; j\rangle$ or its dual belongs to s''.*

Proof. [→] Since s'' is semantically well founded and $s'' \subseteq s$, there is a foundation series S^* for s such that $s'' = s^*_\beta$ for some β and $s^*_{\beta+1} = \rho_p(s^*_\beta)$. Suppose for contradiction that neither $\langle Tr, r; j\rangle$ nor its dual belongs to s''. By the definition of the closing-off operation, $\{s'', \langle Tr, r; j\rangle\}$ is evaluated at $s^*_{\beta+1}$, so $\sim(r < \{s'', \langle Tr, r; j\rangle\})$, contrary to the assumption.
[←] Suppose for contradiction that $\langle Tr, r; j\rangle$ or its dual belong to s'' but $\sim(r < \{s'', \langle Tr, r; j\rangle\})$. So for some foundation series S^* for s, $\langle Tr, \{s'', \langle Tr, r; j\rangle\} \rangle \in s^*_{\beta+1}$ but $\langle Tr, r; j\rangle \notin s^*_\beta$. Since $\langle Tr, \{s'', \langle Tr, r, j\rangle \in s^*_{\beta+1}$, either (a) $\langle Tr, r; j\rangle$ or its dual belong to s^*_β, or (b) $s'' \subseteq s_\beta^*$. Case (a) is ruled out by assumption, so $s'' \subseteq s_\beta^*$. But then, neither $\langle Tr, r; j\rangle$ nor its dual can belong to s'', contradicting the original assumption.

Lemma 2. *$\langle Tr, p; i\rangle \in s_{\eta(s', p)+1}$ iff $\langle Tr, p; i\rangle \in s'$.*

Proof. [→] Suppose $\langle Tr, p; i\rangle \notin s'$. By the definition of η, $\eta(s', p) \leq \beta$, for some β such that $\langle Tr, p; i\rangle \notin s_\beta$. Since the foundation series is cumulative, $\langle Tr, p; i\rangle \in s_{\eta(s', p)+1}$.
[←] Suppose $\langle Tr, p; i\rangle \in s'$. By the definition of η, $s' \subseteq s_{\eta(s', p)+1}$. So $\langle Tr, p; i\rangle \in s_{\eta(s', p)+1}$.

Theorem 3. *μ is a homomorphism of s into the Burgean model M based on the interpretation function V that agrees with s_0.*

Proof. μ is clearly a homomorphism with respect to nonsemantic predicates and constants. It remains to be shown that the interpretation of 'true' is homomorphic under μ, that is, that

$$\langle Tr, p; 1\rangle \in s_{\alpha+1} \text{ iff } \mu(p) \in (Tr_{\alpha})+,$$
$$\langle Tr, p; 0\rangle \in s_{\alpha+1} \text{ iff } \mu(p) \in (Tr_{\alpha})-.$$

Each of these can be proved by induction on a. I can then prove these two claims for an arbitrary a by strong induction on the partial well-ordering <. The proof is straightforward for the connectives, quantifiers, and nonsemantic atomic propositions. For the atomic semantic cases, I must show

(1) $\langle Tr, \{s',\langle Tr, q; 1\rangle\}; 1\rangle \in s_{\alpha+1}$ iff $[Tr(\mu(q)), \eta(s',q)] \in [Tr_a]+$,

(2) $\langle Tr, \{s',\langle Tr, q; 0\rangle\}; 1\rangle \in s_{\alpha+1}$ iff $[Tr(\mu(q)), \eta(s',q)] \in [Tr_a]+$,

(3) $\langle Tr, \{s',\langle Tr, q; 1\rangle\}; 1\rangle \in s_{\alpha+1}$ iff $[Tr(\mu(q)), \eta(s',q)] \in [Tr_a]-$,

(4) $\langle Tr, \{s',\langle Tr, q; 0\rangle\}; 1\rangle \in s_{\alpha+1}$ iff $[Tr(\mu(q)), \eta(s',q)] \in [Tr_a]-$.

First, I must prove the following lemma by strong induction on <*:

Lemma 3. *If* $\mu(q) <^* [Tr(\mu(q))\eta(s', q)]$, *then* $q < \{s',\langle Tr, q; i\rangle\}$.

Proof. Assume that $\mu(q) <^* [Tr(\mu(q)), \eta(s', q)]$. It follows that $\mu(q) \in [Tr_{\eta(s',q)}]+/-$. By induction, I can assume that, for all $\mu(p) <^* \mu(q)$, the lemma holds for $\mu(p)$. The proof proceeds by separate cases: q atomic, q a negation, and so on. I will give only the atomic semantic case: $q = \{s'',\langle Tr, r; j\rangle\}$. So $\mu(q) = [Tr(\mu(r)), \eta(s'', r)]$. $\mu(q) \in [Tr_{\eta(s'', r)+1}]+/-$, and $\mu(q) \in [Tr_{\eta(s', q)}]+/-$, so $\eta(s'', r) \leq \eta(s', q)$. Either $\mu(r) \in [Tr_{\eta(s'', r)}]+/-$ or not.

(a) If $\mu(r) \in [Tr_{\eta(s'', r)}]+/-$, then $\mu(q) \in (Tr_{\eta(s'', r)}]+/-$ as a result of Kleene closure, not as a result of closing off. Therefore, $\mu(r) <^* \mu(q)$, and so, by induction on <*, $r < q$. Therefore, either σ' or the dual of σ' belongs to s'', and by the definition of η, $s'' \subseteq s_{\eta(s'', r)+1}$. Since $\eta(s'', r) \leq \eta(s', q)$, $s'' \subseteq s_{\eta(s', q)+1}$. By Kleene closure, $\langle Tr, q; i\rangle \in s_{\eta(s', q)+1}$. By Lemma 2, $\langle Tr, q; i\rangle \in s'$. So $q < \{s',\langle Tr, q; i\rangle\}$, by Lemma 1.

(b) Alternatively, if $\mu(r) \notin [Tr_{\eta(s'', r)}]+/-$, then $\mu(q) \notin [Tr_{\eta(s'', r)}]+/-$. Since $\mu(q) \in [Tr_{\eta(s', q)}]+/-$, $\eta(s'', r) < \eta(s', q)$. By the definition of η, either $\eta(s'', r)$ is the outer measure of s'', or r is evaluated at $s_{\eta(s'', r)+2}$. Therefore, either $s'' \subseteq s_{\eta(s',q)}$, or σ' or the dual of σ' belongs to $s_{\eta(s',q)+1}$. In either case, it follows that either $\langle Tr, q; i\rangle$ or its dual belongs to $s_{\eta(s',q)+1}$. Therefore, by Lemma 2, either $\langle Tr, q; i\rangle$ or its dual belongs to s', and thus $q < \{s',\langle Tr, q; i\rangle\}$ by Lemma 1.

The proofs of cases (2) and (4) of Theorem 3 are similar to (1) and (3), respectively, and have therefore been omitted.

Proof of case (1). [→] Assume $\langle Tr, \{s', \langle Tr, q; 1\rangle\}; 1\rangle \in s_{a+1}$. Since s_{a+1} is semantically well founded, $\langle Tr, q; 1\rangle \in s' \cap s_{a+1}$. Since $\langle Tr, q; 1\rangle \in s'$, by the definition of η, $s' \subseteq s_{\eta(s',q)+1}$, so $\langle Tr, q; 1\rangle \in s_{\eta(s',q)+1}$. Moreover, since $\langle Tr, q; 1\rangle \in s'$, $q < \{s', \langle Tr, q; 1\rangle\}$, by Lemma 1. Thus, by induction on $<$, $\langle Tr, q; 1\rangle \in s_{a+1}$ iff $\mu(q) \in [Tr_a]+$. So $\mu(q) \in [Tr_a]+$. There are two cases: (1) $\eta(s',q) \leq a$ and (2) $\eta(s', q) > a$.

(1) $\mu(q) \in [Tr_{\eta(s',q)}]+$. By the Kripke construction, $[Tr(\mu(q)), \eta(s', q)] \in [Tr_{\eta(s',q)}]+$. Since $\eta(s',q) \leq a$ and the hierarchy is cumulative, $[Tr(\mu(q)), \eta(s', q)] \in [Tr_a]+$.

(2) $\mu(q) \in [Tr_a]+$. By the Kripke construction, $[Tr[\mu(q)], a] \in [Tr_a]+$. Since $\eta(s', q) > a$, $[Tr(\mu(q)), \eta(s', q)] \in [Tr_a]+$.

[←] Assume that $[Tr(\mu(q)), \eta(s',q)] \in [Tr_a]+$. This entails that $\mu(q) \in [Tr_{\eta(s',q)}]+$. There are two cases: (a) $\eta(s',q) < a$, (b) $\eta(s', q) \geq a$.

(a) By induction on a, $\langle Tr, q; 1\rangle \in s_{\eta(s',q)+1}$. By Lemma 2, we have that $\langle Tr, q; 1\rangle \in s'$. By Kleene closure, $\langle Tr, \{s', \langle Tr, q; 1\rangle\}; 1\rangle \in s_{\eta(s',q)+1}$. So $\langle Tr, \{s', \langle Tr, q; 1\rangle\}; 1\rangle \in s_{a+1}$.

(b) $[Tr[\mu(q)], a] \in [Tr_a]+$. So $\mu(q) \in [Tr_a]+$, and therefore $\mu(q) <^* [Tr(\mu(q)), \eta(s', q)]$. By Lemma 2, $q < \{s', \langle Tr, q; 1\rangle\}$. By induction on $<$, $\langle Tr, q; 1\rangle \in s_{a+1}$. Since $\eta(s',q) \geq a$, $\langle Tr, q; 1\rangle \in s_{\eta(s',q)+1}$. By Lemma 2, $\langle Tr, q; 1\rangle \in s'$. By Kleene closure, $\langle Tr, \{s', \langle Tr, q; 1\rangle\}; 1\rangle \in s_{a+1}$.

Proof of case (3). [→] Assume $\langle Tr, \{s', \langle Tr, q; 1\rangle\}; 0\rangle \in s_{a+1}$. There are two relevant cases: (1) $\langle Tr, q; 0\rangle \in s'$, and (2) $\langle Tr, q; 0\rangle \notin s'$.

(1) The proof here is similar to that of the left-to-right direction of case (1).

(2) By the definition of a Burgean situation, if a is a successor, then either $\langle Tr, q; 0\rangle \in s_{a+1}$ or $s' \subseteq s_a$. In either case, $\eta(s', q) \leq a - 1$. If a is a limit ordinal, then for some successor $\beta < a$, $[Tr, \{s', \langle Tr, q; 1\rangle\}; 0\rangle \in s_{\beta+1}$. By the same argument, it follows that $\eta(s', q) \leq \beta - 1$. So $\eta(s', q) < a$. Therefore, $\eta(s', q) < a$. By induction on, a $\mu(q) \notin [Tr_{\eta(s',q)}]+$. By the closing off construction, $[Tr(\mu(q)), \eta(s', q)] \in [Tr_{\eta(s',q)+1}]-$. So $[Tr(\mu(q)), \eta(s', q)] \in [Tr_a]-$.

[←] There are again two cases: (1) $\mu(q) \in [Tr_{\eta(s',q)}]-$, and (2) $\mu(q) \notin [Tr_{\eta(s',q)}]-$.

(1) Similar to the proof of the right-to-left direction of case (1).

(2) If $\mu(q) \notin [Tr_{\eta(s',q)}]-$, the construction of M guarantees that $\eta(s', q) < a$, since only indices lower than a are closed off in $[Tra]-$. By induction, $\langle Tr, q; 1\rangle \notin s_{\eta(s',q)+1}$. Lemma 2 guarantees that $\langle Tr, q; 1\rangle \notin s'$ and the definition of η entails that either (a) $\langle Tr, q; i\rangle \in s_{\eta(s',q)+2}$

or (b) $s' \subseteq s_{\eta(s',q)+1}$. By Kleene closure, clause (2) (in case (a)), or the closing-off operation ρ (in case (b)), $\langle Tr, \{s', \langle Tr, q; 1\rangle\}; 0\rangle \in s_{\eta(s',q)+2}$. Since $\eta(s', q) < a$, it follows that $\langle Tr, \{s', \langle Tr, q; 1\rangle\}; 0\rangle \in s_{a+1}$.

Appendix C On schematic generalization

The solution to liar-like paradoxes developed in Chapters 5 and 7 depends on a kind of context-sensitive limitation on the expressiveness of natural language. It has often been argued that the postulation of such limitations is self-defeating, since the theory being proposed cannot, by its own lights, be expressed with sufficient generality. I hope to show that this objection can be met by proposing a distinction between two kinds of generality: schematic and quantificational.

I begin with an objection to Burge's solution posed by D.A. Martin.[1] Although we cannot express higher-order liars in natural language, we certainly can do so by means of explicit quantification over Burgean propositions. We can, for instance, construct a self-referential proposition (λ_1):

(λ_1) $\neg \text{true}_1(\lambda_1)$.

(λ_1) says, in effect, that (λ_1) is not true_1. This proposition is untrue_1 and true_2. Similarly, for each ordinal α, there is a liar proposition λ_α. We can introduce a function term '$\lambda(x)$', designating, for each ordinal α, the liar $\lambda\alpha$. Now consider the token ($\mathcal{A}$):

($\mathcal{A}$) $\forall x \in \text{ON}\ \text{true}(\lambda(x))$.

Each liar λ_α is $\text{true}_{\alpha+1}$ but there is no level at which all are true. How, then, can we interpret the occurrence of the predicate 'true' in ($\mathcal{A}$)?

The problem,of course, is that, in interpreting ($\mathcal{A}$), we want to use a level that is the ordinal of the class of ordinals. The idea that there is an ordinal of the class of ordinals can be shown to be inconsistent; in fact, this was the first of the set-theoretic paradoxes to be discovered, the Burali–Forti paradox. Thus, in order to solve Martin's problem, something must be said about the solution to the set-theoretic paradoxes in intensional contexts. I shall simply insist that the domain of the model being used to interpret ($\mathcal{A}$) be a set. Then there is always some ordinal number β greater than any ordinal α occurring in the domain

[1] D.A. Martin, Seminar on the liar paradox, University of California, Los Angeles, October 14, 1985.

of token ($\mathcal{A}$). We could assign the ordinal β to the occurrence of 'true' in ($\mathcal{A}$).

The occurrence of the variable 'x' in the token ($\mathcal{A}$) would have to be relativized to some set, say κ (it seems natural to assume that κ is a rank V_κ in the *ZF* hierarchy). We could then assign to the occurrence of 'true' in ($\mathcal{A}$) an ordinal number β that is larger than κ and that belongs to the next highest rank, κ_1. There would then be no token $\lambda(\beta)$ that falls within the range of the quantifier in ($\mathcal{A}$), and therefore no reason for denying that ($\mathcal{A}$) is true$_\beta$. This idea accords well with the view, expressed by Charles Parsons, that the distinction between sets and classes is not an ultimate, ontological one, but merely one of differences of perspective. As Parsons points out:

> It is a general maxim in set theory that any set theory which we can formulate can plausibly be extended by assuming that there is a set that is a standard model of it. [This implies] that we could not produce a discourse in the language of set theory such that it could be interpreted as true if and only if the quantifiers ranged over absolutely all sets . . . . It seems that a perspective is always possible according to which your classes are really sets.[2]

This sort of theory can also shed a great deal of light on the significance of the hierarchy of extensions of 'true' in Burge's solution. We could introduce a nonindexical truth-predicate, applicable only to Burgean propositions, and then define the context-sensitive truth-predicate discussed in the Section 6.1 as follows: a token x is true$_\kappa$ if and only if $(\exists y_\kappa)(x$ expresses y_κ and y_κ is true). The variable 'y_κ' ranges over propositions that can be made up from ordinals belonging to κ. There can be no liar-like propositions, since *b*-propositions cannot be self-referential. No proposition belongs to its own universe of discourse, since its index (fixing that universe) cannot be less than itself. Liar-like sentence tokens are possible, for example:

(L_0) ~ $(\exists x_0)$((L_0) expresses x_0 and x_0 is a true *b*-proposition).

The variable 'x_0' ranges over propositions containing no indices whatsoever. *(L_0)* therefore expresses a true proposition, since the only proposition it expresses does not belong to the universe of x_0.

This approach lacks the flexibility that can be achieved by defining a primitive truth-predicate predicable directly of tokens. It corresponds quite closely to Tarski's original hierarchy and to construction C1 in Burge's paper. Therefore, it cannot incorporate the notion of *grounded truth* as developed in Kripke's paper. We cannot have

[2] C. Parsons (1974b), pp. 10, 11

significant self-application of truth and falsity. For example, the second disjunct of

$$2 + 2 = 4 \text{ or this sentence is true}$$

expresses a false *b*-proposition, according to the theory under consideration. Consequently, we are forced to rise quite high up the hierarchy to interpret quite unproblematic discourses. In the case of epistemic predicates, as we saw in Chapter 4, such true self-applications are essential to developing a theory of common knowledge in game theory. For this reason, we cannot do without context-sensitive predicates, as well as context-sensitive variables.

The introduction of context-sensitive set variables raises a new difficulty for the Burgean solution, however. Throughout the formal theory presented in Section 6.1, I made use of a great deal of variables ranging over ordinal numbers. According to the Parsonsian addendum to that theory just presented, all of the occurrences of such variables must be relativized to some particular level in a hierarchy of ranks. How then can it be claimed that what was presented in that section is a general theory of the semantics of 'true'? There will be tokens in which there are occurrences of 'true' that must be assigned ordinal numbers of higher types than that to which the variables in my theory are relativized. Haven't I failed to say anything about the interpretation of such tokens?

The time has come at last to discuss what Burge has called the "schematic" uses of the semantic predicates(and by extension, of set-theoretic variables). A very similar idea was also expressed by Charles Parsons in responding to a similar problem: the charge that his account of the paradoxes lacked complete generality: "The generality which such a discourse as this paper has which transcends any particular set as range of its quantifiers must lie in a sort of systematic ambiguity, in that indefinitely many such sets will do."[3] A very similar idea of the use of ambiguity of a kind was suggested in an early work of Bertrand Russell: "Mathematical Logic as Based on the Theory of Types."[4] In that work, Russell distinguished between 'all' and 'any': "Given a statement containing a variable x, say '$x = x$', we may affirm that this holds in all instances, or we may affirm any one of the instances

[3] C. Parsons (1974a), p. 28n13.
[4] Russell (1908).

without deciding as to which instance we are affirming."[5] "In the latter case, according to Russell, our statement (such as 'Let *ABC* be a triangle, then the sides *AB*, *AC* are together greater than the side *BC*') our statement is "absolutely ambiguous." "We do not affirm any one definite proposition, but an undetermined one of all the propositions resulting from supposing *ABC* to be this or that triangle."[6]

If a normally context-sensitive predicate or variable can be used in a way that is intentionally ambiguous in this sense, it ought to be possible to introduce a symbol that announces this intention. Let us therefore understand 'true_α' and 'x_κ' to represent such intentionally ambiguous (schematic) uses of the context-sensitive predicates 'true' and the variable 'x'. We can then develop a logic that governs the use of such expressions.

In the case of schematic predicates, we can assert logical truths, such as '$(\forall x)(\text{true}_\alpha(x) \text{ or} \sim \text{true}_\alpha(x))$', or general laws of semantics, such as

$$(\forall x)(\forall y)(x = \text{Neg}(y) \rightarrow [\text{true}_\alpha(x) \leftrightarrow \text{false}_\alpha(y)]).$$

In both of these cases, we treat the various occurrences of 'true_α' and 'false_α' within a statement or a connected discourse as being linked: intuitively, we are to think of them as being assigned the same (unspecified) level in the hierarchy (namely, α). If we wish to include two schematic occurrences of semantic predicates in the same discourse that are not linked in this way, we will have to introduce syntactic distinctions, like 'true_α' and 'true_β'.

Let 'rooted_α' abbreviate 'true_α or false_α' If a token is rooted_0 (if, e.g., it does not contain any semantic or other level-indexical language), then we can say that the token is rooted_α, since whatever is rooted_0 is rooted_α, at all levels α. We can even assert the unrestricted Tarski schema for such rooted_0 tokens, like a token of '2 + 2 = 4':

$$\text{true}_\alpha(\text{'}2 + 2 = 4\text{'}) \leftrightarrow 2 + 2 = 4.$$

If a token is not rooted_0, we cannot say that it is rooted_α.

We can have a rule that allows us to deschematize an assertion. For example, if we can assert '$\text{true}_\alpha(\varphi)$', then we can assert '$\text{true}(\varphi)$', since whatever level is assigned to the occurrence of 'true' in the second assertion was already encompassed by the occurrence of 'true_α' in the first. In other respects, such as the application of theorems of first-order predicate logic, we can treat 'true_α' and 'rooted_α' as we would

[5] Ibid., p. 64.
[6] Ibid., p. 65.

any other predicate.[7] (I will discuss semantic evaluations of tokens including 'true$_\alpha$' and 'rooted$_\alpha$' a little later.)

Just as occurrences of the schematic predicate 'true$_\alpha$' do not have to be relativized to a level, since they ambiguously represent occurrences of 'true' at any arbitrary level, so occurrences of the schematic variables 'x_κ', 'y_κ', and so on do not have to be relativized to any particular type in the hierarchy of ranks. All of the general laws and the resulting theorems of the predicate calculus can be asserted using such context-sensitive variables. Moreover, we can add a rule enabling us to deschematize assertions. If we can assert '$(\forall x_\kappa)\varphi$', we can deduce '$(\forall x)\varphi$' using the nonschematic, context-sensitive variable 'x'. Let us call this rule "SE," for schematic elimination.

The crucial restriction on the axiom schemata that must be made (in an axiomatic logic) is that the axiom schema '$[(\forall x)\varphi \rightarrow \varphi_{[t/x]}]$' must be restricted to cases in which the term 't' is not a schematic variable. Similarly, in a natural deduction system, the inference rule of universal instantiation (elimination) must be restricted in order that universally quantified nonschematic variables not be instantiated by schematic variables. Such an inference would invalidly move one from a restricted to an unrestricted kind of generalization: all nonschematic variables are indexically relativized to a level, while schematic variables are not. For obvious reasons, variables of existential quantification may not be instantiated with schematic variables by the rule of existential instantiation (elimination). In the case of natural deduction systems, the inference rule SE must not be used within a conditional or indirect (reductio) derivation.

Finally, I would like to discuss the semantics of tokens involving the use of schematic predicates and variables. Let us reconsider the problem raised by D.A. Martin at the beginning of this appendix. The token ($\mathcal{A}$) asserts that every liar proposition is true:

($\mathcal{A}$) $\forall x \in \text{ON}\ \text{true}(\lambda(x))$.

As we have seen, the variable 'x' must be indexed to some rank V_κ in the *ZF* hierarchy. Suppose we try to state ($\mathcal{A}$) schematically:

($\mathcal{A}$*) $\forall x_\kappa\ \text{true}_{\kappa+1}(\lambda(x_\kappa))$.

Now we want to evaluate token ($\mathcal{A}$*).

(σ) true($\mathcal{A}$*).

7 In second-order logic, we will have to restrict the rule of universal instantiation in order to prevent instantiating a predicate variable with a schematic predicate.

What level can be assigned to the occurrence of 'true' in σ? It is clear that no level can be assigned to it, since if we assign level β to the occurrence of 'true' in (σ), we will be overlooking the fact that ($\mathcal{A}$*) implies that $\lambda(\beta)$ is $\text{true}_{\beta+1}$. Should we then express the evaluation of ($\mathcal{A}$*) as:

(σ') $\text{true}_{\beta}(\mathcal{A}^*)$?

However, if it is inappropriate to assign any particular level to the occurrence of 'true' in σ, it can hardly be correct to assert ambiguously, as (σ') does, a token of the form of σ for every level that can be assigned to 'true'. It appears that a semantics of schematic tokens is impossible.[8]

We must take seriously the idea that ($\mathcal{A}$*) is ambiguous, that there is not some one thing that ($\mathcal{A}$*) expresses. If ($\mathcal{A}$*) does not express any one thing, then an evaluation (whether context–sensitive or schematic) that treats ($\mathcal{A}$*) as a single object of evaluation will be incorrect. Let $f(y)$ be a function that assigns the index y to the variable 'x' and the index $y + 1$ to the first occurrence of 'true'. We can then express a positive semantic evaluation of ($\mathcal{A}$*) by means of the following formula:

(σ*) $(\forall y_{\tau})\ \text{true}_{\tau}(<$'$\forall x$ true$(\lambda(x))$', $f(y_{\tau})>)$.

The schematic token (σ*) talks about not one thing (e.g., the token ($\mathcal{A}$*)), but a multiplicity of things: the various Burgean propositions that ($\mathcal{A}$*) ambiguously (schematically) expresses. Note that (σ*) itself involves a schematic variable and a schematic predicate. As Charles Parsons conjectured, "One cannot express wherein the systematic ambiguity lies except in language that is subject to a similar ambiguity."[9] Or as Tyler Burge put it, "There is no deschematizing the schema."[10]

[8] Tyler Burge suggested at one time that we say that . is $\text{true}_{\kappa+1}$. I cannot see how to give a meaning to that notation, unless it means that ($\mathcal{A}$*) is true_{β}, for all β greater than 0, in which case it fares no better than (σ').

[9] C. Parsons (1974a), p. 28n13.

[10] Burge (1979), in Martin (1984), p. 116.

Bibliography

Aczel, P. 1988. *Non–well–founded Sets*. Center for the Study of Language and Information, Stanford, Calif.

Anderson, C.A. 1983. "The Paradox of the Knower." *Journal of Philosophy* 80:338–55.

Armbruster, W., and Böge, W. 1979. "Bayesian Game Theory." In *Game Theory and Related Topics*, ed. O. Moeschlin and D. Pallaschke. North Holland, Amsterdam, pp. 17–28.

Asher, N. 1986. "Belief in Discourse Representation Theory." *Journal of Philosophical Logic* 15:127–189.

Asher, N., and Kamp, H. 1986. "The Knower's Paradox and Representational Theories of Attitudes." In *Theoretical Aspects of Reasoning about Knowledge*, ed. J.Y. Halpern. Kaufmann, Los Altos, Calif., pp. 131–48.

1987. "Self–Reference, Attitudes and Paradox." In *Property Theory, Type Theory and Semantics*, ed. G. Chierchi, B. Partee, and R. Turner. Kluwer Academic, Dordrecht.

Aumann, R. 1976. "Agreeing to Disagree." *Annals of Statistics* 4:1236–9.

1987. "Correlated Equilibria as an Expression of Bayesian Rationality." *Econometrica* 55:1–18.

Bacharach, M. 1987. "A Theory of Rational Decision in Games." *Erkenntnis* 27:17–55.

Barwise, J. 1985. "The Situation in Logic III: Situations, Sets, and the Axiom of Foundation." Center for the Study of Language and Information, Stanford, Calif.

Barwise, J., and Etchemendy, J. 1987. *The Liar*. Oxford University Press, New York.

Benacerraf, P. 1967. "God, the Devil, and Gödel." *Monist* 51:9–32.

Bernheim, D. 1984. "Rationalizable Strategic Behavior." *Econometrica* 52:1007–28.

Bicchieri, C. 1988a. "Common Knowledge and Backward Induction: A Solution to the Paradox." In *Proceedings of the Second Conference on Theoretical Aspects of Reasoning About Knowledge*, ed. Moshe Vardi. Kaufman, Los Altos, Calif., pp. 381–93.

1988b. "Strategic Behavior and Counterfactuals." *Synthese* 76:135–69.

1989. "Self–Refuting Theories of Strategic Interaction: A Paradox of Common Knowledge." *Erkenntnis* 30:69–85.

Binmore, K. 1987. "Modeling Rational Players, Part I." *Economics and Philosophy* 3:179–214.

1988. "Modeling Rational Players, Part II." *Economics and Philosophy* 4:9–55.

Böge, W., and Eisele, T.H. 1979. "On the Solution of Bayesian Games." *International Journal of Game Theory* 8:193–215.

Brandenburger, A., and Dekel, E. 1987. "Rationalizability and Correlated Equilibria." *Econometrica* 55:1391–402.

Bunder, M. W. 1982. "Some Results in Aczel–Feferman Logic." *Zeitschrift für Mathematische Logik* 28:269–76.
Burge, T. 1978. "Buridan and Epistemic Paradox." *Philosophical Studies* 34:21–35.
1979. "Semantical Paradox." *Journal of Philosophy* 76:169–98.
1981. "Tangles, Loops and Chains." *Philosophical Studies* 41:353–66.
1984. "Epistemic Paradox." *Journal of Philosophy* 81:5–28.
Chellas, B. F.1984. *Modal Logic*. Cambridge University Press, pp. 171–80.
Church, A. 1956. *Introduction to Mathematical Logic*. Princeton University Press, Princeton, N.J., p. 53.
1976. "Comparison of Russell's Resolution of the Semantical Antinomies with That of Tarski." *Journal of Symbolic Logic* 41:747–60.
Clark, H. H., and Marshall, C. R. 1981. "Definite Reference and Mutual Knowledge." In *Elements of Discourse Understanding*, ed. A. K. Joshi and I.A. Sag. Cambridge University Press, pp. 10–63.
Davidson, D. 1967. "On Saying That." *Synthese* 17:130–46.
Donnellan, K. 1957. "A Note on the Liar Paradox." *Philosophical Review*, 66(3): 394–7.
1970. "Categories, Negation and the Liar Paradox." In *The Paradox of the Liar*, ed. R.L. Martin. Yale University Press, New Haven, Conn., pp. 113–20.
Feferman, S. 1962. "Transfinite Recursive Progressions of Theories." *Journal of Symbolic Logic* 27:259–316.
1982. "Toward Useful Type-Free Theories, I." *Journal of Symbolic Logic*; repr. in Martin (1984), pp. 237–89.
Flagg, R. 1984. "Consistency of Church's Thesis with Epistemic Arithmetic: Abstract." *Journal of Symbolic Logic* 49:679–80.
Frege, G. 1978. *The Foundations of Arithmetic*, trans. J.L. Austin. Northwestern University Press, Evanston, Ill., p.4.
1979. *Posthumous Writings*. University of Chicago Press, Chicago, p. 205.
Gaifman, H. 1983. "Infinity and Self-Applications, I." *Erkenntnis* 20:131–55.
1986. "A Theory of Higher Order Probabilities." In *Theoretical Aspects of Reasoning About Knowledge*, ed. J.Y. Halpern. Kaufman, Los Altos, Calif., pp. 275–92.
1988. "Operational Pointer Semantics: Solution to the Self–referential Puzzles I." In *Proceedings of the Second Conference on Theoretical Aspects of Reasoning About Knowledge*, ed. M. Vardi, Kaufman, Los Altos, Calif., pp. 43–60.
Gärdenførs, P. 1978. "Conditionals and Changes of Belief." *Acta Philosophica Fennica* 30:381–404.
1984. "Epistemic Importance and Minimal Changes of Belief." *Australasian Journal of Philosophy* 62:136–57.
1988. *Knowledge in Flux: Modeling the Dynamics of Epistemic States*. MIT Press, Cambridge, Mass., pp. 106–8, 114–17.
Gödel, K. 1931. "Üeber unentscheidbare Sätze der *Principia Mathematica* und verwandter Systeme I." *Monatshefe für Mathemathik und Physik* 38:173–98. English translation by J. van Heijenoort, "On Formally Undecidable Propositions of *Principia Mathematica* and Related Systems I." In van Heijenoort (1967), pp. 596–616.

Gupta, A. 1982/84. "Truth and Paradox." *Journal of Philosophical Logic* 11 (1982): 1–60; repr. in Martin (1984).
Hardin, R. 1982. *Collective Action.* Johns Hopkins University Press, Baltimore, pp. 145–50.
Harman, G. 1977. "Review of *Linguistic Behavior* by Jonathan Bennett." *Language* 53:417–24.
Harsanyi, J. 1967–8. "Games with Incomplete Information Played by "Bayesian" Players, Parts I–III." *Management Science* 14:159–82, 320–34, 468–502; repr. in Harsanyi (1982).
1975. "The Tracing Procedure." *International Journal of Game Theory* 4:61–94.
1982. *Papers in Game Theory.* Reidel, Dordrecht, pp. 1115–70, 1180–1.
Heim, I. 1982. *"The Semantics of Definite and Indefinite Noun Phrases."* Ph.D. dissertation, University of Massachusetts.
Herzberger, H.G. 1982. "Notes on Naive Semantics." *Journal of Philosophical Logic* 11:61–102.
Hintikka, J. 1962. *Knowledge and Belief.* Cornell University Press, Ithaca, N.Y.
1973. *Logic, Language-Games and Information.* Van Gorcum, Assen.
Hodgson, D.H. 1967. *The Consequences of Utilitarianism.* Clarendon Press, Oxford, pp. 38–50, 86–8.
Kamp, H. 1981. "A Theory of Truth and Semantic Representation." In *Formal Methods in the Study of Language*, ed. J. Groenendjik, T. Janssen, and M. Stokhof. Mathematisch Centrum, Amsterdam, pp. 277–322.
1983. "Context, Thought, and Communication." *Proceedings of the Aristotelian Society* 85:239–61.
Kaplan, D., and Montague, R. 1960. "A Paradox Regained." *Notre Dame Journal of Formal Logic* 1:79–90.
Konolige, K. 1985. "Belief and Incompleteness." SRI Artificial Intelligence Note 319. SRI International, Menlo Park, Calif.
Koons, R. 1989. "A Representational Account of Mutual Belief." *Synthese* 81:21–45.
1990a. "Doxastic Paradox Without Self-Reference." *Australasian Journal of Philosophy* 68:168–77.
1990b. "Three Indexical Solutions to the Liar." In *Situation Theory and Its Application,* Vol. 1, ed. R. Cooper, K. Mukai, and J. Perry. Center for the Study of Language and Information, Stanford, Calif.
Kreps, D., Milgrom, P., Roberts, J., and Wilson, R. 1982. "Rational Cooperation in the Repeated Prisoner's Dilemma." *Journal of Economic Theory* 27:245–52.
Kreps, D. M., and Ramey, G. 1987. "Structural Consistency, Consistency, and Sequential Rationality." *Econometrica* 55:1131–48.
Kreps, D., and Wilson, R. 1982. "Reputation and Imperfect Information," *Journal of Economic Theory* 27:253–79.
Kripke, S. 1975. "Outline of a Theory of Truth." *Journal of Philosophy* 72:690–716.
Kyburg, H. 1970. "Conjunctivitis." In *Induction, Acceptance, and Rational Belief*, ed. M. Swain. Reidel, Dordrecht, pp. 55–82.
Levi, I. 1977. "Subjunctive, Dispositions, and Chances." *Synthese* 34:423–55.
1979. "Serious Possibility." In *Essays in Honour of Jaakko Hintikka*, ed. Esa Saarinen. Reidel, Dordrecht, pp. 219–36.

Lewis, D. 1969. *Convention.* Harvard University Press, Cambridge, Mass., pp. 51–5.
Löb, M.H. 1955. "Solution of a Problem of Leon Henkin." *Journal of Symbolic Logic* 20:115–18.
Luce, R.D., and Raiffa, H. 1957. *Games and Decisions.* Wiley, New York, pp. 100–2.
Martin, R. (ed.). 1984. *Recent Essays on Truth and the Liar Paradox.* Clarendon Press, Oxford.
McClennen, E.F. 1978. "The Minimax Theory and Expected Utility Reasoning." In *Foundations and Applications of Decision Theory*, ed. C.A. Hooker, J.J. Leach, and E.F. McClennen. Reidel, Dordrecht, 337–68.
Mertens, J.F., and Zamir, S. 1985. "Formalization of Harsanyi's Notion of 'Type' and 'Consistency' in Games with Incomplete Information." *International Journal of Game Theory* 14:1–29.
Miller, D. 1966. "A Paradox of Information." *British Journal for the Philosophy of Science* 17:59–61.
Montague, R. 1963. "Syntactical Treatments of Modality, with Corollaries on Reflexion Principles and Finite Axiomatizability." *Acta Philosophica Fennica* 16:153–67.
Nash, J. 1951. "Non–cooperative Games." *Annals of Mathematics* 54:286–95.
Olin, D. 1983. "The Prediction Paradox Resolved." *Philosophical Studies* 44:229.
Parsons, C. 1974a. "The Liar Paradox." *Journal of Philosophical Logic* 3:381–412.
1974b. "Sets and Classes." *Nous* 8:1–12.
Parsons, T. 1984. "Assertion, Denial, and the Liar Paradox." *Journal of Philosophical Logic* 13:137–152.
Pearce, D. 1984. "Rationalizable Strategic Behavior and the Problem of Perfection." *Econometrica* 52:1029–50.
Perlis, D. 1987. "Languages with Self-reference, II: Knowledge, Belief and Modality." University of Maryland, Computer Science Dept., College Park, pp. 1–42.
Pettit, P., and Sugden, R. 1989. "The Backward Induction Paradox." *Journal of Philosophy* 86:169–82.
Rapaport, A., and Chammah, A. 1965. *The Prisoner's Dilemma.* University of Michigan Press, Ann Arbor.
Regan, D. 1980. *Utilitarianism and Cooperation.* Clarendon Press, Oxford, pp. 69–80.
Reny, P. 1988. "Rationality, Common Knowledge and the Theory of Games." Unpublished manuscript, University of Western Ontario, Dept. of Economics.
Rescher, N. 1976. *Plausible Reasoning: An Introduction to the Theory and Practice of Plausibilistic Reasoning.* Van Gorcum, Assen, pp. 6, 49–56.
Rosser, J.B. 1937. "Gödel Theorems for Non-constructive Logics." *Journal of Symbolic Logic* 2:129–37.
Russell, B. 1908. "Mathematical Logic as Based on the Theory of Types." *American Journal of Mathematics* 30:222–62; repr. in *Logic and Knowledge*, ed., Robert Charles Marsh, Allen and Unwin, London, 1956, pp. 57–102.
Schiffer, S.R. 1972. *Meaning.* Oxford University Press, Oxford.
Selten, R. 1978. "The Chain-Store Paradox." *Theory and Decisions* 9:127–59.
Shubik, M. 1982. *Game Theory in the Social Sciences.* MIT Press, Cambridge, Mass.
Skyrms, B. 1986. "Higher Order Degrees of Belief." In *Prospects for Pragmatism*, ed. D.H. Mellor. Cambridge University Press, pp. 109–37.

Sobel, J. H. 1975. "Interaction Problems for Utility Maximizers." *Canadian Journal of Philosophy* 4:677–88.

Sorensen, R. A. 1986. "Blindspotting and Choice Variations of the Prediction Paradox." *American Philosophical Quarterly* 23:337–52.

1988. *Blindspots.* Clarendon Press, Oxford, p. 328.

Stahl, D. 1988. "On the Instability of Mixed–Strategy Nash Equilibria." *Journal of Economic Behavior and Organisation* 9:59–69.

Tan, C.T., and Werlang, S. 1988. "The Bayesian Foundations of Solution Concepts of Games." *Journal of Economic Theory* 45:370–91.

Tarski, A. 1956. "The Concept of Truth in Formalized Languages." In *Logic, Semantics, Metamathematics*, J.H. Woodger, trans. Oxford University Press, New York.

Teller, P. 1976. "Conditionalization, Observation, and Change of Preference." In *Foundations of Probability Theory, Statistical Inference, and Statistical Theories of Science*, ed. W.L. Harper and C.H. Hooker. Reidel, Dordrecht, pp. 205–59.

Thomason, R. 1980. "A Note on Syntactical Treatments of Modality." *Synthese* 44:371–95.

Ushenko, A.P. 1957. "An Addendum to the Note on the Liar Paradox." *Mind* 66:98.

Van Fraassen, B. 1984. "Belief and the Will." *Journal of Philosophy* 81:231–56.

Van Heijenoort, J. 1967. *From Frege to Gödel.* Harvard University Press, Cambridge, Mass.

Wright, C., and Sudbury, A. 1977. "The Paradox of the Unexpected Examination." *Australasian Journal of Philosophy* 55:41–58.

Index